Praise for
The Wingman's Path to Positivity
by Michael S. Gross

The Wingman's Path to Positivity contains it ALL! It's packed full of inspiring ways to truly practice positive thinking and living—including all the times that it doesn't feel positive at all. This full-hearted and deep-life-living book creates a profound path and map for every Wingman and Wingmate in this world.
    -SARK, author/artist PlanetSARK.com

The Wingman's Path to Positivity contains the age-old truths we all experience when seeking enlightenment. We all create our futures so there are no coincidences. Our consciousness creates our future. Reading this book can become a road map for your future. So, make your journey a lot easier and read about the wisdom Michael has to share with us all.
    -Bernie Siegel, MD author of
    365 Prescriptions for The Soul and *A Book of Miracles*

Michael Gross is an American author, life coach, and motivational speaker. He is the author of *The Wingman's Path to Positivity*, a combination of Law of Attraction, Positive Psychology and old-school common sense.

Michael is available for select speaking engagements.
To inquire about appearances, please contact
michael@beyourownwingman.com.

The Wingman's Path to Positivity

by Michael S. Gross

Tasfil Publishing, LLC
New Jersey, USA

Copyright © 2020 Michael S. Gros
The Wingman's Path to Positivity
MichaelGross@Tasfil.com

Published 2020 by Tasfil Publishing, LLC
www.Tasfil.com
Voorhees, New Jersey 08043 USA

Paperback ISBN: 978-0986258091

Library of Congress Control Number:
Pending

ALL RIGHTS RESERVED
No part of this publication may be reproduced, stored in a retrieval system, or transmitted in any form or by any means, electronic, mechanical, photocopying, recording, scanning, or otherwise, except in brief quotations embodied in critical articles and reviews, without the prior written permission.

The author of this book does not dispense medical advice or prescribe the use of any technique as a form of treatment for physical, emotional, or medical problems without the advice of a physician, either directly or indirectly. The intent of the author is only to offer information of a general nature to help you in your quest for emotional or spiritual well-being. In the event you use any of the information in this book for yourself, which is your constitutional right, the author and publisher assume no responsibility for your actions

This book is considered a memoir. All names, events, and incidents are reproduced here in accordance with the author's memory. Some names and identities have been changed to protect the privacy of the individuals involved.

Dedication

To my granddaughter, Penelope,
and the next generation,
may these practices help you begin
a lifetime of thinking, seeing, feeling, and believing
in yourself, your dreams and your unlimited potential.

And to my wife, Janet; there is no Wingman's Path without you

Contents

Welcome to the Wingman's Path
Introduction

1.	A Wingman Minute	1
2.	The Darkness Revisited	5
3.	The Epiphany	9
4.	The Masters	14
5.	Taking Action	18
6.	Getting My Windshield Cleaned by Jimmy	21
7.	Talk-N-Angels	24
8.	Be Your Own Wingman	27
9.	A Wingman Minute	31
10.	Congratulations to Me!	36
11.	Boys' Weekend	39
12.	*Mea Culpa*	44
13.	Father's Day	48
14.	The Summer of My Discontent	54
15.	Welcome to the Game	58
16.	The Rules of the Game	62
17.	The Continuum	67
18.	My Old Friend Vance	74
19.	I'm A Lucky Guy	79
20.	The Macy's Lady	82
21.	Hocus Pocus, Change My Focus	86
22.	I'm Embracing my Challenges	91
23.	The Four Questions	98
24.	Lime-Green Cars	104
25.	My Eighth-Grade Self	108
26.	William and Ronja	114
27.	Miss New Jersey	119
28.	Here Comes Da Judge	124
29.	A Message from the Dalai Lama	127
30.	Weekend at Bernie's	131
31.	And Down I went	138
32.	Zen Master Jung Bong Mu M	143
33.	Bidding War	147

34. One Amazing Year	151
35. My Buddy Coop	158
36. Wing Dog Down	162
37. It Happened One Morning	166
38. My Dearest, Jan	173
39. Swan Lake	178
40. The Monk's Trail	184
41. Wingman on a Motor Scooter	189
42. The Destiny Café	195
43. Perfect Emptiness	200
44. The Miracle of Cha Am	204
45. The Brimfield Flea Market	210
46. I Forgive You, I Forgive Me	216
47. A Jammy Bastard	222
48. My Vibration has a Twang	227
49. An "Out of Buddy" Experience	233
50. A Deep(ak) Disappointment	237
51. Guess Who Came to Dinner	243
52. Today…	247
53. Travel Day	252
54. Sunrise, Amed, Bali	256
55. Thank You	259

Recommended Reading
Acknowledgements
About the Author

Welcome to the Wingman's Path

Thank you so much for picking out this book...Or maybe, it picked you. Either way, you now have in your hands a map detailing an easy-to-follow route that I call the *Wingman's Path to Positivity*. By following it, you can win the Spiritual Lottery, which is like winning a regular lottery, only better.

What?

When people imagine winning the lottery, they usually see a great deal of money coming to them. They think that money will bring them the happiness and freedom they've been wanting. But, although some research suggests lottery winners *do* have higher levels of satisfaction in their lives, other studies prove wealthy people are no happier on average than the rest of the population. Even worse, many are often significantly less happy.

There are no such crazy contradictions when it comes to hitting the Spiritual Lottery. When you win it, you no longer seek happiness; you *become* happiness. You let go of your worries about money, love, health, your job, and your life in general. You don't see limitations. And you don't hear "no" every time you ask.

Don't get me wrong. Winning the Spiritual Lottery doesn't mean you'll live challenge-free. But it does mean you'll see the challenges you do face differently. Instead of roadblocks or obstacles to achieving your goals, you'll see them as events unfolding to provide you with opportunities to grow, to learn, to better clarify your desires, and to become more confident in your power to manifest your goals.

Now you're probably wondering if I have manifested everything I want. No, I haven't. But that's because when I achieve one goal, I find another. And then another. Have you found that as well? I think it's the human condition: we always need a reason to do, be, or have something new to go after. When we successfully manifest one desire, we find another target to shoot for. We move from goal to goal and challenge to challenge, thus giving credence to the old adage: *Life is a journey and not a destination.*

The Wingman's Path to Positivity has helped me enjoy the journey *and* each destination along the way. And I do it with ever-growing passion, clarity, and appreciation. When you enjoy the journey like that, then you've won the Spiritual Lottery!

Introduction

Admittedly, I'm no genius. But I have figured out a way to manifest a life of my choosing. Perhaps it was dumb luck or trial and error, but when I stumbled upon a one-minute practice of finding and focusing on the positives in life, a new world opened up for me.

My transformation has been truly remarkable. Before finding the Wingman's Path, I was an ordinary guy living an ordinary existence. But then something happened, as you'll soon learn, and I responded by allowing myself to become a victim of circumstances. I ended up in a dark place for a long time.

I appreciate that dark place now because that darkness is what inspired me to get to where I currently am. I've gone from being homeless, to owning a home, and back to being homeless again. Only this time, I am homeless by choice: I've made the world my home, and I'm exploring it country by country. I've replaced my own pain and suffering from losing family members and loved ones, jobs, homes, cars, and many other possessions, with an abundance of clarity, calm, understanding, love, prosperity, and happiness.

I did it all by practicing what I call *Wingman Minutes* each day. These one-minute practices are the stepping-stones that make up the Wingman's Path. Taking the time to do them is the essential work required to follow the Path. And following the Wingman's Path is what made me hit the Spiritual Lottery.

The good news is that the path is easily duplicated. That is why I wrote this book: to detail each step I took and how I came to discover it, so by the end of this book, you, too, will know the Wingman's Path. You will recognize your ability to live a life of your choosing.

Can you imagine that, living life by your rules? Because you can. You just need to allow this book to be your map, your Yellow Brick Road, to achieving your goals. Actually, not your Yellow Brick Road. Use this book to follow your own Wingman's Path.

1
A Wingman Minute

I know myself well. I learned at a young age, that if something wasn't easy, I wouldn't do it. Meanwhile, the Universe taught me that what I look for, I find. So, I looked for a simple plan to improve my life. And I found it: practice positivity for one minute each day.

It doesn't get much easier than that, does it?

Although, as one client said, "it's still easier not to."

Actually, that particular client was a young man who had started an IT company a year before coming to me. He told me he was depressed, "drinking booze and smoking weed" every day, nearly divorced, and about to close his business and declare bankruptcy. After our first session, I gave him a one-minute practice to do. The next morning, we exchanged texts.

Since then, his company has grown into a 30-million-dollar business, and he is still happily married to the same woman. His change came about for the same reason mine did: he changed his thoughts to more positive ones. And that's what I hope to do for you with this book: help you bring more positivity into your life.

Why? What's so special about positivity?

Thinking positive thoughts makes you feel good. And the better you feel, the higher the vibrational frequency you emit out into the Universe. Because like attracts like, high-frequency thoughts, ideas, people, and events will then come back to you. It's the Law of Attraction.

> **If you want to find the secrets of the Universe, think in terms of energy, frequency, and vibration.**
>
> ~attributed to Nikola Tesla

The exercises in this book, these Wingman Minutes, are what I've used to become more positive, thus raising my vibration, which is what has helped change my life dramatically. Together, my wife, Janet, and I have created a life of travel, connectivity, and service by doing something every day that helps us raise our vibration. For me, that begins each morning when I video and post on social media a Wingman's Path daily practice. No matter where I am in the world, the practices have enabled me to share a spark of positive energy with my Wingmates on the Wingman's Path to Positivity.

Those sparks have ignited truly amazing adventures and encounters. As our lives unfold, as Janet and I help bring more energy, more love, more joy, more happiness, and more magic into our lives, we get to bring it into the lives of our family, friends, and loved ones. When they are inspired to do the same, that energy, love, joy, and happiness extends into neighborhoods, the local communities, towns, countries, and even all over the world.

That power isn't just ours. It's everyone's.

Imagine what could happen if we all spent time every day practicing positivity! When we can all do that, we will be able to create some pretty incredible things. Who knows? Perhaps we will even be able to create world peace, just from one minute of positivity each day.

Now you may think I'm getting a little bit carried away with the idea of world peace from just one minute of thinking happy thoughts each day, but I've seen what these Wingman practices can do. I know what happens when people start feeling better about themselves.

So, the first question on the Wingman's Path, then, is to ask: What frequency am I emitting into the Universe? Not sure? That's OK. That's actually a question I receive frequently.

How do I know if I'm sending out a positive vibration?
The answer is: if you feel good. Our emotions tell us what our vibrational frequency is. The happier and more positive we feel, the higher our vibration is. Similarly, the less happy and more negative we feel, the lower our vibration.

Which leads me to another frequently asked question: *Is positivity always a feeling of constant elation?*

For me, it is *not* a feeling of constant elation. It's more a feeling of confidence, clarity, and calmness in knowing I can handle anything that comes my way.

Simply put, you know you're sending out a positive vibration when you feel good. The better you feel, the higher your vibration. Paying attention to how I felt is what made the Wingman's Path so powerful for me; I learned how to utilize my thoughts, feelings, and actions as indicators of my vibration. The more consistently I practiced thinking thoughts that led to feeling better, the more I recognized my ability to control my vibration and either raise it or keep it high.

That's right. I learned I have control over my vibration, which means I have control over whatever situation or circumstances I find myself in; because I choose how I am responding to it.

There is nothing either good or bad, but thinking makes it so.
~*Hamlet*, William Shakespeare

We always have a choice as to how something affects us. We can choose to find the positives and be solution-oriented. Or we can choose to focus only on the negatives and get stuck in a downward spiral.

I found that if I shift my thinking to view my situation in a more positive light, the easier it became to feel good whatever was going on. Why? Because the Law of Attraction is constant. The Universe always, always, *always* matches our vibration and sends back to us exactly what we are sending out. That's how positivity can turn around negative situations.

And it all starts by simply asking yourself: "What frequency am I emitting out into the Universe?" Then trying to feel your vibration, your emotions. Once you recognize where you are vibrationally, my Wingman Minutes will help *you* raise your vibration, which will help you start moving in a more positive direction toward achieving your goals. When you do that, the people you connect with will feel that higher vibration and become inspired to raise *their* vibration and work toward manifesting *their* desires. That's how we can change the world together.

And that's how the Wingman's Path works. It's a roadmap you follow based on your emotions.

As you read each chapter, you will discover how I stumbled upon and learned to use the Wingman's Path. I will discuss how a particular practice came to be, and then I will end each chapter with a Wingman's Path practice for you to do.

Simple, right? Exactly how I like it.

So let's get started.

A Wingman Practice:

Observe Your Vibration

For one minute, repeatedly ask yourself: "What is my vibration?"

As you do, think about the energy you are sending out into the Universe. Are you sending out a feeling of confidence or desperation? Of love or indifference? Of hope or hopelessness?

You don't have to answer the question, you just need to ask it. Your feelings will give you the answer.

2
The Darkness. Revisited
October 2009

Let go. Terminated. Fired.

I began looking for the Wingman's Path back in October of 2009, only I didn't realize what I was doing at that time. I just thought I was getting fired. I wasn't surprised about losing my job. The CEO had been terminated a few months earlier, so the handwriting was on the wall. But knowing that didn't make it any easier to deal with.

I owned a big old Victorian house, with a big new mortgage.

I was scared, nervous, in debt, and worried.

"Maybe it's a blessing in disguise," a work-friend had told me.

"If it is," I answered, "it's a really good disguise." I certainly did *not* see it as a blessing, and at that time, I did not believe that *everything happens for a reason*.

But then I had a flashback to 25 years previously. *That* was when I had my first real taste of misfortune. It happened on Friday, May 3, 1985. Ironically, the following Monday was supposed to begin "my week"—I was poised to become a very wealthy man.

At that time, I was a stockbroker with EF Hutton, a large investment brokerage firm. Through hard work, good luck, and some very talented associates, I made a very nice living managing union funds. We managed them so well, in fact, that nine more unions wanted to give us money to manage.

Lots of money.

Each of those unions had meetings set up that coming week—not really meetings, more like competitions. They had invited us, along with two other money managers, to make persuasive presentations as to why they should choose us to manage their funds. At the end of the presentations, they would select a winner.

The thing is, we were the heavy favorite. The unions were so impressed by how well we had managed some health and welfare funds, they just wanted to hand us the money. But unions don't work that way. They were required to receive information from three different companies. It didn't mean we couldn't lose, but with us being the heavy favorite, and nine different unions selecting from the presentations, we were certain to win at least five or six of them. More likely eight or all nine.

Yes, I was about to become very wealthy.

But then, life took an unexpected turn. I still remember the headlines from that Friday:

E.F. HUTTON GUILTY IN BANK FRAUD:
PENALTIES COULD TOP $10 MILLION

It was devastating. The unions didn't cancel or change the meetings set for the presentations; we were just uninvited. Imagine that! They wanted those meetings because of how well we had done in the past, but because of the headlines on *that one day*, and because bank fraud is a felony, they could not have us manage their money.

However, the incident ended up just being a headline. (And even if the story had been true, no bank would be a witness against their biggest client.) In other words: there were no charges, no trials, and no prosecutions. There was no crime.

Shortly afterward, EF Hutton made some deals, and everyone was made whole. No harm, no foul.

The financial world moved on. EF Hutton moved on. The banks moved on. It was quickly forgotten...but not by me. I was shattered.

If the headline had come out two weeks earlier, or two weeks later, nothing would have changed. I would have been made a wealthy man.

But the headline came out *that* Friday, the Friday before the unions made their decisions about who would handle their money. So the unions invested with others. I lost out. Timing is everything.

Looking back, you could say that, really, nothing had changed for me that week: I still made a nice living; still lived in my nice house and drove my fancy car.

But something had changed. I changed. I became a victim in my own mind. And then I allowed myself to fall into a depression where I lost everything. I ended up homeless, living out of my car, and sleeping on friends' couches.

And then my car was stolen.

Ouch.

I went from top to bottom in record time. And I would wallow in that muck for a long time. It was a blessing in disguise, though. A really good disguise.

What?

How can I say that? Because from those ashes, this Phoenix rose. Or should I say, this Wingman rose?

But I'm jumping ahead. Let me take you back to where this chapter began, with me being fired. You remember, don't you? I was scared, nervous, in debt, and worried. I had been trying to be more positive in my life, had even been doing positivity practices like saying affirmations, but I wasn't ready to handle losing my job. It's like I had moved forward an inch or two into a happier life, and then got smacked backward by 10 miles.

Fortunately, something kept me from returning to the depths I fell into back in '85. It was the understanding that the Universe matches whatever vibration I send out and returns more of the same. Back in 1985, after the unions dismissed us, the vibration I sent out to the Universe was one of failure. So it brought me more to fail at in life.

This time around, I knew I had to change my vibration. That's not easy to do when you're facing major adversity. Hell, it's not easy to do when things are going well. But it's not impossible.

So, I looked around for a little help, and I realized the Universe had already supplied it to me in the phrase from my work-friend that kept going through my mind: *It's a blessing in disguise.*

That's right, the words spoken by my work-friend became the first practice on my path to create the life of my choosing by being positive. As I re-visited the phrase and said the words *it's a blessing in disguise*, I laughed at my original response that it was *a really good disguise*. Laughing felt good.

Laughing means you're feeling better, which means your vibration is shifting. And remember: the better you feel, the higher your vibration. So I kept repeating the phrase and feeling good while I did it. Soon enough, I discovered my mind was searching for any blessings that might come from losing my job. As I sifted through the rubble of my trampled mind, I searched and, even better, I began to believe there were possible blessings.

A Wingman Practice:

It's a Blessing in Disguise.

For one minute, say out loud or quietly to yourself: "It's a blessing in disguise."

As you do, think of your current situation and think about what good might possibly come from it. Don't worry if you can't come up with anything, just keep saying *it's a blessing in disguise* for one minute. Neuroscience will tell you, you don't even have to believe it when you first start saying it, but if you continue to say it, sooner or later, your brain will eventually wrap around it, and you will begin to believe it. And that's when it finally starts to sink into your subconscious and begins to influence your behavior in the way you want. Finally.

Remember, try to go beyond just thinking it. Try to practice the *feeling* of it. When I speak of energy, vibration, or frequency, what I mean is, how does it feel? More important than the thoughts you think or the words you speak, is the feeling you are feeling. Because what you're feeling is the vibration you are sending out.

> By the way...when doing this, or any practice, my goal is always to feel just a "li'l bit better." Just a li'l bit. I'm not looking to jump from pissed to blissed immediately. I'm just looking to get a little momentum going in the right—that is a more positive—direction. When you get really clear that the game of life is vibration, you quickly realize the value of momentum. And your thoughts can create that momentum, a li'l bit at a time.

The beauty of saying, *it's a blessing in disguise,* is that your mind stops focusing on how terrible everything is and starts moving in a positive direction, if only for one minute.

Congratulations! You're now on your way to manifesting a better life.

3
The Epiphany
Thanksgiving, 2011

Thanksgiving, 2011, is when the Wingman's Path truly became evident to me. I had been trying to find positives in my situations, trying to hang on to positive phrases, for some time because they helped me feel better; they kept me from spiraling downward in negativity. It was on that Thanksgiving, though, when I caught a real glimpse of their power.

For it was on that Thanksgiving morning when my car died as I returned from my walk in the woods. And so began my day of giving thanks.

My car dying wasn't a total surprise. The car had been giving me problems since I had purchased it three years before. I had promised myself to sell it the moment the warranty was up, but my habit of procrastination kept it in my driveway. Realizing it was no longer under warranty, a flood of negative thoughts invaded my mind.

I'm an idiot. How could I be so stupid? I knew this would happen sooner or later, why didn't I sell this car three months ago as I had promised myself?

There's nothing quite like the torture of beating yourself up. The more you do it, the easier it becomes. And the momentum can be devastating. Thankfully, as I sat in my car, pissed off at the world, I realized I had better do something quickly to change my energy if I was to have an enjoyable Thanksgiving. I had a houseful of people coming over, and I wanted to feel joy, not self-loathing and anger.

I then asked a question out loud that has since become my mantra. "What would my Wingman say?"

Because I had been walking with a trusted friend and real-life Wingman, I didn't have to wait long.

"Well," he said sarcastically, "you were looking for a sign about your car, you certainly got one."

Hmmm. Not exactly what I wanted to hear, but not a bad start either. As mentioned, I'd been having issues with this car. You could say each one was a sign I'd ignored up to this point. One of the many lessons I've learned on my path to being my own Wingman is that when you have a situation that you avoid dealing with, it only gets bigger. Truer words were never said concerning my car. Once you accept that fact, you'll discover you procrastinate less. It's just that for some of us, yes, I'm talking about me, it takes a long while to accept it.

I knew it was time to turn to my internal Wingman and ask again. I sat quietly and breathed deeply to let something flow to me. What I heard from within came quickly and clearly. *Practice what you preach, find the positives.* Although there were other times in my life when I had turned to my internal Wingman, never had I received such a clear answer. It seemed surreal. I actually *felt* the answer.

But, how could I see a positive when I'm sitting in my broken-down car that needed to be towed, on Thanksgiving, and would cost more money than I currently had in the bank to get it back on the road?

Well, obviously, I could *not* start by being thankful for my car, so I looked around for other things to appreciate and, of course, found a few.

1) My car was in a very safe spot in a parking lot in my hometown. It didn't break down on the road, where I would have to deal with it immediately. Seeing as it was Thanksgiving, this was certainly a positive.
2) No one was hurt.
3) A friend was with me and could drive my dog and me home.

Wow! Did I just come up with three positives? Watch out world, I'm on my way.

4) I knew I had some time to think of the best way to handle this ordeal.
5) It was Thanksgiving, and being that I'm a pretty thankful guy, it was one of my favorite days of the year. I would forget about this for today and focus on all I had to be thankful for. I would enjoy my day today. (This may seem a bit like procrastination, but in fact, it was perfect time management, as there wasn't much else that could be accomplished

on Thanksgiving, anyway. And trying to find a tow-truck driver or get in touch with the dealership would be a futile waste of time.)
6) As my friend had mentioned, the truth is I had been looking for a sign, and I received one. It was time to take notice of it.

Right then, a plan came into my mind. I would have the car towed to the dealership on Friday, have them fix it, and even though the car is out of warranty, have them help me with the cost because they knew how problematic it had been since day one. I was so excited and sure about my inspired plan that I also decided they would want to do right by me and would buy the car back from me at fair wholesale market value.

Then, I remembered something: my daughter, who had just moved to Philadelphia, no longer needed her car and was looking for a way to save money. She would be thrilled if I would take over her payments. We could share the car, thus saving us both money.

Wow! Being thankful got me into such a positive frame of mind, I was having so much fun, I was almost glad my car broke down. NOT!

Folks, let's not get crazy here. I'm in no way saying that at that time I was glad my car had broken down. I am saying that when you can learn to find something, anything to be positive about, somehow, you begin to find more things to be positive about.

Perhaps it's true, as Dr. Wayne Dyer often said:

**When you change the way you look at things,
the things you look at change.**

Or perhaps, science has a better explanation. According to Newton's First Law of Physics, the Law of Inertia, an object in a constant speed of motion stays in that constant speed, and an object at rest stays at rest unless something else interferes or acts upon it.

In other words, when you are in a negative (e)motion, a negative frame of mind, you tend to stay in a negative (e)motion unless you do something about it. Which is what I did by switching my focus to finding the positives.

After playing my find-the-positives game, I was able to put my car troubles out of my mind and enjoy my Thanksgiving holiday.

The next day, amazed at how happy I had become knowing everything would work out, I put my plan into action. I had the car (I was already viewing it as *the* car, not *my* car) towed to the dealership and waited for the dealership's call on the following Monday. I just knew they would agree with all I had asked for.

I was excited to speak with them and looking forward to seeing the results of my positive energy. So imagine my surprise when the service manager said, "Hi Mike, I'm sorry, but the car is no longer under warranty so we won't help with the cost, and, unfortunately, we know this car too well, we don't want to buy it back."

Huh? What went wrong?

Isn't that what people ask when they "try" practicing the Law of Attraction? The difference, so you understand, is I wasn't trying. I *knew* I was coming from a positive place. I could feel it. I wasn't "faking it 'til I made it." I wasn't just thinking the words. I was *actually feeling certain* that everything was working out for me. As a matter of fact, I was so upbeat, his words didn't really hit me. Maybe I was in shock, but I told him to fix it anyway and to call me when it was ready. This turn of events was so unexpected that I started laughing. The cost of fixing the car, and the fact that I didn't have enough money to pay for it, never entered my mind.

Exactly one hour later, a woman who had been a health insurance client of mine a few years prior, called.

"Hi Michael," she said. "I don't know if you remember me, but when I was with my previous employer, you did our health insurance. I'm with a new company now, and we just got our renewal. I was hoping you would review it for us."

"I'd be happy to," I replied. "Who do you work for now?"

Her answer nearly floored me. "I work for a small law firm that specializes in lemon laws for automobiles."

My smile went ear to ear. "Before we talk health insurance,' I said. "Can I tell you my story?"

Seriously, no more than one hour had passed since my conversation with the car dealer.

As it turned out:
- I got the car fixed.
- I got $3,500 back.
- I got fair market value for my car.
- I took over my daughter's lease, saving us both money.
- I learned the power of consciously practicing positivity.

That's it, wrapped up nice and easy for you.

A Wingman Practice:

Find the Positives.

Take one minute right now and find something, anything, to be positive about. See how many positives you can come up with and let positive momentum build. As you fill your list, you surround yourself with a more positive vibration, you will feel better and begin to attract more positive energy.

People often ask me, how? *How do I find the positives so easily when there are so many negatives in my life?*
As my own Wingman, I now know the answer. Practice!
A positive attitude does not happen overnight. But if you begin practicing tonight, I assure you, tomorrow will look a little bit better.
My car breaking down on Thanksgiving is a perfect example of how to live my be-your-own-Wingman philosophy, and how to start living your life on the Wingman's Path. You start by finding something positive, anything you can be thankful for.
As demonstrated in my Thanksgiving story, when you can keep your vibration high and consistently find positives, the way you see the world, and the way the world responds to you, changes.

4
The Masters

So there I was, after Thanksgiving in 2011, feeling pretty sure of myself. I had connected with my inner Wingman. Others might call it your wiser self, your higher self, Source, the Universe, God. Whatever it was, I had made the connection. I felt like *Da Man*. But I wanted more, and I expected more.

I was certain I would be receiving wisdom, guidance, and divine insight from my inner Wingman on a regular basis. That it would just flow to me when I needed it. Anytime I had a decision to make, I could just check in with my newfound connection and receive spiritual enlightenment.

Instead, every day, at least once per day, I would ask: "What would my Wingman say?" And every day, I waited. And I heard nothing.

I grew frustrated. I couldn't believe it. I had felt the connection! Where was he? And why could I no longer connect with him?

I began reading anything and everything about the non-physical to figure out what I was doing wrong. I truly wanted to find out the best way to access divine guidance so I could live my life according to it.

While the idea of spirits, life forces, angels, or ghosts never really held any interest for me, I had always been fascinated with mythologies and religions. So that's where I initiated my research, which led me to Joseph Campbell and his book, *The Hero with a Thousand Faces*, a discussion of the epic trials and tribulations one must overcome in order to achieve the goal of self-knowing.

Campbell opened the doorway for personal development books for me. Soon, I was fascinated by the whole genre, including spirituality, self-help, and the Law of Attraction. From Joseph Campbell, I went to other modern masters like Wayne Dyer, Abraham-Hicks, Deepak Chopra, the Dalai Lama, Paulo Coelho, Thich Nhat Hanh, Eckhart Tolle, James Redfield, Don Miguel

Ruiz, Rhonda Byrne, Neale Donald Walsch, Louise Hay, and Dr. Bernie Seigel, who actually became a friend as well as a mentor.

I became captivated by their words and influenced by the references they all made to the many early great masters from religion, science, the arts, spirituality, business, and philosophy who came before them. So, I started reading them as well: Jesus, Buddha, Albert Einstein, Shakespeare, Thoreau, Emerson, Sir Isaac Newton, Andrew Carnegie, Henry Ford, Napoleon Hill, Lao Tzu, Gandhi, etc. The list went on and on.

The more I read from these modern masters, from the greatest leaders and thinkers throughout history, the more the message became clear. For every one of them, no matter when they lived, or in what field they excelled, all from different times and different worlds, using dissimilar words and languages, all seemed to say exactly the same thing:

I create my own life, and I can create the life I desire.

That's it.

You, me, your neighbor, your lazy-ass cousin, your beautiful daughter, the man in the coffee shop, each and every one of us create our own life and, hence, can create the life we desire.

It is the foremost lesson that has been repeated from each and every one of these great teachers. Seriously. The more I read, the more I recognized how often that same lesson had been written.

It had been written a thousand different ways, over thousands of years by our most brilliant scholars, mentors, intellectuals, and gurus. And their words became well known. So well-known, that we constantly see them in our everyday life. From bumper stickers to business offices, yoga centers to gymnasiums, little artisan gift shops to your doctor's office, reggae bars to coffee houses, we see and hear their words. And whether your background is religion, or science, or business, or theater, or philosophy, we all know their words and can quote them.

Do any of these sound familiar?
Thought: The mind is everything. What you think you become.
Emotion: You can do anything if you have enthusiasm.
Action: Be the change that you wish to see in the world.
Faith: All things are possible for one who believes.

What struck me as strange, though, is that we all know these great words, but very few of us actually live by them. We throw them out at cocktail parties and tell others they should learn from them, but for most of us, they've become a cliché. We may say them often, but we don't *hear* them, and we definitely don't live them.

Why? Why, if the Masters of our Universe, those that we hold in the highest regard, have been telling us these simple words for years, why don't we live them?

While reading one day, the answer hit me. We might hear them, but we don't quite understand what they're telling us. And why is that? Well, as I was struggling over a wordy passage one day, I wondered if perhaps the straightforwardness of these brilliant lessons got mixed up in the longer writings. I know I often had trouble with them. As I would force myself to read and re-read, my eyes would glass over, and often I would fall asleep. The books were too religious, or scientific, or philosophical or frankly, just too long-winded for me. I couldn't easily comprehend them.

I continued trying because I knew I was on to something. Listen, I'm no scientist or mathematician or philosopher for that matter. However, I do understand probabilities. It seemed to me, with every great master telling me that what I think about I become about, I thought it wise to get control of the thoughts I was thinking and that I should think more positively.

But there had to be more. I still wanted to know how to access divine guidance when I needed it. And with all those words filling up those brilliant books, the answer had to be in there for me to learn. I felt it, and so I kept struggling to read the works of genius.

This is where my Wingdog, Monty, came in handy. Every day I would walk with him in the woods for an hour. So I decided to get audiobooks and listen to a chapter over and over and over again while I walked him. I would listen until I actually understood it. But for me to do that, to truly understand the chapter, I had to simplify it. I had to break each piece down to the lowest common denominator. And so I began to reduce these great works into small games and exercises. How? By seeking the message from within chunks of the text as if it were a treasure hunt. And once I found it, I would "practice" it by thinking it, saying it, and feeling it.

Thus began what would eventually become my daily practice and my advancement along what I now call the Wingman's Path.

The most important thing was that I allowed myself to have fun with the idea. That's why I made it a game to do a positivity practice each day. The more I played the game, the more I became unconsciously competent at seeing positives, at seeing solutions, and at seeing what was going right in my situation and building from there.

I still thought there had to be a way to access diving guidance whenever I needed it, but while I searched for it, this was a close second. By committing to learning what the Masters of our Universe have been saying for so long, and by simplifying it down so I could understand it, I began living their message.

I urge you to do the same. Have fun with it. Practice it. Enjoy it.

A Wingman Practice:

What I think, I become

Repeat to yourself for at least one minute: "What I think, I become."

As you repeat the phrase, remember that these words, or words similar to them, have been spoken by many of our greatest leaders, thinkers, and achievers throughout time. Knowing that should help you feel the importance of them.

5
Taking Action

I enjoyed my new routine. Every morning I would wake up, go to the woods with Monte, and while I walked, I would listen to audiobooks from the world's Masters. But as often happens in life, I got knocked off my path. It happened without warning. There was no drama, no fanfare. It just kind of faded away—the way it does when you're going to the gym and exercising. You miss one day, and it's no big deal. But then you miss another, and another, and suddenly you realize you haven't worked out in three weeks. That's what happened to me.

My morning practice had become inconsistent because we no longer had the woods to ourselves. The walks with Monte, which initially had provided me wonderful solitude in the woods, had changed. Many other dog lovers had recently discovered our utopia, and we were often accompanied by them.

Not that I didn't enjoy the company. I did, and I made some good friends along the way. It was still my favorite part of the day. But, instead of practicing my connection to the Universe, I was connecting with my physical community, neighbors, and friends.

I hadn't even realized the change had happened until a few months went by, and I noticed I had become spiritually flabby. Similar to how the lack of physical exercise will turn muscle into fat, once you stop practicing positivity, negativity gets a hold of you. And before you recognize it, boom! You're falling down that rabbit hole.

What's a Wingman to do?

The good news was, I acknowledged my falling off the positivity wagon. Clearly, my morning walks were no longer the time I was able to practice.

But finding a new time takes effort and self-discipline, two things I was sorely lacking.

Enter the Universe. Help came in the form of an email from a friend asking if I wanted to join him at something called a Law of Attraction Meetup. Have you ever heard of Meetup.com? I certainly hadn't at that time. It's a website you can join to find people gathering together for any reason they invent. It started back in 2001 after the September 11 terrorist attacks as an open invitation to defy the instinct to hibernate in our homes. It grew exponentially as mommies, hikers, computer people, singles, and anyone with a common interest started planning play dates, happy hours, expeditions and get-togethers. To my delight and surprise, there were meetups for people to discuss the Law of Attraction and learn from each other.

I did want to join him. So we drove about 30 minutes to a Starbucks coffee and joined in. After attending that one, I went to another one in New York City, and then to a third one a bit closer to me. Each one was informative, friendly, and extremely enjoyable. Only they weren't that accessible to me as either their location or the days they would hold the meetings, was inconvenient for me. I realized it was time for bold action, so I started my own meetup.

The decision to create it was easy. I was looking for something that would get me back to my positivity practices. I recognized my need for more practice and for a better understanding and improved consistency in my spiritual learning. Regular meetings with like-minded people seemed like just the thing to help me fill those needs by holding the meetup on a weekly basis. My thinking was that since I would be facilitating the meeting, I would be forced to have an agenda. In setting up an agenda, I would need to spend time researching what I wanted to discuss. I thought the homework was an ideal solution for getting me back on my spiritual studies.

And it was. As I said to a good friend who was joining me for those first meetups, "I don't care if only you and I show up. Because no matter what, at least you and I will discuss the Law of Attraction for at least 90 minutes every week."

But it wasn't only the two of us. That first week five people showed. And each week through the summer, it grew in attendance. It grew so much, I had to change the meeting place to a larger venue. Clearly, I wasn't the only person thirsting for more clarity about the way our Universe works.

I was back on my Path. I may not have been practicing daily, but by making sure I was prepared and organized to lead my meetup, I was studying and learning more about the Law of Attraction, the Power of Positivity, and my ability to create a life of my choosing. All it took was being open to an invitation, setting an intention, and taking the first step.

That being said, it was also obvious to me that I had a long way to go to achieve my goal of being able to create that life of my choosing. If I could lose my focus so quickly that I stopped practicing without even realizing it, clearly, more work was needed. But, I had taken my first step.

A journey of a thousand miles begins with a single step.
~Lao Tzu

A Wingman Practice:

Take Action

Think of a desire you want to manifest and, for one minute, repeat to yourself the quote from Lao Tzu: "A journey of a thousand miles begins with a single step."

While saying it, think of a single step you could take today to move you in the direction of achieving your goal. Now see yourself taking it.

While saying the words, I want you also to envision yourself achieving your goal. How would you feel in accomplishing it? Would you feel proud of yourself? More confident? Would you walk a little taller? That feeling is the vibration I want you to practice sending out into the Universe.

6
Getting My Windshield Cleaned by Jimmy, the Gas Station Attendant

I was in action. Starting my meetup was a great first step. By making certain I was prepared each week to run the meetup, I was back to reading and listening to the different Masters again. It felt good to be back.

Once you begin moving in the direction of your desire, something always shows up to help you continue moving in that direction. You just have to take notice of it. It shouldn't be surprising—that's the way the Law of Attraction works. But, for some reason, I, like many others, don't always take notice of it. I take that first step, and then stop. Even when I have a little momentum going for myself, I will grind my progress to a halt by focusing elsewhere. Thankfully, this time when I got back on my Wingman's Path, my universal Wingmates had my back. They sent me Jimmy and made certain I learned from him.

It happened one Friday evening. My wife and I were driving to meet some friends for dinner when I stopped to fill my car up with gasoline. Now we were in New Jersey, where you never pump your own gasoline. It's a state law that only an employee of the gas station can do it. That's how my next practice came to be. For it was there, I had the opportunity to be served by Jimmy, a young man who clearly makes a practice of going above and beyond.

Not only did he do his job of filling my gas tank, but he did it promptly, with courtesy and a smile. In today's society, that in and of itself would have exceeded any expectations. But then, he asked if he could clean my windshield. I was so surprised, I didn't answer him immediately. When I finally said *yes*, he did so with a cheerfulness that had my wife and I discussing it long after we were back on the road.

Jimmy's service got me thinking about the times in my life when I had gone above and beyond for someone else. As I remembered different moments, both small and large, the emotions of those flashes in time were sensed in my body. It was as if I were experiencing them once again, and they felt wonderful.

The next day, when my wife returned from running errands, I naturally asked about her day.

"I had a really great day." She grinned as she told me. "You know our discussion from yesterday? Well, today, I got the opportunity to exceed expectations, and I delivered." She was beaming, and I couldn't wait to hear more.

Jan described being at the drive-through window at the bank when an elderly man pulled into the parking lot, got out of his car, and proceeded to ask people how to get to a particular address in our town. No one, including my wife, knew where it was.

"He looked so forlorn," my wife said, "I thought I'd look it up on my GPS. But as I started telling him how to get there, I could see he was confused. So, I offered to drive there, and he could follow me." My wife's grin was now spreading wide across her face. "He was so appreciative. It made me feel so great."

"Wow!" I exclaimed. "You were like Jimmy at the gas station. You went above and beyond as a Wingman."

And so, by driving a couple miles out of her way, my wife turned an ordinary Saturday into an exceptional feeling. She also delivered me my next practice along the Wingman's Path.

It's another easy practice. At least once each day, I look for an opportunity to go above and beyond. It's not just about helping others. It's about doing more than you're expected to do, whether at work, at home, or just for yourself.

Napoleon Hill, the bestselling author of *Think and Grow Rich*, said it best:

"Render more and better service than you are paid for, and sooner or later you will receive compound interest from your investment. It is inevitable that every seed of useful service you sow will sprout and reward you with an abundant harvest."

While the business side of you may understand that you will be "rewarded with an abundant harvest" by going above and beyond, I will tell you the most important part of this practice is the vibration you will be sending out. When you do more than necessary, it produces a feeling inside of your soul: a feeling of pride, of achievement, of a job well done.

Here's the thing, though: going above and beyond is not a simple practice you can do in one minute. Rather, it is a state of mind that you must develop so that it becomes a part of everything you do.

Like every other practice on the Wingman's Path, you will be able to develop this habit by making certain to do one extra thing each day. Maybe it's making an extra call, helping someone in need, or just cleaning up. The step itself is not important. It's the taking of the step that is.

By the way…going above and beyond only works if you do so with a positive mental attitude. Let my experience with Jimmy, the gas station attendant, be a reminder to keep a smile on your face, an optimistic feeling in your heart, and a sense of happiness in your soul as you travel further than you are expected to go.

A Wingman Practice:

Be A Better Wingmate

1. Repeat to yourself for one minute: "Be a better Wingmate." While saying it, practice the feeling of seeing yourself going above and beyond expectations or of "rendering more and better…"

2. Get into action. Today, do something above and beyond what you normally do. As you do, say to yourself with a smile, "I love doing more than expected."

7
Talk-n-Angels

As I progressed along the Wingman's Path, I continued to find it surprising how the Universe would regularly lay out breadcrumbs for me to follow. Often, they would be there in the form of a mishap or an unintended occurrence. Thus was the case when I called a business contact named Robert, and, when hitting his name on my cell phone, accidentally tapped the name directly above his, Rita.

Rita was a friend I had worked with in the corporate world. We were terminated from the company around the same time, and Rita had decided to go in a different direction. Although she was excellent at what she did and had been offered similar positions at other companies, Rita followed a different calling. She recognized her divinity and had become an angel channeler, spiritual advisor, and Reiki master. She also began hosting a radio show called *Talk-n-Angels*.

I'm not sure why I still find it so surprising when the Universe rises up to meet me. I mean, I've seen it happen time after time. When I set my intention, and emit a frequency that resonates with what I want, the Universe always matches the vibration I'm sending out. Each and every time, the Universe will send me back *exactly* the same frequency that I am emitting. No exceptions. And yet, no matter how far I've progressed on my Wingman's Path, no matter how certain I am that it will happen, every time it does, I'm still like a kid who wakes up in a candy store. I love it.

That's what the *Talk-n-Angels* radio show was to me: the candy store. Here I was, learning about being a Wingman, about helping others and myself, and the Universe sends me Rita and her show. As we spoke on the day of that fortuitous phone call, Rita invited me to be a guest on her show and talk about my Law of Attraction meetup group.

I had great fun on the show, and we had great chemistry. So much so, that after the show was over, Rita invited me to be her co-host for the foreseeable future. So yes, once again, my universal staff came through. I proclaimed myself to be the poster boy for the Law of Attraction. I sent out a vibration looking for new situations to keep me moving in that direction. And Rita's show was exactly the type of opportunity I was looking for.

I accepted her invitation and became the co-host of the *Talk-N-Angels* radio show. My job was to bring more Law of Attraction into the conversations. It was another reason to study, research, and prepare to discuss what I was learning on a weekly basis.

Even better: not only did I need to be prepared to discuss how to manifest desires and create a life of my choosing, but we would often interview bestselling authors, speakers, and gurus in the world of self-help, Angels, Law of Attraction, Meditation, and positive energy. It was fantastic! Each week brought me a chance to raise my vibration and better understand the spiritual laws of our Universe.

My Wingman's Path became better lit with each twist and turn I took on it. Momentum built. I found myself in fewer circumstances that encouraged me to turn back and skip my positivity exercises. Instead, I was more motivated to do a practice every day. I was moving in a positive direction, and it became easier and easier to continue to do so.

Connecting with Rita locked my vision in. I was now able to see how advancing along this path would get me to where I wanted to be. As long as I stayed focused on being as positive as possible, more positive things would come my way. I still didn't have divine guidance speaking in my ear, but I could feel where I was being guided. The better I felt, the better the place I was led.

Only I had a slight problem. Yes, I had been given an exciting opportunity to further my education, and I found a problem with it: the name of the show! *Talk-n-Angels*? The idea of speaking with angels was so foreign to me that I initially couldn't even say the word *angels*. Perhaps it was my religious upbringing or my business background, but the notion that there were angels seemed pretty insane to me.

But, while I may not have believed in angels, I wasn't going to let that fact get in the way of a great opportunity. For if there is one thing my journey has taught me, it's that it is extremely important to remain open to opportunities, even if they're not exactly what you want them to be. As I've frequently found while coaching others, it's so easy to allow ourselves to get closed off. We've been doing things the way we do them for so long, we can't fathom the possibility of there being other ways to do them, let alone better ways.

Often, we look for very specific opportunities to help us with a problem or reach a goal. Being specific closes us off from the many other potential positive situations, some—or at least one—of which, could be better than anything we could imagine. Those opportunities come our way cloaked in circumstances that make them less obvious to us. But, vibrationally speaking, opening yourself up to the idea of other opportunities and taking on a new one, even if it's not one you specifically desire, will lead to more opportunities, which will lead to more and more.

So, to soften my hesitation over the name, I created a new practice: "I am open to opportunities coming my way." I used it to celebrate the manifestation of co-hosting the radio show and to help raise my vibration regarding the show in general. Raising it in general included finding acceptance of the name, which led me to embrace the name, which you'll learn about soon.

A Wingman Practice:

Open to New Opportunities

For one minute, repeat out loud or to yourself: "I am open to opportunities coming my way."

As you say the words, try to feel receptive to ideas and opportunities coming your way. You don't have to know what they are, just be open to the concept that they are there and coming to you. The more open you are, the more open your vibration will be. This will help you begin receiving more opportunities. And, the more opportunities that come your way, the better the odds of the exact situation you're looking for, or something better, will present itself.

8
Be Your Own Wingman

I had not realized how large Rita's audience was. Nor did I realize how many people in my own backyard were in the angel community. It was a community I knew nothing about at first. But each week, through my conversations with Rita, questions from listeners, and interviews with authors, it became more apparent to me that my Law of Attraction path was parallel to Rita's Angel path. The paths had their differences, but they certainly moved in the exact same direction.

But let me step back for a second and clear something up. Although I've been using the term *Wingman* since the beginning of this book, it wasn't until my association with Rita that the word stuck, and the Wingman's Path actually received its name. That came about only because I learned to understand angels in a new light.

As I mentioned, I was uncomfortable with the word *angel*. Since the basis of Rita's show was to discuss a different Guardian Angel each week, I opened myself up to learn about them. Only, because of my aversion to the word, I began to refer to them as "our invisible friends with benefits," granting that because of their divinity, the benefits were far greater than the physical ones I once associated with the phrase.

The jump to begin using the term *Wingman* happened a few weeks after starting the show. I was still in the health insurance business at the time and had taken a call from a client who had already learned about my newfound position as the co-host of *Talk-n-Angels*.

"Do you believe in Angels?" he asked in such a way that I got the feeling he was questioning whether his company should continue to do business with me.

I understood his concern, but I also knew the reality of what I was living.

"David," I answered. "I believe in Wingmen." *Wingmen*, I understood. And Angels were great Wingmen.

That was the first time I had used the word *Wingmen* when describing angels. And from there, the term Wingman just took off.

> The term wingman originated, at least in modern times, from the United States Airforce. Originally, the word referred to the pilot of the plane flying next to, but slightly behind the lead plane in the traditional V-formation. That pilot would be on the lookout for any trouble the lead pilot wouldn't be able to see as easily. In today's more modern lexicon, the word wingman is used to describe someone who is helping his or her friend in whatever situation that may arise, often social. I still remember my daughter, when going out one evening with her friend, proudly proclaiming, "I'm the wingman tonight," which meant she was going to help her friend meet new boys.
>
> Regardless of how you look at it, a wingman helps another to be successful on their chosen mission. A wingman is someone who has your back.

Wingman can be defined a few different ways, but my favorite definition comes from my friend and mentor, Dr. Bernie Siegel. Bernie is the best-selling author of *Love, Medicine and Miracles* (among other books), a spiritual guru, and a retired surgeon. He has helped millions of terminally ill patients take control of their lives with the healing power that stems from the human mind.

I was fortunate to meet Bernie when Rita and I had interviewed him on the show. While looking at his bio, I realized he lived in the same town as my sister. We became friendly enough after the show that whenever I would visit my sister, which was often, I would visit with him. One time, as we were taking a walk with his dogs around his neighborhood, he looked at me and said, "Mike, do you know what a Wingman is?"

Smiling, because I was certain I knew of every possible definition, I replied, "Yes, Bernie I—"

I never got to finish because it quickly became obvious he'd asked a rhetorical question.

"A wingman," Bernie explained, "is an angel in heaven with only one wing, who grasps onto another one-winged angel, so they can then fly together."

Wow! Didn't expect that one.

What I found even more unexpected came three days later. I had returned home and was flipping through the sports section of my newspaper when I came upon my horoscope. Now, although I love reading the sports section, I rarely read my horoscope. But this caught my eye:

> **Sometimes you feel like a one-winged creature looking for another one-winged creature to fly with. But you really do have two wings. You just need a teacher who can give you flying tips.**

My horoscope, coming on the heels of Bernie's words, certainly seemed like a message. Although I wasn't quite sure what it meant. So I decided to go where I always go when I'm looking for clarity: to my wife, Janet. I showed her my horoscope and recalled Bernie's interesting Wingman definition.

She thought for a moment and then gave me her interpretation. "Before you began on your Wingman's Path, you would often defer to others—what *they* thought, what *they* wanted, what *they* felt. Rather than take responsibility and have faith in yourself and your own judgments and decisions, you would look to others, instead of within yourself. You often didn't trust yourself to fly solo. Maybe you felt like you only had one wing, and therefore could only fly by embracing another. You have now truly become what you have set out to be, your own Wingman. But, like many of us, you still fall back on old habits such as the thought that you need another to 'fly,' but you no longer do. Perhaps, it is time to recognize, as your horoscope points out, you really do have two wings. You just need someone to remind you every now and then."

How about that? It was like Glenda, the good witch from Oz, telling Dorothy she could have gone home anytime. But just like Dorothy, I had to learn it on my own by following my own Yellow Brick Road, my Wingman's Path.

How about you? Do you sometimes fall back into old, insecure, and limited thinking and forget you have two wings? We all do. Being your own Wingman means you trust in the decisions you make, and you have confidence in your ability to create the life you want to live, even though it doesn't always adhere to the expectations of others. Don't get me wrong, we can all use and value the physical Wingmates in our lives, whether they're male or female. We can always, always use a good Wingmate in our lives. But, like my horoscope suggested, and the Wingman's Path has taught me, I *can* fly solo. I can create my own happiness, and I can feel confident in whatever path I choose.

A few years later, Jan and I decided to practice what we preach. We sold our house and were going forth on an adventure traveling and living around the world. I let fear and doubt creep in more and more frequently as we planned on becoming nomads and taking off on our big journey. My vibration took a hit. (Yes, even having been on the Wingman's Path for many years, I still allow fear and convention to take over once in a while.)

So, there I was, clearing everything out of my home office, looking for some divine sign that I was making the right choice. We were moving all our stuff to a storage facility, and as I was cleaning out my desk, I reached up to a shelf well above me. I pulled out reams of paper, and a tiny bag, no bigger than 2 inches, came falling to the ground. Tumbling out of the bag was a very small ceramic angel I didn't know I even had. As the bag floated to the floor, the angel hit my desk, and one of the angel's wings broke off. I picked it up and smiled; I had my sign. There, in my hand, was a one-winged angel. Happily, I knew how easy it was to make it, like me, whole again. Glue for it, focus for me. I just needed a little time back on the Wingman's Path.

A Wingman Practice:

I'm on the Path

For a full minute, repeat: "I'm on the Wingman's Path to positivity, to raising my vibration, and to creating a life of my choosing."

As I completed my preparations to start the new era of my life as a nomad, those words became my tagline. I say them every day as I video a practice and welcome people to the Wingman's Path. I've noticed every time I say these words, I'm smiling. And when I'm smiling, I'm always feeling better, which always means a higher vibration.

Try it! As you say it, imagine walking joyfully toward the life of your choosing. Practice the feeling of knowing you are on your way.

9
A Wingman Minute

Doing the radio show was like finding a friend to join you on a great adventure. I was rooted on the Wingman's Path now, and I had Rita as a wonderful Wingmate. Each week would bring something new, an original idea for improving my spirituality or learning more about how to manifest any desires I might have.

I couldn't wait for Wednesday nights. I would start preparing for the show each Tuesday, always excited to talk with Rita and our listeners. Unfortunately, my self-discipline during the rest of the week still needed some work.

"Ask, and it is given." And so I did. I was looking for something to elevate my consistency, and once again, the Universe delivered, this time with both barrels providing two answers to make sure I received the message.

The first answer arrived on the radio show. We would often be asked by publishers to interview authors who had just finished a new book. One of them was Donald Altman, a psychotherapist and former Buddhist monk who had just released his book entitled, *One Minute-Mindfulness*. Rita had received his book before the interview and gave it to me to read after our conversation. Although I thoroughly enjoyed our conversation, and the idea of practicing for only one minute was certainly appealing to me, the book ended up on my nightstand waiting to be read. Every once in a while, I'd find myself flipping through it.

Somehow, the idea got into my subconscious. Perhaps it was through osmosis, most likely from reading the cover, *One Minute Mindfulness*, over and over as I would get in bed each night, but I began to think about the concept of practicing for just one minute every single day. Could one minute make that much of a difference?

And then the Universe delivered the second answer on Super Bowl Sunday. I'm a big fan of professional football, and I always look forward to the Super Bowl. But I never go to Super Bowl parties. I like to focus on the game without a lot of distractions, and I love the commercials! As you probably know, many companies bring out new commercials during the Super Bowl. But if you're at a party, that's often the time most people like to chat. Not me, I'm a Super Bowl commercial nerd.

It was a great game that year, coming down to the last two minutes. But despite the intrigue of the game, the commercials are what really captured my attention. For it was on that day that the power of a minute really clicked for me. I realized every commercial, every single one of them, all advertising for one of the most successful businesses of our time, each from the biggest and best-known companies spending millions and millions of dollars, each one lasted one minute or less. Sixty seconds was the maximum length.

It got me thinking about these businesses and advertising as a whole. Here they were, looking to grab my attention for just one minute, in the hopes that when I bought my next beer, car, snack, computer, dinner, or whatever, I'll purchase their product. In only a minute! And that's where I connected the dots back to Altman's book. These wonderfully prosperous companies were spending millions of dollars to appeal to my conscious mind for only one minute, in the hopes of getting into my subconscious mind forever.

And they were very successful at doing so.

Now, I'm not a scientist or a mathematician, but I do understand probabilities. And with these commercials being hugely efficient, and with every great master telling me that what I think about I become, I reasoned it would be wise for me to practice thinking positive thoughts for one minute a day at least.

In fact, I decided right then and there, that I should do my own commercials. I should deliberately set aside one minute every day to think a thought that would be beneficial for me. A thought that would help me be more positive. I would use that minute to get that thought into my subconscious.

I could do that. Or so I thought.

I quickly learned that even when trying to focus on a single thought for just one minute, I could be distracted by many other different thoughts. The commercials on television definitely kept my attention better than the commercials in my own head. I was like that dog in the animated movie *Up*, the one who gets distracted easily and exclaims, "Squirrel!" I couldn't believe I wasn't able to do it. I mean really, it was just one minute and one thought.

But it was so difficult to hold onto that one positive thought that I started doing some research. Boy, was I surprised! No one knows how many thoughts we have in a day, but everyone agrees it's a lot. According to the National Science Foundation, we have about 50,000. And the folks at the Laboratory of Neuroimaging, University of Southern California think it's closer to 70,000. Regardless, of who is right, that's a lot of thoughts in one day!

I didn't think I had 150.

Now supposedly, 95% of those 50,000 to 70,000 thoughts are exactly the same thoughts we thought yesterday, and—what is most fascinating to me—about 80% of our thoughts are negative.

Wow!

That means, for most people, on average, only 20% of our thoughts are positive, and the other 80% are negative ones we keep repeating day in and day out.

I understood why it was awfully difficult for me to get some positive momentum going: four out of five thoughts in my brain were negative!

We have met the enemy, and he is us.
~Pogo

Awfully difficult, but not impossible.

Here's what I wound up doing: I decided to pick a positive thought to repeat, then set my timer to one minute. I called it my *practice.*

In the beginning, as I would say the words and think the thought, negative thoughts would flood my mind. Of course, they would! If, on average, 80% of all our thoughts are negative, that meant for every positive thought I had, four negative thoughts would come back to me. And in those beginning days, that's how it seemed to work. It went something like this inside my head:

I can do this.
No, you can't.
You're just going to quit.
You've tried before and failed.
Don't be a putz.
You are a putz.
What's for dinner?

On and on it went.

However, I kept at it. I would take my cell phone, click on the clock, and go to the timer, then set it for one minute and see if I could focus on the same positive thought the whole time. Most of the time, I couldn't make the full minute. Guess what? It didn't matter. The fact that I was practicing was all that mattered.

Let me repeat, *the fact that I was practicing was all that mattered.*

But then I realized the more I practiced, the longer I could hold onto those positive thoughts. First, it was just five seconds, then ten seconds, then fifteen, then twenty, then thirty...And pretty soon, I was able to do it! I could keep my focus on one positive thought for one full minute. I'd high-five myself each time I did it.

I was so excited, I played with the math. Let's say I was on the low end of thoughts each day—something my wife might agree with—and I averaged 50,000 thoughts. By practicing for just one minute, I was increasing the number of positive thoughts I was having, and thereby decreasing the number of negative thoughts. If I started with 40,000 negative thoughts and 10,000 positive thoughts, maybe tomorrow I could have 10,500 positive thoughts, and only 39,500 negative ones. And on and on until I reached what Malcolm Gladwell calls the tipping point. Sooner or later, I would reach the juncture where I would have more positive thoughts than negative thoughts.

Now that's a thought worth thinking!

I can't tell you how this could be scientifically measured, but I can tell you that's how I experienced it. And it felt great.

A Wingman Practice:

Practice Being Positive

For one minute, say out loud or to yourself: "I can practice being positive for one minute each day."

Try to tap into the belief that you can practice being positive for one minute each day as you repeat it. Saying this over and over will assist you in believing in yourself and your ability to stay on the Wingman's Path. As you do, you will notice improved confidence in your ability to focus.

10
Congratulations to Me!

I was feeling pretty proud of myself. I knew I had just come up with a big piece of the puzzle. I had a plan. Even better, it was a simple plan: for one minute each day, I would practice being positive. It seemed very wise to me to have created a well-organized plan to break down my mission of spiritual enlightenment into one-minute practices. I felt so smart. And I knew this strategy would enable me to stay disciplined, focused, and consistent.

Accept the challenges so that you can feel the exhilaration of victory.
Attributed to George S. Patton

I called these daily practices my Wingman Minutes because they always connected me with a higher vibration; they always helped. I felt the exhilaration of victory, one minute at a time, each time.

Yes, my vibration was improving daily, maybe not by leaps and bounds, but I had now found a method of continuously moving forward. I acknowledged to myself that I would not be able to go from pissed to blissed immediately, but as long as I was moving in the right direction, I felt pleased. Pleased with my progress, pleased with myself, and pleased with the world.

The force was with me.

Congratulations to me.

I felt so good about myself that after my morning walk one day, I started saying, "Congratulations to me." I congratulated myself for some of the recent positives in my life:

Doing my daily Wingman Minute practices.
Overcoming so many challenges.
Physically exercising.

A good business meeting I had the day before.
Eating healthy for the past few days.

And then I continued by stating congratulations over and over for anything and everything.

Waking up.
Taking my dog for our morning walk.
Drinking water.
Filling my car up with gas.
Brushing my teeth.
Eating something that wasn't healthy but tasted great.
Being on time for an appointment.
Breathing.

Each and every thing, whether it was big or small, I congratulated myself for doing it. It felt great.

Then one day, on another morning after I had finished my walk, I started doing some physical exercises in a pavilion in front of the woods. Seeing as there were no cars in the parking lot, and I thought I was by myself, I started screaming, "Congratulations" at the top of my lungs. I quickly recognized how wonderful it felt to do a Wingman Minute out loud.

Unexpectedly, a woman then walked out of the woods about 25 feet from me. Feeling a tinged embarrassed, I quickly yelled my apologies and continued my practices in a quieter mode. She didn't answer, and I couldn't think of anything I might say at that moment that would make a difference, so I said nothing. I did note to myself that when doing these practices, while it could be beneficial doing them out loud, it might be best if I did them when I was by myself.

I finished up both my physical exercise and my Wingman practices and got in my car. As I proceeded down the long driveway out of the park, I saw a friend walking up. He's a child psychiatrist, and we often talk about different techniques to practice positivity. He took off his headphones as I approached, so I slowed to a stop and opened my passenger-side window.

"I just want you to know," he said. "I've been forewarned; there's a crazy person up there."

"Guilty as charged!" I responded, and we both had a good laugh.

I once again reminded myself: in the future, make certain I'm alone when doing any of my practices out loud.

Later that evening, when Jan and I were going to a party, we were perfectly on time. I said, "Congratulations, we're perfectly on time." She gave me a wifely eye roll—you know the one: it basically says, *Are you kidding me?*

Now usually, when I'm on the receiving end of an eye roll, it's with good reason. However, this time I explained how I'd been saying congratulations about anything and everything because it kept my vibration moving higher and higher. Even these small, little, no big deal, being on time accomplishments were to be congratulated.

Especially these small, little, no big deal, being on time accomplishments. It's the small ones that help you consistently build up momentum.

That next Monday, I was doing a presentation to a small business and mentioned my new practice of self-congratulations. They loved it. We ended the event by walking around for five minutes congratulating each other and ourselves. The energy in the room increased by leaps and bounds, and I knew I had taken a big step along the Wingman's Path.

A Wingman Practice:

Congratulations

For one minute, say out loud, if you're by yourself, or quietly to yourself if not: "Congratulations!"

Think of any successes you've had recently. It could be something you've accomplished at work, or even just the fact that you woke up and brushed your teeth. The point is that while saying, "congratulations," you practice that feeling of completing a job well done. That's the frequency you want to be emitting out into the Universe.

Just the word *Congratulations* has very high vibrational powers. Even if you're not feeling it, say it anyway for the one minute. Remember, neuroscience tells us you don't have to believe it, you just have to say it, and your brain will wrap around it, and slip this vibration into your subconscious.

11
Boys' Weekend

I was feeling pretty good. And the more I found to congratulate myself for, the better I felt. Although I was still struggling financially, I was proud of myself for not letting it get me down. I knew I was on the path to better days.

So, it was in that frame of mind that I was getting together with a group of my high school buddies. One of my friends had a cabin at Elk Mountain, up near Scranton, Pennsylvania, and eight of us, friends since high school, were heading there for a guys' weekend. We were all looking forward to skiing, hanging out, watching football, playing some poker, and just catching up.

It's amazing that we'd been able to stay connected for so long—we'd managed to remain friends for almost 40 years. Through marriages, children, and business successes, we'd been there for all the fun times. That's when it's easy to stay friends: when everyone's feeling like a winner. But these friendships have endured tougher times as well: funerals, sicknesses, divorces, lost jobs, and business failures. Those are the times when friendships are tested, and bonds are either strengthened...or broken.

We'd been together long enough that when someone would say something that pissed you off, you give him some leeway. You let things go. Even though we didn't all share the same beliefs or ideas, the old familiarities reminded us to be a little more open, a little more understanding of what each of us had been through. We could see life through each other's eyes, which is certainly easier to do when you're in a good place, when the space between your ears is feeling peaceful.

And as I said, I was in a pretty good place.

I was driving up with my buddy Al. Al was a good friend who had jumped around from job to job until about five years previously. It was then that he found a business and began to flourish. And I mean *flourish*.

We were two hours into the drive, about halfway there, when Al dropped a bombshell. "Dude, I just got a check yesterday for $1,000,000."

A million dollars! I heard those words, and for the next minute, I heard nothing more. I felt the green-eyed monster of jealousy rise up inside me. I let Al's success bring me right back to my perceived failures. Despite his joy, I wanted to kick the door open and immediately go hide and lick my wounded pride. But, being that we were going 70 miles per hour on I-95, all I could do was sit there and pretend to be a good friend.

As soon as he said it, my first reaction was: *Why not me? I want a million dollars.* But then I immediately thought of the commandment, *Thou shalt not covet thy neighbor's goods.*

There was no question I was covetous though, and the energy I was sending out was one of envy. Thankfully, I'd become much quicker at recognizing my vibrational changes and understood the implications of my bitterness. I knew if I didn't change how I was feeling, I was certain the Universe would, as always, match the frequency I was emanating and send back more for me to feel envious about. Since I was going to be spending the weekend with my old friends, many of whom were very successful, I knew I had to change that vibration quickly, or my fun weekend with friends would soon collapse under the weight of my negative energy.

So here's what I did: I celebrated Al. I celebrated his joy at receiving a million-dollar check.

Yes, my eyes were green with jealousy. Here I was looking for work, struggling to pay my mortgage, and my friend had seemingly struck pay dirt. Celebrating his joy was not going to be easy. But I knew it was necessary in order to change my vibration. Because here's the thing: when you're covetous, it means you're experiencing lack and unfulfilled desires. And so the Universe sends you back more lack, more to feel resentful about. But if I could somehow practice feeling his elation, practice sending out a sentiment of pure joy for him, then the Universe would respond in kind and send me back more to be joyous about.

Had the conversation happened a year prior, I would have fallen into a dark place. After my previously mentioned financial failures, anytime I heard about another's financial success, my vibe would tank. Immediately. I'd feel like a failure, crawl into my bed, and not come out for a week. And when I did, I would snap at my wife, kick the dog, and just been an all-around miserable guy to be near.

Instead of going down that rabbit hole, I asked Al what he was going to do with the money. He said one fourth would go to meet payroll, one fourth to paying off business loans, one fourth to pay off his mortgage and his two sons' college loans, and one fourth to savings.

As he spoke, I could feel his relief, his gratitude, and his bliss, so that is where I started my celebration.

I practiced the feeling of how relieved he felt to be able to meet his payroll.

I practiced the feeling of how thankful he seemed to be able to pay off all his business and personal loans.

I sensed his exuberance at putting so much money in savings.

And I practiced feeling his joy. The feeling did not come to me easily. That's why I call it practice, because it takes work to change a vibration. But work I did. And I could feel my energy shift, ever so slightly.

That was cool. I recognized the power of my vibration and embraced the challenge of taking back control of my life by controlling how I responded to things. I detected a smile creeping across my face. Oh yeah, this was definitely a Wingman Minute practice.

The rest of the ride seemed to fly by. The traffic opened up, we quieted down, and I continued to practice feeling Al's happiness at receiving the check.

When we got to the house, I had bounced back and was again in a really good place. We were the last to arrive, and it was great being among old friends. But unfortunately, I had more work to do. Everyone seemed to have something I desired. A great job, beautiful cars, vacation homes, great health, wonderful relationships with their spouses and children. The list went on and on, and I could perceive my jealousy starting to wrangle its way back into my thoughts. Hmmm. This practice wasn't going to be easy. I could tell this one would take some continued effort.

We drank, watched movies, and played poker deep into the night. Eventually, I fell asleep on the couch in the living room. I woke up before anyone else and went for a morning walk. As I was trekking through the cold frozen woods around the house that morning, I deliberately thought of each friend, and individually celebrated him by reflecting on something positive about him.

Don't get me wrong; my friends are not Mother Teresas. Like all of us, they can be a pain in the ass at times. And there are certainly things about each of them that irritate me, just as I am sure there are things about me they think are a pain in the ass and irritating. But that morning's practice wasn't about the negatives; it was about focusing on the positives, about feeling the love for them.

And so the love I felt. As I walked, I would deliberate on each friend and come up with something I could praise:
- How he built a life around his strengths.
- How he has a great relationship with his children.
- How he never gets rattled and sees the good in each of us.
- How he's living life on his terms.
- How tough he is and how he's made it through some difficult times.
- How he always comes up with a new idea, and always keeps moving forward.
- How great it was that he has a new job and was making good money.

Talk about raising your vibration! I felt great! My energy was high, and my heart was full. I started thinking...what would it feel like if we did this all the time? If we did it with our kids, our spouses, our co-workers, our in-laws, our neighbors, and anyone else who crosses our path?

> **Everything is energy and that's all there is to it. Match the frequency of the reality you want and you cannot help but get that reality. It can be no other way. This is not philosophy. This is physics.**
> ~Darryl Anka – Bashar
> "Ides of March"

A Wingman Practice:

Celebrate Others

Start with someone you know, you like, and who has something you desire. It can be a friend, a relative, or even a co-worker. What does that person have that brings up a jealous feeling in you? Maybe it's the perfect family, a loving spouse, a wonderful job, great health, or financial security. Who it is, is not important. Whatever it is, is not important. That you raise your vibration by thinking of their joy at having it, is.

Eliminate your jealousy by celebrating their happiness at having it. Practice the sensation of experiencing their pleasure, gratitude, and bliss and feeling really joyous for them. Repeat positive statements like: "I love that Joe has his dream job. I love that he feels secure and empowered to follow his dreams." And practice emitting out into the Universe those feelings.

It might take some time, but the more you practice rejoicing in their elation, the more your feelings of resentment will dissipate, and the more you will be producing a vibration of pure joy.

Then, as you change the energy you emanate out into the Universe, from one of jealousy to one of pure joy, the Universe will match it and begin to send you back reasons to feel joy as opposed to more reasons to feel envious.

12
Mea Culpa

What a great step I had just taken. Celebrating others became my go-to practice. It was so easy. Wherever I was, I would look for someone who had something I desired, and I would celebrate them. It seemed so simple. However, I soon learned that jealousy is an emotion that rises quickly within me. Before I even recognize it sometimes, I'm emitting a covetous frequency, one that rapidly drives my vibration straight into a negative rabbit hole.

Literally, it was the following week after my Boys' Weekend that the green-eyed monster visited me again. It was as if the Universe wanted to make certain I absorbed my lesson by pounding it into my head. And then for good measure, threw in a bit of public embarrassment. I learned that replacing feelings of envy with feelings of celebration for others would take time to master. Oh, and that I better practice.

It started on the Monday night after my Boys' Weekend, when I attended a Law of Attraction workshop in New York City. I had been to it a few years earlier, before I had discovered my path. It was mobbed back then, with about 70 to 80 people there, and it had felt too touchy-feely for me during that first visit. But, now that I had been building my own group, I decided it would be wise to go back. After all, Craig, the gentleman who runs it, must be doing something right to have such a good following.

This time, there were about 50 people in attendance. All practicing being positive. It was beautiful. The only problem was me.

I had timed my day terribly and got stuck in New York City traffic. My hour-and-a-half ride took close to four hours. I came in with attitude, and it wasn't an attitude of gratitude.

I was pissy. So much so, that between my outlook and my concern about the traffic, I left a bit early. My poor planning had put a damper on the whole experience.

Over the next few days, though, I realized how much I had gained from Craig's meeting. I had a good positive feeling from it, and I also got a few ideas and practices I could utilize with my people.

What could be bad, right? Seemed like a win-win all around.

Except, as co-host of the *Talk-n-Angels* radio show on Wednesday evening, I mentioned, I didn't like it on air. And while we weren't Oprah, we did have a following. My comments were just plain wrong. And I heard about it from some listeners, including Craig.

Here's a man who was helping people, successfully doing workshops, and I was being negative. What I realized after the fact was... it wasn't "it" I didn't like. It was me.

I was jealous of Craig, and his very successful event. And I felt bad about feeling jealous. Then I felt worse because I had said something unkind about a nice man doing wonderful work—on the radio. Talk about a buzz kill.

Of course, I emailed my apologies and mentioned my *mea culpa* on the show the following week. But I still found myself going back to it, like a scab you can't stop picking. I was no longer bothered by my jealousy. I was upset that I had allowed it to affect my behavior in such a pitiful way. I couldn't get away from it and kept beating myself up about it, which was just killing my vibration.

So I asked: "What would my Wingman say?"

But I didn't need my Inner Wingman to answer this question. I responded to myself, "Change your focus. Move on. Put it behind you."

Hmmm. Easier said than done.

Though, I made changing my focus and putting the incident behind me my goal. I knew what needed to be done as a first step. After all, I had just learned *that* lesson one week prior. I immediately began celebrating Craig and his joy at running such a successful event. How fun it must be to run such a great meeting filled with positive energy. And run it so well that everyone, even someone who left pissy and irritated from his meeting, benefitted.

I was celebrating Craig, feeling his joy when the Universe tapped me on the shoulder and asked, "Can you take it one step further?"

"Can I take it one step further?" I asked. "Take what one step further?"

The very next thought in my head concerned the Law of Attraction, and it made me question: does my being at Craig's meeting where he had 50 people, mean I'm closer to my having my own meetup having 50 people?

Whoa! Way Cool!

I celebrated me: me being in the presence of something I wanted. Doesn't that make sense? Perhaps it was a bit of a stretch, but I started practicing the idea anyway. The more I practiced it, the more I believed it.

I had just added a second part to my celebration practice. How awesome is that? Not only was I now celebrating Craig's joy at having a successful meeting, but I also celebrated that by my being there, I was that much closer to having my own successful meeting.

Two celebrations for the price of one. Talk about a win-win.

And then, I added a third win. I thought back to my buddy Al, and his million-dollar check. I thought about our drive, and that by him being a close friend of mine, and me being with him the same day he received that check, I was that much closer to my own million-dollar check.

Wow! That was definitely the frequency I wanted to be emitting out into the Universe. A feeling of knowing a million dollars was coming my way.

Why?

Because when you match the vibration of your desire, it becomes your reality.

It seems so easy. But even as I practiced celebrating Craig, Al, and myself, negative energy seeped in. It was difficult to let go of how disappointed I was in myself regarding how I acted toward Craig, and I had a hard time really believing a million dollars was coming my way. But I continued to practice consciously for one minute every day. And soon I noticed with each practice, I felt a little better.

I continued practicing by thinking of Craig, rejoicing in his joy from having such a fabulous Law of Attraction meeting, and of Al, and his check. And I learned something new in the process: by celebrating another's victories, I stop resisting my own.

It's now easier for me, not easy, but easier, to see someone who is happy, or has something I desire, to celebrate him or her. That way, I instantly begin to match the frequency of the reality I desire. However, I haven't completely eliminated my jealous feelings. They still come up, and when they do, they hit quickly, and they hit hard. But I now have a tool to combat the energy that in the past would have dropped me into an emotional tizzy, where the vibration I was sending out was dreadful. It definitely takes practice. And so I do.

Give it a try today. This practice will speed up your progress by helping you stop any negative vibrations you are sending out around jealousy.

A Wingman Practice:

Celebrate Others, Part 2

Celebrate the fact that you know people who have what you want. Cherish the fact that via the Law of Attraction, what you desire is now on its way to you. Focus on that happy feeling and practice sending that energy out into the Universe for one minute.

Interestingly, I no longer use the word *jealous*. It's a negative word that brings up negative feelings. Instead of saying, even jokingly to a friend, "I'm jealous of you," I say instead, "I celebrate you." I urge you to give it a try.

13
Father's Day

My *Celebrate Others* practice took me to a new level in my quest for spiritual evolvement. Everywhere I went, and everyone I saw, I would practice it by looking for something I would like and then praising it. I would celebrate that person's joy in having it, and I would celebrate my being close to it, which meant via the Law of Attraction, it was on its way to me. The practice felt wonderful and made for an awesome winter.

The following spring went by quickly. My journey seemed easy, as I constantly found someone to celebrate. Jealousy still reared its ugly head from time to time, but I was amazed at how adept I became at eliminating that destructive reaction.

In general, I was operating on a higher frequency. When something happened that turned my mood downward, I found myself bouncing back a bit quicker. I was feeling so good, I wanted to test the waters more. Yes, I was creating a happier life, but I wanted more. I started visualizing the possibilities of designing a life of my choosing. I would often ask myself, "What do I want to do with the rest of my life?" and I allowed myself to believe anything I wanted would be feasible.

With Father's Day approaching, I decided to experiment and set my intention to have a fantastic Father's Day. As I'd been fighting a bit with my son, I thought that was a reasonable goal. So I practiced by imagining having dinner where he, my daughter, and I would be laughing together. I remained consistent in my positivity practice, believing I could achieve anything I desired, and it worked. One thing led to another, and my vision of a nice Father's Day expanded and manifested into a sensational Father's Day week.

It began with my son calling and asking me to fly out to Los Angeles with him. He intended to take film classes at UCLA while finding a job and an opportunity to build his life there.

I'd found the Wingman's Path to be filled with practices on being a better Wingman to myself and to others. But not really to my son. My son and I had not always seen eye to eye, and often, in my disagreements with him, I'd learned some valuable lessons—like patience. Most of the time, his thinking seemed extremely flawed to me, and when I'd offer to help, he would decline loudly. At times, I'd get so frustrated, I'd just want "to smack some sense into him" metaphorically. So the idea that I could support him at such an exciting time in his life was especially gratifying for me, and the fact that it was happening the week of Father's Day made it even more special.

The second amazing manifestation for my Father's Day week happened after I left my son in LA. I flew up to San Francisco to have breakfast with Susan Ariel Rainbow Kennedy, better known as SARK. Susan is a best-selling author and one of the world's best visionary and transformational leaders. Now she is also someone I call a friend and mentor. But back then, I barely knew her. We'd first met when Rita and I interviewed her on our radio show after she wrote her book, *Glad No Matter What.* Later, I met her in New York when I attended one of her workshops. Since I was going to be in California, I thought it would be fun to meet up with her there. So, I sent her an email seeing if she was available and she was.

I remember thinking, could it really be this easy? Oh yeah...ask, and it is given. She was available and happy to meet me for breakfast!

Phase three of my dream Father's Day week had me attending the World Series of Poker in Las Vegas, which had been a life-long dream of my brother's and mine. My brother and I had always discussed going but never got around to it. He passed away about eight years prior, but I knew he would be there with me in spirit, and I was looking forward to feeling his presence. I had chills thinking about him and me in Las Vegas. I could feel myself winning the tournament. Playing in the World Series of Poker had long been on my bucket list, and I was now fulfilling that dream.

The week went beautifully. My time with my son was fantastic. We set up his apartment, leased him a car, and got him registered for classes at UCLA. In between, we talked warmly and checked out some of the fun sites.

I then flew up to San Francisco for my breakfast with SARK. The reality of sitting at an outdoor café, speaking about the Law of Attraction with her, had me smiling ear to ear. We discussed how words could help me change how I feel about any given situation, and how I feel about said situation would determine the outcome.

My vibration could not have been higher as I boarded the plane to Las Vegas.

As I stepped onto the plane, I felt an odd sensation. Maybe it was the whole Father's Day week, but I felt my father around me. It was a strange feeling, made even more so, when, at the moment I arrived at my seat, there sitting face up, was a $.25 piece, a quarter. Whenever I see a quarter in a strange location, I think of my dad. It started one day when I was walking in the woods. For some reason, I was thinking of my dad, or actually, it was more like I felt his presence, and when I looked down, there was a $.25 piece right in the middle of a dirt trail. While we didn't have the closest relationship back when I was younger and he was alive, I am thankful for his presence and appreciate him being in my life now.

So it was no real surprise when, as I dozed off to the Allman Brother's "Mountain Jam," that in my slumber, I received the following message from my Dad:

> "You're doing great," he said. "They [my children] can handle life. You're doing great. Don't worry so much about it. You pushed my buttons just like yours are now being pushed. And then you blow up and move on. Focus on how you've helped and what you've learned. It's now time for you to move on. Think about where you are right now and how much you now understand. It seems a great deal more than before.
>
> "Be thankful for that. Be appreciative of that, and enjoy everything you've now learned. Keep practicing as best you can. Don't stop because something gets in your way. There is nothing wrong with taking a break from it. There is nothing wrong with feeling bad. As a matter of fact, feeling bad can be a great day. It can help you think about what you really want and help provide real clarity. Focus. Enjoy it.
>
> "Don't get so tied up and wrapped up and worried about it. Enjoy what happens, and keep on practicing to be the person, or better, the Wingman you want to be. By the way, I love the Wingman. Great idea for helping you get clarity on helping others. Keep helping, it will not only help you be happy, but will help others be happy as well. Just keep practicing being a Wingman.

"Look for progress, not perfection. Practice asking *How can I help you?* Those five words will get you started on a beautiful path, and you will not believe how happy you can be. How can I help you? It's as simple as that."

Talk about shifting your perspective! It couldn't have happened at a worse time.

From the moment I landed, I was unable to focus on playing poker.

Flying back from Vegas broke, busted, and feeling just plain beat up, I was in no mood to discuss the Law of Attraction and its many merits. I was far from *Glad No Matter What* (SARK's book title), nor did I want to think any positive thoughts. I was down, depressed, and disappointed. I was so certain I was going to win my way into the World Series of Poker. I couldn't believe I was flying home broke.

Any brilliant words of wisdom for me now, Dad? I thought to myself with dripping sarcasm. I was pissed. *If you can communicate with me when I was flying out here, why couldn't you help me out at the tables?*

Closing my eyes, trying to sleep, I thought back to those words: "There is nothing wrong with feeling bad. As a matter of fact, feeling bad can be a great day. It can help you think about what you really want and help provide real clarity. Focus. Enjoy it."

What I really wanted was to punch someone in the face. What I really wanted was to have won a bunch of money. What I really wanted was to throw up and forget the entire week.

And that's when it hit me: what I got was a real opportunity to learn. I received the lesson I'd been preaching but obviously hadn't been learning.

It's easy to talk about changing your thoughts and shifting your attitude when things are going your way. It's when you feel like I did at that moment, on my flight home from Las Vegas, that requires real practice. And let's face it; this wasn't anything really serious, such as the death of a loved one, the breaking up of a family, or a severe illness. It was just a loss of money.

I was the self-proclaimed poster boy for the Law of Attraction. Friends had told me I inspired them by living it. Yet there I was, allowing a situation to make me a victim. Instead of thinking about my fantastic week, I was focused on my miserable ending.

"But Master," I said out loud, "If I can create that entire week, why can't I create my desired ending?"

"Ah, Grasshopper, if you created the entire week, then didn't you, in fact, create the ending?"

I had to admit I created the ending. I had arrived in Vegas unable to keep my focus on winning. And I never got my focus back on winning. So, I lost, big time.

Or did I?

It was right then and there, 30,000 feet up, I found the positive in my getting crushed and destroyed on the green felt tables of my dreams.

> **The only person you are destined to become is the person you decide to be.**
> ~attributed to Ralph Waldo Emerson

I had always hoped and expected poker would be my destiny. But at that moment, I conceded I was wrong. Right then and there, my true purpose revealed itself to me. My objective was clear: I had found the Wingman's Path to winning the Spiritual Lottery, and now I would help others find their way to the Wingman's Path. I would help others achieve their goals, release their pain, and be happier. With that as my purpose, I had to remain on the path so I could teach, while I continued to learn the Wingman positivity practices that would lead to my spiritual evolvement.

And one of those lessons was happening right then: it was to recognize that you must persist in practicing even when, especially when, life is kicking you in the stomach, and all you want to do is crawl under a rock and lick your wounds (which is the exact place I wanted to be).

With perfect timing, an exercise I had read about in SARK's *Glad No Matter What* book popped into my head. Hmmm....how synchronistic.

SARK had described it as Pollyanna's "Glad Game," from Eleanor H. Porter's classic, best-selling 1913 novel, *Pollyanna*. I changed it slightly and named it *High Five*. It's simple. You make a list of the five best things from the previous 24 hours, or in this case, the prior week. Even if you're currently not in a good place, you do the practice nonetheless. Maybe you can only come up with three things that weren't terrible. Whatever, you still do the practice.

Why?

Because it gets your mind moving in a more positive direction, and keeps you advancing on the Wingman's Path to positivity, to raising your vibration, and to creating a life of your choosing.

As my plane descended into Philadelphia, I contemplated my High Five from my Father's Day week:

1) Spending time with my son and helping him get set up in Los Angeles. I had been able to see life through his eyes as he moved on his own to a new city for the first time. While he was nervous and excited, I only felt his excitement.
2) Having breakfast with SARK at the precise moment my son called to tell me about hitting a pole with his car—the same pole I had repeatedly warned him about. The timing couldn't have been better, as SARK and I had been discussing Law of Attraction, and I realized how my constant reminders to my son may have actually helped create him hitting that pole.
3) Searching for and finding the lesson in the darkness, for when I can learn something in my failures, they become my successes.
4) Understanding that I created this entire week, which demonstrates that I can create anything I desire.
5) Proving to myself that because I could practice at that moment, for even just one minute, was evidence that I could accomplish anything I set my mind to.

As I contemplated my top five, my list expanded to include one more: I now had a purpose and a worthwhile ambition to focus on.

A Wingman Practice:

High Five

High Five! Think of the best five things from your past 24 hours. If need be, stretch your time limit. Or, if things are currently going poorly, come up with three things that weren't lousy. The objective here is to get you thinking about your situation in a more positive way. Then the more you focus on the positives, the more momentum you'll gain, and you'll realize you have even more good things to focus on.

Now that's worthy of a High Five.

14
The Summer of My Discontent

I loved my new High Five practice. Each morning, as I walked with Monty, I would think about the previous day and try to come up with five things I was happy about or thankful for. Despite that, I could not shake the disappointment of my Las Vegas experience. It cast a pall over my summer. It didn't make sense to me. I had created a fabulous week, one where I had spent time with my son, had breakfast with SARK, and played poker in Las Vegas during the World Series of Poker.

I even found my wonderful purpose. I should have been on top of the world. But I wasn't.

I had been so certain I would win my way into the tournament, make it to the final table, and then win a great deal of money. I had felt prepared and confident. My desire was clear and undeniable. But it didn't happen. I couldn't accept that it was just because I'd lost focus. I couldn't understand why I couldn't get it back and win.

My daily practices were helping, but there was no denying my displeasure over losing. Sure, I had found my purpose. But after a while, I began to think that wasn't reason enough. Truth be told, I don't think I was completely ready to give up on my dream of winning the World Series of Poker. Or possibly, I didn't want to admit I wasn't quite good enough at the game of poker. Or maybe it was simpler than that? Maybe it was just that I had lost a bunch of money, and I was pissed.

I think it was a combination of all three. Poster boy needed more practice.

One day, when speaking with my wife, she said, "maybe you did win and don't realize it. Maybe had you done really well, you would have forgotten about The Wingman's Path and become too focused on playing poker. I don't know about you, but I can't imagine how that would have been good for our marriage." Then she added the proverbial, "I'm just saying." And you know when someone, especially your wife, says, "I'm just saying," they're not. And she definitely was not, just saying.

Hmmm... so if she wasn't *just saying*, perhaps I should think about the idea that maybe she had a point. Maybe it was good that I lost. Don't you just hate when people say something like that? I know I do. Although it was my wife who said it, so I had to consider that it was possibly an all-too-familiar blessing in disguise.

Years ago, when my wife had suggested that I get professional help, I had done so. To be truthful, however, it wasn't my wife's recommendation that got me to see a therapist. It was a request from my CEO, back before he was fired, and I was subsequently let go. Actually, it wasn't a request, it was more of a demand.

You might remember: I was in the health insurance business. I worked for a small firm in New Jersey, that was trying to grow into a large, national company. During that time, the World Series of Poker had just started gaining popularity. Everyone, from celebrities to athletes to average guys like me, was jumping in hoping to win the tournament. We hailed it the *ultimate competition*.

Now, despite having played poker and holding my own since I was nine years old, I never knew anyone could play poker for a living, much less make a fortune doing it. So yeah, the idea of being poker's newest celebrity millionaire caught me in its grasp. And living a stone's throw from Atlantic City, made it easy to scratch that itch.

As time went on, I was spending more and more time at the poker tables, and less and less time at my office. I wasn't winning enough to quit my day job, though, so I still had to work. I did get a large client from being there, but my CEO wasn't happy. He gave me a mandate: go see a therapist about my poker playing and get back to work. It wasn't a suggestion; it was a demand.

When my wife, who is a psychotherapist, heard my boss' demand, she jumped on it like a bee to honey. I was getting hit from both ends, so I surrendered.

However, if I had to go, I decided I would use it to my advantage. As I told my therapist at our first meeting, "my boss wants me to see you, so that I stop playing poker. But I'm here to figure out why I'm not winning big at poker."

We met every week for a while. At one point, I had mentioned: "Poker rooms were my classrooms for life." I'll never forget her answer: "Then start learning from them."

During the summer of my discontent, after my unfortunate showing in Las Vegas, I finally took her advice. Once again, I was at a green felt table, and once again, the results were the same.

As I stood up from the table, disgusted, overtired, and broke, a gentleman sitting next to me said, "The next best thing to playing and winning is playing and losing. The main thing is to play."

Excuse me, asshole.

The phrase is actually a fairly famous poker saying attributed to Nick "the Greek" Dandalos, who, in 1949, played head-on poker for five months straight with Jonny Moss. They played in the lobby of the Binion's Casino in Las Vegas, breaking only for sleep. Their game attracted so much attention and publicity that Benny Binion, the owner of the casino, was inspired to begin the renowned World Series of Poker.

Sometimes, the phrase is longer:

The next best thing to playing and winning is playing and losing. The main thing is to play.

I had read and heard the saying before and always thought it senseless. I'd been around enough poker rooms, and seen enough people lose, that I can assure you with 100% certainty that when people are walking away after losing their money, they're not thinking, *this was great, almost as good as winning.* They're disappointed, hurt, irritated, pissed, frustrated, angry—everything I was that night.

As I drove home in the early morning darkness, the quote kept teasing me. *The next best thing to playing and winning is playing and losing. The main thing is to play.*

Thank you, Nick Dandalos.

I did have to give him some credence. I mean, yeah, I'd been playing poker since I was a kid and truly thought it was my destiny to win the World Series, but Nick Dandalos certainly knew more about the game than I did. And he had majored in philosophy in college, so he probably knew more about life. That's when I understood what he meant. As I exited the Atlantic City expressway, as the darkness turned to dawn, I finally learned the lesson from all those poker-room classrooms.

It wasn't about poker. It was about life.

Life. The next best thing to playing and winning is playing and losing. The main thing is to play.

I couldn't stop saying it. Suddenly, it made perfect sense. I felt myself smiling. "Life, the next best thing to playing and winning is playing and losing. The main thing is to play."

The more I said it, the better I felt. Of course, you want to win at life, but even when you're losing, the important thing is that you're still playing.

"Life, the next best thing to playing and winning is playing and losing. The main thing is to play."

Can you feel the difference in the energy of that statement when you add the word *life*? I felt it. I may not have been winning at life at that moment, but I was still playing, and that was the next best thing.

Feeling better, I recognized the importance of my statement. It had completely stopped the sinking momentum of my vibration. And any time you can stop yourself from falling further down the rabbit hole, you make sure to do so. It's the first rule of holes, or, as they say in the United Kingdom, it's Healey's First Law of Holes:

If you find yourself in a hole, stop digging.

I put the shovel down.
Lesson learned. At long last, I understood.

A Wingman Practice:

The Game of Life

For one minute, repeat the phrase: "Life, the next best thing to playing and winning is playing and losing. The main thing is to play" and try to tap into a playful feeling with it. See how it improves your mood.

15
Welcome to the Game

With my newfound clarity, my vibration had jumped to a new level. I was in the game of life, and the frequency I was now emitting was one of enjoyment. And the more joy I felt, the better life got.

Change that, it wasn't life that got better, it was me. I got better at playing life.

Don't you find that always to be true? That whatever it is you're doing, when you enjoy it, you do it better?

When you enjoy playing, you play better.
When you enjoy your work, you work better.
When you enjoy exercising, you exercise better.

When I enjoy laughing, I laugh better.
When I enjoy thinking, I think better.
When I enjoy learning, I learn better.

If you're a salesperson, do you find when you enjoy selling, you sell better?

If you're a teacher, do you find when you enjoy teaching, you teach better?

If you're a writer, do you find when you enjoy writing, you write better?

The answer seems pretty simple then, right? Just start enjoying whatever it is you are doing. I was so excited I couldn't wait to share my discovery to live a better life. I wrote a blog and shared it with my peeps. Immediately I received back two responses.

The first was from an old classmate: "No Shit Sherlock. Who doesn't know that?"

Maybe I wasn't on to anything so special. But wait—that old classmate, while perhaps knowing it, certainly wasn't practicing it. Instead of enjoying his life, he seemed to be mad at everyone all the time and was living his life that way. It wasn't a pretty sight. He was living a miserable existence where he never went out, was constantly on drugs, and hadn't worked in the past couple of years. He was unhappy, and I got the feeling he wanted to make me feel unhappy as well.

The second response was better. It was from my friend, Stan, the owner of a successful commercial real estate business.

"Mike, I love it," he wrote. "Anything that can help me do more business, I'm all for. But how do I do it? I've got an expensive mortgage and quotas to be met. I'm always anxious and worried, especially at the end of the month when deadlines loom. How do I stop worrying so much and better enjoy the selling process, so I get better at selling?"

Selling, teaching, writing, doctoring, building, etc... whatever your game is, the more you practice enjoying it, the better you get at it. The challenge that so many of us face, however, is we don't want to practice. We just want to play the game.

> **We're sitting here ... I'm supposed to be the franchise player, and we're in here talking about practice. I mean, listen, we're talking about practice. Not a game. Not a game. Not a game. We're talking about practice. Not a game. Not the game that I go out there and die for and play every game like it's my last. Not the game. We're talking about practice, man.**
> ~Allen Iverson

Like Allen Iverson and my No-Sh#t-Sherlock classmate, we just want to play the game. But if you knew, really knew, that all you had to do was practice *enjoying* the game of life for one minute each day and your life would be better, wouldn't you sign up for practice immediately?

I did know it. That's why I kept my discipline rolling and consistently and consciously practiced finding positives on a daily basis. My friend Stan understood it, too. And he was looking for help. He wanted to make his life better and if practice at finding the positives was what it took, he was all in. He became my first client.

We set up a plan. I emailed him a practice to do for one full minute every morning. We would also meet at his office each week to discuss whatever was going on in his life. If things were going well, our conversation would be about practices to keep improving his energy. If he was anxious, and his vibration was taking a hit, we'd examine exercises to turn things around.

As I keep saying...what you send out, you receive back. If you're sending out anxious energy, the Universe will send you back more reasons to feel anxious. So, my job with Stan was to help him keep his vibration high, no matter what the circumstances—despite his mortgage, expenses, reaching his quota, or anything else that would make his vibration suffer from anxiety or stress. Together, we worked on getting him to emit a happy, joyful, and successful frequency as he conducted business. The more he did, the more business he could bring in, which would increase his happiness, which would bring in more business, and the cycle would continue.

The sequence is obvious, right? It's fantastic when things are going our way. It's lousy when they're not. If we remain focused on the fantastic, it only gets better. If we remain focused on the lousy, it only gets worse. You see it daily, whether in life, in business, or even when watching a sporting event on television; you can usually tell which team has the momentum on its side.

The key is to keep practicing bringing in positive energy for one minute *every day*. Of course, we all know how easy it is to stop your routine, how it often becomes either mentally tiring or just physically boring, be it going to the gym, sticking to a diet, practicing seeing positives, quieting your mind, or whatever it is you do. That's why it's important to keep your discipline rolling as best you can.

And, just like going to the gym, if you take a vacation day, or even a week, as soon as you realize you haven't been practicing, you get back at it. You missed the gym the last few days? No worries, head on over. Just had a great Philly cheesesteak with fries and a milkshake? It's OK, just jump back into your healthy eating plan. Stopped practicing your positivity? Put a timer on for one minute and start counting your blessings.

You just pick up the ball and start practicing immediately.

Nike said it best with their ad slogan: *Just Do It*.

I know you've heard it a thousand times before. But it's true - hard work pays off. If you want to be good, you have to practice, practice, practice. If you don't love something, then don't do it.
~Ray Bradbury

If you really want to get good at your game, at your game of life, then you have to practice finding the good, finding the positives. The good news is that on the Wingman's Path, you only need to practice for one minute a day to get back in and stay in your groove.

But for that minute, practice like you mean it.

A Wingman Practice:

Keep the Discipline Rolling

For one minute, say out loud or to yourself: "I'm keeping my discipline rolling."

While repeating it, picture yourself successfully living a life of your choosing. Feel proud of yourself for consistently practicing for one minute each day. It's a fabulous vibration to be sending out.

16
The Rules of the Game.

During one of our meetings, Stan revealed he would like to do more business on the golf course. The idea made sense to me: golf is a great way for business people to connect. Spending four quality hours with valued customers in a peaceful setting can take your interaction beyond just a conversation. By watching them handle themselves on the golf course, you can learn more about people than you could in a lifetime of business meetings. Do they play by the rules and control their emotions? Or do they hit a bad shot and blow a fuse?

And that was where Stan's challenge presented itself. As he explained to me, he was a very good golfer, but when he'd hit a bad shot, sometimes he'd get upset, which could lead to a flurry of worse shots. His mood would rapidly change, and he would go from smiling, gregarious, and sociable, to sullen, brooding, and bad-tempered.

Because of his inability to control his emotions, Stan had stopped playing golf with clients. He didn't want to risk losing a client or potential client because of his meltdowns. But, he knew he was missing out on tremendous opportunities; his business prospered when he played well. Vibrationally that made sense: when he emitted a frequency of happiness and success, his fellow players and business associates enjoyed being and working with him. But when he played poorly and emitted a frequency of anger, frustration, and worse, the other golfers were less inclined to want to make deals with him.

But, no matter how good you are at something, mistakes can happen. The most skilled surgeon still loses a patient once in a while. The All-Star quarterback sometimes throws an interception. The best salesman doesn't make every sale. No one ever succeeds 100% of the time in anything. It's what happens after the interception that counts the most.

The Wingman's Path

> **It's easy to grin when your ship comes in, and you've got the stock market beat. But the man worthwhile, is the man who can smile, when his shorts are too tight in the seat.**
> ~Judge Smails, *Caddyshack*.

My job was pretty clear: Stan wanted me to help him keep his perspective as he played because he believed that would help him increase his business. I was excited. I mean, this was right up my alley. Golf is like any other of life's games: keeping positive is of utmost importance. Many great golfers have the right physical attributes—eye-hand coordination or a perfect swing—but the real game of golf is played mostly between your ears. Even the best professionals hit a bad shot once in a while. A bad shot in golf is like any harmful occurrence in any other business. But it's what happens in your head after the bad shot that often determines your success or failure.

> **The test of success is not what you do when you are on top. Success is how high you bounce when you hit the bottom.**
> ~George S. Patton Jr.

Stan and I decided to play golf with two mutual friends so I could see first-hand how he handled the game. I wasn't exactly sure how I would approach this challenge, but I knew the answer was not in teaching the mechanics of the game. Instead, I observed how he spoke and behaved. As our day progressed, it became obvious why his business suffered when he was playing poorly. I didn't need to be a detective to notice how Stan's mood changed any time he hit what he considered a bad shot.

When we got to the ninth hole, I received my answer as to how to help Stan. The hole was a relatively short, par three. Billy, a scratch golfer, and by far the best golfer among us, led out. He hit a six-iron into the sand trap. From his perspective, it was a very disappointing shot, but you couldn't tell from his attitude. He was unflappable. Looking at him, you would never know if his shot was good or bad. It was apparent to me that Billy's calm demeanor was one of the reasons he was so good.

Stan, using a five-iron, hit his ball into the same trap and immediately became petulant.

Then it was then Jack's turn. Jack is an average golfer, a 17- handicap, and therefore much worse than Stan. He teed his ball up, took one practice swing, and proceeded to hit the ball straight up about 100 feet, but landed only about 20 feet from where we stood. Stan, breaking out of his self-imposed misery, stated in a somewhat helpful fashion, "Don't worry about it."

You could tell Jack was a good friend of Stan's. With a smirk, he sarcastically answered, "OK, Stan. Thanks, I'll try not to."

We finished the hole then stopped for lunch. Billy had saved par by hitting a beautiful shot out of the sand trap about 12 inches from the cup. Jack hit his second shot to the edge of the green, from where it proceeded to roll about 25 feet and stop about four feet from the hole. It was his best shot of the day, and he confidently followed it by sinking his putt for par. Stan, unfortunately, had gotten into his own head and ended the first half with a double bogey.

As we sat down to burgers and beers, I asked Jack about his response to Stan.

"I'm outside," he replied. "I'm with my friends on a beautiful day playing golf. Does it really matter what type of shot I hit?"

Bingo! Jack's answer was Stan's lesson. Jack had changed the rules. He didn't need to have a great score to enjoy his day of golf; he was just happy to be out with friends. The score wasn't important, only that he was playing golf with friends.

When I pointed this out to Stan, he retorted that Jack wasn't that good of a player, so a bad shot isn't as meaningful. I agreed with him but then pointed to Billy, who was a better golfer than Stan, and who had hit the same poor shot into the sand trap.

"He didn't let it affect him. And," I added, "More to the point: while today we were just playing golf. When you're with clients, golf isn't even the game you are playing. The game you are playing is business, golf is just the platform you're using to play your game."

Change the rules. I loved it. It became my new practice anytime I wasn't enjoying whatever "game' I was "playing." I would just change the rules the way Jack had. He changed the rules of playing golf: the rules went from playing his best game to being outside with friends, enjoying the day.

This practice not only helped me, but it also helped Stan. He changed the rules as well. He quickly realized that when he was playing golf with clients, it wasn't golf he was playing. It was business. From that point forward, anytime Stan hit a bad shot, I had him say, "I'm changing the rules."

I'm happy to report that Stan's golf game has improved, and he's doing more business than ever. Even better, he's not irritating as many people with his peevishness when things don't go exactly as planned.

How about you? Are you:

- A sales rep who just had a sales call but didn't get the sale?
- A single person who's had another bad date?
- A person who looks to their external circumstances for their happiness?

If so, how can you change the rules so you can enjoy what you're doing more?

Perhaps...

- The sales rep can recognize that her sales are based on a percentage of how many clients she sees, versus how many sales she makes. If, for every five sales calls she makes, she averages one sale, then instead of worrying whether she gets the sale, she can congratulate herself for making the sales calls. She knows the sales will automatically follow. She now celebrates just going on a sales call because she knows for every five sales calls, she'll get one sale. Which one of the five doesn't matter.
- The single person who has a bad date can change the way he rates dates. Perhaps he could celebrate the good dinner, or entertaining movie, or something else about the date. Just because the main purpose of the date, the woman wasn't the perfect love match, will no longer matter. If he changes the rules so that if any part of the date was good, then he always has a good date. By doing so, he changes his vibration from negatively thinking about dates to positively thinking about dates. The change in vibration absolutely helps him have better and better dates.
- And the person who looks externally for happiness and complains that if something or someone else would change, then she would be happy, can change the rules about her beliefs. Instead of saying, "If only my boss would recognize all I do," she can decide to celebrate her good work for herself. She can change the rules and decide to find her happiness by looking inside, rather than outward.

Perhaps you can change the rules to play something, play a game, play an instrument, play with a friend, or even better, play at work. I'm not saying to regard your work as frivolous; when I say *play at work*, I mean enjoy your work today. Change the rules of your work so you can enjoy what you have chosen to do to earn a living, just for today.

Or make your own rules of being happy even easier the way my friend Cliff does. His rule of happiness is simple. He says: "If I wake up today and take my first breath, I'm going to be happy."

Change the rules. You'll be amazed at how good you'll begin to feel.

A Wingman Practice:

Change the Rules

Remind yourself that it's your life, your game, and you make the rules. For one minute, repeat: "I'm changing the rules."

As you do, think of different ways you can change the rules in your life so that you always feel like a winner.

17
The Continuum

As summer turned to fall, I was *Keeping My Discipline Rolling* and *Changing the Rules* so that I always found some reason to be happy. I was getting more and more clarity about my vibration, and I began to find evidence of how whatever I was sending out was, in fact, helping to create my reality.

I was also beginning to believe, really believe, that I had stumbled upon a path to a better feeling place, to a higher spiritual plane. Do you know what I mean by really believing? It's like an inner knowing.

> So...have you been practicing? Have you been following the Wingman's Path? If you have, then perhaps you, too, are starting to believe that you can bring more positive energy into your life, that you can raise your vibration, and that you can actually create a life of your choosing.

When I first began this journey, I wanted to *see* the path. I wanted direct divine guidance or some definite steps to take to achieve a happier life. But I discovered it wasn't like that. The path is more like a series of coincidences, where with each new practice I did, a new teacher or lesson appeared.

Of all my teachers, the one who had the most lessons for me to learn was my son. Perhaps it's a generational thing, but many of my practices seemed to have been developed throughout my relationship with him. Perhaps you won't be surprised, then, when I tell you my next "class" would be conducted when he returned from California that fall.

"How many times do I need to learn the same lesson?" he asked as we sat down to breakfast one morning.

Was I hearing correctly? Was my son actually asking me a question about life? Was all of my Wingman research and practices coming to full meaning with a loved one? Was my son finally interested in my Wingman philosophy? Was he ready to embrace my one-minute practices? I wanted to savor the moment as my mind ran in ten different directions.

But then I laughed as the waitress came by to take our order. I laughed, not because I knew the answer, but because my wife had just asked almost the exact same question 16 hours earlier. I know when I hear something, see something, or read something repeated within a short timeframe that there is a message for me to receive. And it will continue to repeat until I do get it.

"Cheese omelet, well-done home fries, rye toast, and coffee," I ordered, happy for the chance to get my thoughts together while my son spoke to the waitress. I needed to reflect on what had happened the day before. It started when my wife went to the gym for her Zumba class in the morning. While there, she ran into a friend and, feeling invigorated, hit the treadmill for an additional 30 minutes. When she got home, not surprisingly, her knee was sore. Three hours later, on the couch with her leg elevated and a pack of frozen vegetables on her knee, she asked the same question I've heard from her for the last 16 years: "Why won't I ever learn?"

I was about to chime in with my Wingman's Path wisdom, but she raised her hand in the air, palm facing me as if to say *stop*. "It was rhetorical, honey," she said. "I really don't need an answer."

And now, my son was basically asking the same question. I was in Daddy Wingman Heaven. But I knew I needed to tread carefully, as my wife's reminder had suggested.

You see, as I had been uncovering more and more of the Wingman's Path and developing the Wingman practices, I began seeing my ability to practice and find more practices as gifts, of sorts. After my experience with Stan, I attracted more clients and was able to serve them with those gifts. I became adept at helping them see the future they wanted to have, and then customizing simple practices to help them make that future a reality. It was a win-win situation for both my clients and myself because as they got what they needed, I had constant opportunities to practice. Just as with my clients, the more practicing I did, the more I was able to see the future I wanted, and the path to crafting it.

The challenge is that often my gifts became curses—like when I'm sitting with friends or family, and they're sharing their latest challenge. When I'm in a coaching session with a client, they've asked and paid for my help. When I'm sitting with friends or family, they usually haven't asked, and almost always don't want to hear it.

Regardless, I sometimes (maybe more than sometimes?) persist in offering my unsolicited help. Why? With my new education about energy and vibration, it begs the question, Why? Why don't I stop giving advice when it's not wanted? *Why don't I ever learn?*

Perhaps it's because I find it difficult not to speak up when I see a friend or loved one walking into a tsunami. But for whatever reason, I just can't help myself sometimes. Regrettably, I do it more with my son than with any other living human being. It annoys him to no end, and usually, the conversation ends with us not speaking at all. I hate when that happens. It's become a real challenge for me not to push, even though I know the more I do, the more he resists.

Maybe it was time for me to vibrationally recognize the patterns in my conversations with him, and with others, that make me want to speak up. That would be a great first step to breaking this habit I have of speaking too much, of going too far with my wonderful, but sometimes unwelcome, guidance.

At that moment though, as the waitress delivered our breakfast, I was feeling pretty good. After all, one of my strongest desires had been to have these types of talks with my son, to be able to help him understand that he can be, do, or have anything he desires. And this morning, over eggs and potatoes, we were actually having one of these conversations. You can imagine how wonderful I was feeling. Until, without realizing it, I once again pushed too far. But it was my little dance of constantly pushing too much with him that led to my next step on my path. Hopefully, it will help shine a light for you as well.

It's about wanting too hard. Have you ever desired something? Silly question, of course you have. But have you ever desired it so much that you felt like you *needed* it? Yet, the more you wanted it, the further you seemed to push it away?

As I chewed my toast that morning, I reassessed my situation. Was I helping bring my son closer, or pushing him further away? Was my vibration one of confidence or desperation? Aha!

Where was I on the Continuum of wanting versus allowing?

Continuum was the name I had given it. I first read of it in Dr. Wayne Dyer's book, *Change Your Thoughts – Change Your Life: Living the Wisdom of the Tao* (Hay House, reprinted. 2009). He spoke of having a desire and becoming desireless, or "Letting go and letting God." When I first read it, I didn't understand it. But that day, as I pushed my Wingman Practices to my son who didn't want to hear them, it smacked me right in the face.

Ohhhh, I get it.

It's the line between wanting (having a desire) and allowing (becoming desireless).

Do you understand what I mean as to the difference between wanting and allowing? Have you ever desired something so much, that you tried too hard to make it happen? That's the situation I found myself in. I felt like... a school girl dissecting every part of her conversation with the boy she has a crush on. Or a salesman waiting to hear from a prospective client. Or someone who's craving a new relationship or job so much, they come across as desperate. Or a parent who wants their child to listen to them so badly, they don't stop talking long enough to hear what their child has to say.

Has this ever happened to you, perhaps at a job interview, a sales call, or a first date? Perhaps the Continuum practice can help.

Here's how to practice it:

1) Recognize your desire.
2) Acknowledge your desired outcome.
3) Here's the tricky part...Become aware of where you are on the Continuum of wanting versus allowing. Do you want it so badly that you're actually resisting it, almost forcing any other outcome than that which you desire? Or are you allowing it? How is your vibration around your desire? The best way I've found to identify where I am on the Continuum is to stop and recognize how I feel. Do I feel happy, content, confident, or optimistic about where I am concerning my desire? Or do I feel frustrated, anxious, or disturbed that my goal has yet to be reached? Remember, Our feelings are like a GPS, letting us know if we're on the right track.

But what about making it happen?

I'm not arguing with taking action. What I'm doing is exploring the possibility of going too far. Of trying too hard. It's the difference between being confident and being defensive. Of expecting it, as opposed to begging for it.

Let's take a job interview as an example. Making it happen is:
- getting the interview.
- researching the company.
- meeting the prospective employer and hearing all about the job.

- letting them know why you are the perfect candidate, and how you can help them.

Trying too hard is:
- going on and on after you've said your piece.
- turning a great interview into a therapy session.
- talking too much and listening too little.

It's not always easy to recognize where you are on the Continuum, especially when you're talking and talking and talking. It takes practice to recognize your vibration by tuning into exactly how you're feeling during your conversation.

I know I certainly need more practice. Particularly because of my desire to have these conversations with my son. For me:

Making it happen is:
- sitting down to breakfast with him.
- letting him know I can help him with these types of questions.
- being prepared when he asks.
- having a great answer that he actually hears.

Trying too hard is:
- not shutting up and listening.
- going on and on. And on. And on.
- bringing up five different practices when one is all that is asked for.

I have found when I have a desire, it helps me to stop and notice where I am on the Continuum between wanting and allowing.

Wanting -- Allowing

When I am able to stop and think, I can practice feeling where I am on this Continuum. Doing so helps me recognize whether I'm making it happen, or allowing it to happen. Or am I squeezing so hard, I'm forcing it away, and not allowing it to be at all?

Let's use the example of my breakfast to put all of this together.
1) Recognize your desire: I wanted a good breakfast.
2) Acknowledge your desired outcome: I chose the food and placed the order.
3) Become aware of where you are on the Continuum of wanting versus allowing: although I was hungry, I felt confident my

desire would be fulfilled, so I was content to wait (allow) it to show up on the table.

Now, imagine me nagging the waitress about when my food would be out and becoming a pain in the ass to her. How would my breakfast experience be? Or, how about taking it a bit further: imagine if I walked back to the kitchen to take charge. At that point, I might be thrown out and would never get my breakfast. Clearly, I would have gone to the wrong side of the Continuum.

I discovered the more I practiced figuring out where I was on the Continuum, the better I got at quickly recognizing the difference between wanting and allowing. I already knew what wanting something so badly felt like. Now I was learning about allowing and how to compare the two feelings.

And so I practiced. Constantly. Each and every time I had a desire, I would practice feeling where I was on that scale between wanting and allowing. Was I trying too hard? Or was I trusting it would happen?

How many times have you heard, "just allow it," or "trust that it will happen"? How many of those times did you just want to punch someone in the face? Yeah, that's how I felt sometimes. So I knew I needed to make living what I saw as a paradox easier.

I looked at the words I chose. *Allowing*, *permitting*, and *trusting* are all good words that many use, but they are difficult for me to live when I have a strong desire. When I wanted something, I would go after it. But so often I would be in the same type of situation as I was in with my son that morning at the diner, wanting it so badly that I was pushing it away.

And then it hit me. I remembered another time in my past when I got extremely lucky and earned a big account that paid me a great deal of money (this was before my life hit the rocks). A friend asked me how I had acquired it. I answered, "I'm not sure, I feel like I just invited it in." I had never uttered those words prior to that, or after that, until my discovering the Wingman's Path.

Inviting! Yes!

I decided, whatever I desired, I would simply invite it into my life. I thought of it as if I were having a party and wanted all my desires to attend. Anything I sought, I invited. Whether I was ordering a pizza or craving a big corporate client, I would take a step back, and in my mind, invite it to come to me.

You can do it too. What do you want? A house on the beach? Invite it. Better health, a new partner, a new car, more money? Whatever you want, just invite it as if you were inviting a friend to your house for dinner...And start cooking.

But back to my breakfast with my son...I'd like to tell you I was smooth and in control with my son that morning. That I identified when I was pounding too hard and pulled back just enough to have him wanting to hear more, hanging on my every word. The truth is, I did push a bit too far, but I also recognized it. In the end, we didn't fight; we had some good conversation and a great breakfast. I took it as a step in the right direction.

A Wingman Practice:

The Continuum

Think about a desire you want to manifest. Invite it to happen. Say it out loud. "I invite (my desire) into my life." Now feel where your emotions are on the Continuum between wanting it and allowing it. Are you making it happen, or are you forcing it so hard you're pushing it away and not allowing it to materialize?

Practice it. Say the words "I invite (my desire) into my life." Now, feel where you are:

Wanting---Allowing

It's not easy to put it into words, but after practicing for a bit, you will be able to distinguish what allowing feels like in comparison to wanting too hard. By inviting your desires into your life, you will soon be better able to manifest those desires.

18
My Old Friend Vance

The Law of Attraction never quits. Right after I started practicing my new word, *inviting*, I began to receive invitations from different friends for different events. One such invitation was for Jan and me to join a very close friend and her son, Mario, at the Ringling Brothers Circus. We thought it might be a fun night seeing it through his young eyes, so agreed to go. Things somehow changed, though, and it wound up that just me and my young friend, Mario, went to the *Greatest Show on Earth.*

We decided to go early to watch them set up. As we walked around, enjoying the many sights and sounds, we ran into Vance, who had been working for Ringling Brothers since 1984. I had met him about 18 years earlier when I saw the circus with my children. While he seemed to have put on a few pounds, he looked majestic in his circus garb.

Mario was so happy to see him, but after visiting with him for a bit, I was saddened to realize Vance still was unable to escape the same issues he'd been carrying around for the past two decades. Like so many of us, Vance had been conditioned from a young age to respond a certain way to his circumstances and was unable to pull away from those issues that kept him stuck.

Since discovering the Wingman's Path, it's become easy for me to spot when someone is still tied to some past limiting belief. We've all been there. And of course, it's easier to spot it when it's not ourselves who are stuck; when it's not us who have given up on breaking the old chains that bind us. As Mario and I hung around with Vance, I thought of Henry Ford's words:

Whether you believe you can do a thing or not, you are right.

It seemed Vance had just given up, and definitely believed he couldn't do otherwise. I knew differently, and even Mario noticed and asked me about it.

I told him that Vance is really no different than many people: he'd been conditioned to believe something that was untrue about himself. I then explained that because of words we hear or heard when we were young, or other types of conditioning we received, we often stop believing in ourselves.

How about you? Because of something you may have heard when you were younger, have your dreams been quashed? *You'll never amount to anything. You're a bad kid. Your brother is much smarter than you. You're good for nothing. I wish you weren't born. You're a moron. You're worthless.* And on and on...

More often, it's not the words we hear from others, but rather the words we tell ourselves that really destroy our self-esteem and stop us from moving in the direction of our dreams. Those words matter.

> Have you ever seen the movie *Ocean's Eleven* with George Clooney and Brad Pitt? In one scene, Andy Garcia, who plays the owner of the hotel/casino, tells Julia Roberts, "In my hotel, someone is always watching."
>
> It's the same with your subconscious; it's not watching, but it is always listening. And, when your subconscious hears something repeated over and over, it believes it. Whether good or bad, your subconscious will have you believing it. So yeah, as it turns out that the old playground taunt *Sticks and stones will break my bones, but names will never hurt me,* is not actually true. Names do hurt, especially when they become so ingrained in your brain that you say them to yourself.

Too often in my discussions with clients, friends, and business associates, I notice many people use words that sabotage their attempts to get to where they want to be. Have you ever said these words to yourself?

- I can't...
- I don't have time to...
- I'm such a loser.

- Everyone else is so much ... (better, smarter, faster, thinner, more successful) than me.
- I have to...

Or, my personal favorite:
- I'm so stupid.

These statements are like stakes driven into the ground, with heavy chains attached to us that only allow up to reach the point where we believe we can't pull free. And we're right. For when we believe we can't, we can't.

Which brings me back to Vance. Seeing him, I wanted to show him that the chain that was holding him back was nothing more than a thin rope and that he could break it with one strong step forward. But it was clear to me I could not help him. Though, hopefully, this message can help you break free of those deceptive shackles that are keeping you stuck.

You see, Vance is an elephant who had developed a *conditioned response*—that is, he was trained to believe an untruth about himself. When he was very young, he was attached to a stake in the ground by very heavy chains. He was unable to pull himself free, and after trying and failing many times, he gave up. At that point, his keepers would use a thin, light rope to "chain" him into place. Vance might pull against it, but as soon as he feels any kind of resistance from the rope, he stops because he believes his efforts are futile, and he just gives up.

Vance's conditioning reminded me of my own that reared its head a few years back when I was at a big fancy birthday dinner for a friend. I had written a poem for him, which I read aloud. As I finished ode reminiscing about the good old days, which everyone seemed to enjoy, his brother stated loudly, "I didn't know Michael could read, much less write."

While everyone laughed, I felt the sting. He was just being funny, but to me, his words struck true. I wasn't very good at reading when I was growing up, and certainly not at writing. But those were conditioned responses—obviously, I can read and write. I don't know how the beliefs began, or when they infiltrated my mind, but I do know I believed them for a long time, and anytime I tried to write, I failed. Until I broke free of the belief that I wasn't able to.

So now I ask you, have you been conditioned to respond a certain way? Are you holding onto harmful memories or beliefs? Is the chain holding you back really just a slender rope, yet you believe it is unbreakable?

If I could break free of my chains and write this book, then I'm certain with enough practice you can break free of yours as well. After all, it's not a big thick chain, it's just a slender rope, and just like Vance, you may not even realize it. The words we tell ourselves would not have much impact on us if we only said them once or twice. But that's the thing, once these words get into our subconscious, they come out often, easily, and way too quickly. And much like with me when my friend's brother announced my self-limiting belief at the party, the more you hear them, the more you believe them.

Why would we choose to do that to ourselves?

The answer is simple: we don't choose, at least not consciously. Somehow, somewhere these negative thoughts got implanted in our brain, and when something triggers that memory, those damaging thoughts become words that flow out of our mouths and, unfortunately, reinforce those same negative thoughts back into our minds. It's a vicious cycle that is unfailing. I still find it amazing that after many years on the Wingman's Path, some of those old words still pop into my head so swiftly.

The good news is I now have a practice to eliminate them, or rather eliminate the power they have over me. And with consistent practice, you can eliminate your self-limiting beliefs, too.

How?

First, by deciding to do so. And then, notice the different things you say or do that are harmful to you. You must become your own self-sabotage word-police force. Any time you detect a remark or behavior that is subversive to you, you must be vigilant in fixing it.

When I say something treasonous to the me-I-want-to-be, I instantly say, "Cancel, cancel, delete, delete," and then go about correcting the thought with a new one.

When I say, "I can't." I say, "Cancel, cancel, delete, delete. I can, but I choose not to."

When I say, "I don't have time." I say, "Cancel, cancel, delete, delete. I have all the time I need, but I choose not to."

When I say, "I'm such a loser." I say, "Cancel, cancel, delete, delete. I'm a winner who just happened to lose this time."

When I say, "I'm so stupid." I say, "Cancel, cancel, delete, delete. I'm a pretty smart person who just did a stupid thing."

You must pay special attention to the words you say most often, like "I have to go to work" or "I can't eat that on my diet" as they are equally destructive to your well-being. When one of those comments happen to slip out from my tongue, I now instantly correct myself by saying, "Cancel,

cancel, delete, delete. I choose to go to work" or "Cancel, cancel, delete, delete. I choose not to eat that."

Why is that so important? Because by saying it, I am purging a self-limiting belief and taking responsibility for my actions. The more accountable I am for my own decisions, the clearer I become in creating the me-I-want-to-be.

A Wingman Practice:

Cancel, Cancel, Delete, Delete.

For one minute say the words: "Cancel, cancel, delete, delete."

By repeating them, the next time you say something harmful to yourself, you will be quicker to recognize it, and then you will change your conditioned response to a more positive belief about yourself.

19
I'm a Lucky Guy

It wasn't long after seeing the circus that Mario and I got together again. It started with an emergency phone call from his mom, and it ended with him being the impetus for one of my favorite practices.

His mom was stuck at a meeting and had to work late one night. She called to see if I could pick him up from his afterschool activities, bring him back to my house, and then she would pick him up on her way home. It was a Wednesday night, I had the radio show, and Jan was working. So, we decided that I would bring him with me to the radio station and drop him off after the show.

My usual routine on Wednesday nights was to do my Wingman's Path practices during my drive to the station. It's a thirty-minute drive, which makes for a perfect time to get myself, and my energy, ready for the show. I hoped Mario wouldn't mind doing a practice with me.

> Me: Mario, would you want to do one of my Wingman's Path practices?
> Mario: Maybe. What do we do?

I hadn't thought about practices with children before, so I had no idea if saying something over and over would be too boring for a nine-year-old. But I couldn't back down, now.

> Me: We go back and forth saying to each other: "I am a lucky guy."
> Mario: Ok. I'll start. I am a lucky guy.
> Me: I am a lucky guy.
> Mario: I am a lucky guy.

Me: I am a lucky guy.

Children are so much better than adults at understanding positive vibrations. Soon Mario demonstrated that by elevating things.

Mario: I'm a really lucky guy.
Me: (smiling and laughing) I'm a really lucky guy.
Mario: I'm a super lucky guy.
Me: I'm a super lucky guy.
Mario: We're really lucky guys.
Me: We're really lucky guys.

By this time, we were both laughing and adding new and greater adjectives to our statement. We were ultra-lucky guys, extremely lucky guys, exceptionally lucky guys, unbelievably lucky guys, and supercalifragilisticexpialidociously lucky guys.

We were having so much fun I almost missed our turn. However, there's a soft pretzel store near the radio station, which, surprisingly, still had their lights on. *Surprisingly*, because it's always closed by the time I pass by. My schedule on Wednesday nights was predictable. I would always drive by the pretzel store at approximately 6:10 p.m., ten minutes after their closing time. However, tonight, because of picking up Mario from his afterschool program, it was only five-fifty. Seeing they were opened, I asked Mario if he wanted a pretzel and told him how I never get there when they were open.

Mario said, "Yes, and isn't it lucky that they're still open? Your practice must really work!" I laughed, but his comment certainly made me think about our good fortune.

I pulled into the parking lot, and as we got out of the car, Mario said, "Let's see if we can get more lucky."

Smiling, I agreed. "Yes, let's see if we can get more lucky."

We purchased our pretzels and walked over to the mustard bar. As we were putting on mustard (spicy brown for me), a woman came in, ordered her pretzels, and, as she was paying, dropped a couple dollars of change onto the floor. I was too busy preparing my soft pretzel, but Mario, being the great kid he is, walked over, picked up all the change, and handed it back to her. It was at that moment that this practice became an instant classic and one that I often do. Because, as he handed her the money, she told him, "It's for you, you keep it." He turned his head toward me with a smile that said *I'm a super lucky guy.*

He was actually trying not to smile, but he couldn't hold it in. And neither could I.

We're two lucky guys.

A Wingman Practice:

I'm a Lucky Guy.

Repeat "I'm a lucky guy" (or gal or however you refer to yourself) over and over.

Even if you're getting your butt kicked by life right now, say it anyway. The word has a tremendously powerful vibration. Whether you're feeling lucky or not doesn't matter; just continue to repeat the phrase to yourself. While you're saying it, think of as many reasons as you can that you could consider yourself lucky. And there must be some—you're breathing, right? You can read this book? You're very lucky!

The key is to feel lucky as best you can while repeating the phrase. Sooner or later, your brain will wrap around the phrase, and you'll soon be believing it. And when you start believing it, the Universe will start sending you more and more reasons to believe you're a lucky person.

And maybe you, like Mario and me, can get "more lucky."

20
The Macy's Lady

I discovered the longer I was on the Wingman's Path, the more open I became to seeing my next practice. More important: the more trusting I became that the practice will be there when I am ready to use it.

To recap a little, as you can probably see by now, the Wingman's Path is not visible to the naked eye. It's not even a physical path. It's a path of practices brought to me by teachers who may not even be aware that they have a lesson for me to learn. And it's one best seen, or felt, really, with your gut instinct, or with what some would call your third eye. I've begun to say I use my Wingman Vision because I often see each message easily, with great clarity from an enhanced viewpoint.

Sure, the messages seem to be accidental, but I keep receiving them, so I'm thinking there's something more in play here. Is the Universe sending me communications, or are these signs always there for anyone and I'm just now spotting them? Regardless, one thing seems certain: some person, place, or thing, "coincidentally" happens to shine a light right where I could use one every time I need one, so I can stay on the path. I now expect to discover the practice and keep searching until I do. It's a different feeling than wondering or hoping for an answer. It's like the difference between knowing and thinking. *Seek and ye shall find*, and so I do. I see the light even when it is barely shining.

One day, the light was beaming when I was at Macy's looking for a toaster oven. The light came from a young lady who helped me. She was dressed nicely, as expected. But what wasn't expected was what I learned from our conversation. She was homeless.

The conversation brought me back to my time of darkness, when I was homeless but didn't look it. I had just started working in the insurance business and still had my suits from my earlier investment career. Much like the lady at Macy's, you wouldn't know by looking at me that I didn't know where I would be sleeping that night. I was fortunate that I had a few friends whose homes had couches or spare bedrooms. I would sleep at different friends' homes on different nights.

When you're in that situation, you tend to keep everything in your car. One day, in the middle of a snowstorm, I heard a noise that sounded as if something was wrong with my rear, passenger side tire. I pulled over and got out of the car to look at it. As I did, two guys jumped in and stole my car.

That's right, with everything I owned in it. Wrapped up like a Christmas present for them. I not only felt pathetic, I felt stupid.

And if that wasn't bad enough, I had been delivering insurance papers, with checks for the premium payments, from the Cherry Hill, New Jersey office where I worked, to our home office in Philadelphia. They were in the car also. I had hit bottom.

I called a friend to pick me up and drive me back to my office in New Jersey. I had to go in and tell my boss what had just happened, knowing full-well I would probably be fired for my carelessness.

The good news was I didn't get fired. The bad news was everything else: I had no car, no clothes, and no self-esteem.

My friend had stayed with me and was now driving us back to his place in Philadelphia. When we stopped and waited at the tollbooth for the Ben Franklin Bridge, we noticed that someone in the back of the van had some kind of major physical disability. I'm not even sure how or what we saw, but even in my depressed state at that moment, I noticed it.

When it was our turn to pay the toll, my friend reached out with his three one-dollar bills, the fee at that time, to cross the bridge. The tollbooth operator, ignoring my friend and his fare, looked in at me and said words I've never forgotten: "And you think you have problems," referencing the car that just passed.

I did think I had problems. I was broke, homeless, and hanging onto my job by a thread. But, at that moment, something changed. I realized maybe my problems weren't so bad. Or at least that's what it felt like. The comment became the spark I needed to begin my climb back. I was always so thankful to that man in the tollbooth. But I never saw him again.

However, I did think of him the day I spoke to the Macy's lady. Because similarly to his providing a spark of positive energy for me, I was now able to do the same for her.

I was fresh off my *Lucky Man* practice and mentioned it. She wasn't feeling it, at least until I mentioned how I'd been noticing that my good fortune had been rubbing off on anyone who happened to be around me. Suddenly she came to life. She had that excited look of seeing a branch you might be able to grab onto as wild water is flushing you downstream. I was that branch.

She literally rubbed her arm on mine. I laughed and said, "That won't be necessary, young lady. You'll see. Just by us being here together, with the way my vibration is right now, you will find positive energy coming your way."

I knew she would. Why? Because what you look for you find. And she would now be looking for positives. I was her tollbooth operator. Shining a light when needed, never to be seen again. And it was that moment when I realized what a gift I had given the tollbooth operator. It was the same the Macy's lady had given me: the opportunity to help someone. To be their Wingman.

**You can have everything in life you want,
if you will just help enough other people get what they want.**
~Zig Ziglar

When you help another person, when you are totally focused on helping him or her, you send out a vibration of helping. Just as my Dad had said to me when I was flying out to Vegas. "...Practice asking... How can I help you? Those five words will get you started on a beautiful path, and you will not believe how happy you can be. How can I help you? It's as simple as that."

And the Universe, as always, will match your vibration and send help back to you. It's one of the things I learned on the Wingman's Path. It always works. It happens 100% of the time, so it's not surprising to me anymore. I actually expect it now

And it's pretty simple: you feel helpful, so you send out a vibration of helpfulness. The Universe feels your helpful vibration and sends you back help.

I was back at Macy's a month later with my mom. It's something we often did when I'd visit. I made certain to stop down in the appliance department, but she wasn't there. I asked about her, and the saleswoman there that day said she was working someplace else. She had no other information.

I like to think that things turned around for her. I felt her renewed belief in herself and envisioned it sparking her vibration. I felt honored, and extremely happy, to have held a light for her.

I now practice this vibration by saying to myself, "How can I help you?" Every time I do, I think of that young lady from Macy's and see her happy, smiling, and in joy. Of course, there's no way to know, much like my Toll Booth Operator Wingman didn't know how much he helped me.

Although I do like to think that maybe he feels a little extra spark of positive energy every time I think of him and mentally say *thank you*. But really, the practice isn't about him, and it isn't about her. It's about me, and my emitting a frequency of helping. It's a feeling I now practice.

A Wingman Practice:

How can I help?

For one minute, ask out loud, or to yourself, "How can I help you?"

By repeating it, the phrase will get into your subconscious and be in the forefront of your thoughts whenever you meet someone. As you say the words, "How can I help you?" think of a time you helped someone and remember how it felt. That's the feeling I want you to practice.

I don't believe there's a better feeling in this world than feeling the joy of helping someone. If you let that vibration be with you in your communications, whether personal or professional, you'll find you're quicker to ask others if you can help, and, most wonderfully, you'll begin to feel the pure joy of helping someone.

21
Hocus, Pocus, Change My Focus

Do you ever have something that gets stuck in your craw? Do you know what I mean? Something that irritates or rankles you? Something that colors your viewpoint and changes your energy? Something negative that you have difficulty letting go?

I was reminded of how easily that can happen when speaking with a new client, a young woman who had recently returned from a fantastic six-month volunteer mission helping people. It was the trip of a lifetime where she had made fabulous friends and did really great work. As we spoke of her mission, some issues and troubled feelings came up from a passing comment a friend had made on her last day. She since hadn't spoken to her friend, and the more we discussed it, the more obvious it became that her friend hadn't even been speaking to her when she made the comment.

The comment had nothing to do with her, yet it totally colored her view of this fantastic trip.

But that's how life is at times. Something gets in our head, and we allow it to hang out there. And the longer it hangs out in our conscious mind, the better chance it has to get in our subconscious mind. Then it takes over your attitude and prevents you from seeing things clearly, as it did with her.

It's important to realize what's going on in your thoughts because so very often, the difference between success and failure is totally based on your attitude. And where does your attitude come from? Your thoughts!

Even if you are prepared in every other way, if something changes your outlook, you almost always ensure disappointment. Knowing that, why do we insist on entering into meetings, sales calls, or appointments without first checking our mind-set? And that's just at work. How about checking our mind-set before we spend time with our spouses, children, friends, or relatives?

> Dr. Daniel G. Amen can show you visible proof of how a negative thought changes your brain. In his book, *Magnificent Mind at Any Age: Natural Ways to Unleash Your Brain's Maximum Potential*, (Three Rivers Press, 2009) he discusses Automatic Negative Thoughts—or ANTs. They are thoughts that come into your mind unconsciously and send you into a tailspin. Much like those pesky insects at a picnic, when you have one ANT, many more follow.
>
> The danger in ANTs, he explains, comes from your physiology actually changing every time you have a thought. His brain imaging studies have demonstrated that your brain releases a certain set of chemicals each and every time you have a thought. Positive thoughts produce chemicals that make you feel good. Negative thoughts discharge chemicals that make you feel bad.
>
> But our thoughts go beyond just our feelings. One of his studies showed harmful thoughts actually deactivated a woman's cerebellum, the back-bottom part of the brain that plays an important role in your physical coordination, as well as her left temporal lobe, which when disengaged, makes you more likely to get irritated.
>
> Talk about how your thoughts create your entire reality! It happens every day, in every walk of life. Have you ever had a fight with your spouse or significant other? And you were still thinking about it as you entered your workplace the next day? How many of us have had a bad day at work on a Friday and allowed it to ruin our weekend?

How attitude can impact us, was never more apparent than when I was coaching little league baseball. I discovered early on that when a child struck out, he was much more apt to make an error in the field on his next play. Why? Because he was still thinking about striking out. Similarly, the woman who "couldn't" stop thinking her friend had made a negative comment to her, "struck out" because the attitude her thoughts created was one of hurt and anger. They prevented her from seeing the mission as the successful and good thing that it was.

When we allow our negative beliefs to influence our attitudes, we get bitter and angry, then alienate ourselves from others. In other words, we become the situation that resembles our attitude.

How?

It's all about momentum. A negative thought left to fester uninterrupted will cause you to think more negative thoughts, and more and more and more. If we could stop that destructive thought before it gets too much force behind it, before it gets too much power, then we can stop the influence that thought has over our attitudes, hence over our situations and lives. The funny thing is, we're the ones giving it the power.

Yeah, that's right: you, me, us.

Don't tell me you have not stayed with a thought that felt lousy. We've all done it. Why? I don't know. Maybe it's because sometimes we just want to feel lousy. We allow ourselves to have a little self-pity party. We then cry about how the world is against us, how it just isn't fair. It happens all the time. I've done it, and I'm sure you've done it as well.

And we need to remember the Law of Attraction is always working So if you're focused on a negative thought for long enough, it's going to attract more negative thoughts, and more, and more.

The game, however, is not to allow it to go on for too long. You need to end it before something in you shifts. Otherwise, like the woman after her mission, you end up living in that injurious space for a couple of days, then into a couple of weeks, and into a couple of months, with it perpetually skewing your perception. It can even go for a couple of years or decades. When that dreadful momentum gets going against us, sometimes it's just easier to give up fighting it, as like I did those many years ago.

It may have happened by accident. Maybe you took a wrong turn or slipped onto the wrong path. But it doesn't matter what created the attitude, all that matters is that you get back on track. And to do that, you have to take responsibility for where you are—even if you think someone else did you wrong. Only *you* can decide how you respond or how you will think about a situation, hence how that situation will inform your life. But ultimately, you have to learn to take full responsibility for what you are thinking, so you can be in control of your attitude and your life.

Portia Nelson wrote a fantastic poem about this very thing. It's called "Autobiography in Five Short Chapters" and appears in the introduction of her book *There's a Hole in My Sidewalk: the romance of self-discovery* (Atria Books/Beyond Words; Reprint edition, 2018. In it she speaks of a deep hole in a sidewalk that we all fall into during our journeys through life. Each time we fall into the hole, we have a different perspective of why. If we choose to grow with each misstep, we move from being blameless and helpless to recognizing our responsibility to avoid the hole.

Me, I took a while to learn how to avoid the hole. I spent so much time there, I had cable TV delivered into that hole. I didn't want to get out immediately I wanted to stay, to feel the pain.

I found being in that hole was like being bewitched by the Sirens in Greek mythology. Do you know the story of the Sirens? The Sirens were singing enchantresses capable of luring passing sailors to their islands, and, subsequently, to their doom. Their song was so sweet, if you heard them sing, you would never leave. You get comfortable there. You forget what your original intention was. You begin to focus on why it's so great to be there. You start making excuses as to why you don't want to leave. You begin to believe you don't deserve to get out.

Even those days you do climb out, you expect to fall back in.

What about your angels, guides, and Wingmates?

Oh, they're there. They're still there wanting to help, hoping to help, trying to help. Only when you're in the hole, you shut them out, too. You become hypnotized by your thoughts and believe you are stuck in that low vibration. And a low vibration makes it very difficult to connect with such high vibrational help.

However, you're never beyond hope. Regardless of how strong the negative momentum is behind your thoughts, you can switch the direction of the momentum, even if for just one minute at a time. Honestly, I know if I can just shift my vibration a little bit, momentum will take over, my vibration will start to rise, and I'll be better able to connect with my angels and Wingmates. It's the whole first Law of Motion thing: An object at rest stays at rest and an object in motion stays in motion at the same speed and in the same direction unless acted upon by another force.

Your vibration is an object. If it's going south, you have to become the force that turns it around.

How?

Hocus, Pocus, Change My Focus.

I borrowed that little phrase from a magician friend of mine. Turns out, at all the workshops I do, both corporate and public, this one little phrase gets remembered the most.

It's a great little thought that you can think, or say to yourself, whenever you catch yourself paying too much attention to unhelpful thoughts. That's how I start. Simple, right?

Am I saying, just by thinking, *Hocus, Pocus, change my focus*, that my focus changes?

Yes, I am. And this practice not only works well for adults, it works great with children, helping them to refocus.

Half the time I do it, I start laughing because I'm saying such a silly phrase, as if that in and of itself, will be able to change my focus. But it does. For by saying it, I have a reason to laugh. And laughing always helps swing my momentum in a more positive direction. It's now gotten to the point where, when I say it, I look forward to laughing about it... and totally forget where my focus was. It's become a self-fulfilling prophesy, a blank page, which allows me to begin anew.

And if the grooves in your brain bring you back to that bad feeling place once more, think it or say it again. "Hocus, Pocus, change my focus." And then think of something, anything that makes you happy.

A Wingman Practice:

Hocus, Pocus, Change My Focus.

For one minute, repeat out loud or quietly to yourself, "Hocus, Focus, Change My Focus."

Allow the phrase to get into your subconscious so that when something doesn't feel good to you, the words slip out quickly and easily. And when they do, choose to focus on something that feels good. If the bad feeling comes back to you, and it most likely will, repeat the process. It's as simple as that.

22
I'm Embracing My Challenges

"Wingman in the house!" I called out as I knocked on the front door before entering Rita's home for our Wednesday night radio show. She was in the kitchen, making dinner. We hugged, and she greeted me with a warm, "How are you doing?"

"I'm embracing my challenges," I retorted. We both hysterically laughed and boom! I had a new practice.

You see, despite being the Wingman on the Wingman's Path, challenges continued to come at me. It seems that sometimes life can be a series of challenges; either you're challenging life, or life is challenging you. And that day, life was challenging me, both physically and financially. Earlier that day, I had visited two different doctors for some tests, and my mortgage was due without my having the required amount in my bank account.

How can that be?

We become what we think about most of the time.
~Earl Nightingale

Probably the best lesson I've learned on the Wingman's Path is *What I think about, I become about.* Others might say, "What I focus on expands," but it means the same thing. It's a basic rule of the Universe.

Notice how Nightingale adds, "most of the time"? That's because your predominant thoughts, the ones you think about *most of the time*, are the ones that have the most power. It only makes sense, right? If the Universe acts like a giant mirror reflecting back to me what I am projecting out, then if I'm projecting more thoughts that bring laughter, the Universe will send me back more reasons to laugh. And when I focus on my challenges, I get more to feel challenged about. It's pretty simple, really. But it's a bit of a bummer, too. Because sometimes, it seems impossible *not* to focus on the challenges when they are all around, and you feel surrounded.

What I had discovered, is the *Hocus Pocus, change my focus* practice worked great when I was at the beginning of a negative thought pattern, when I could catch the thought before too much momentum was behind it. But for other thoughts, ones I'd been focused on for extended periods of time (years!), I needed a stronger practice. And that's what I found with *I'm embracing my challenges.*

Before I had entered Rita's house that night, my health and financial issues were not new for me that day. They were both frequently in my mind, were both what I thought about the most. And for some reason, as I stepped through Rita's door, I realized I'd been thinking about them in the wrong way. It'd been thinking about them like they were alligators.

Alligators?

Let me back up a little. When I was asked to speak at a homeless shelter, I led a discussion on how to handle daily struggles and used alligators as a metaphor. "When you're in the swamps with alligators," I said. "It's tough to focus on anything but the alligators. They can kill you. But if you only focus on them, they are all you see, so you can't find your way out of the swamp. However, if you can take just one minute to look elsewhere you'll see possibilities to exit. And if you take one minute the next day and the next…you'll eventually see enough that you can find a path. It's the same with your life. If you can take just one minute, say when you're falling asleep at night or first thing when you wake up in the morning, and do one of these practices, within a week, maybe a month—it might take as long as six months—you'll be amazed at how much better things start to get. You'll notice the alligators less and start seeing pathways out of the swamp. You'll start seeing a better life for yourself. And the better it gets, the better it gets."

The thing is, often those alligators are really just barriers we've built in our minds that have grown bigger and bigger due to our believing in them, to our paying attention to them. And since "we become what we think about most of the time," if we keep noticing and saying "I'm stuck," I'm stupid," "the world is stacked against me," etc., we'll remain there.

What I decided to do instead, as Rita embraced me with a hug to say hello, was to embrace my challenges.

"Wait a second!" Lisa, a participant at a workshop demanded when I brought this embracing part up. "If what you focus on expands, then by embracing your challenges aren't you, by definition of the Law of Attraction and your own words, bringing yourself more challenges"?

"Wow! Great question," I replied. Was I, by practicing embracing my challenges, bringing myself more challenges? It didn't feel that way. I know when I said it to Rita that night, it felt freeing. And as I practiced, it felt more like I was changing my vibration around my challenges. It's weird, but the more I said, "I'm embracing my challenges," the less I seemed to think of them as things working against me. I was no longer "worried" about them; it was more like they became necessary obstacles to my achieving my goal.

"Yes," I answered Lisa, "Except while *you* hear the word 'challenges,' the Universe doesn't hear anything, it operates on feelings, vibrations. And the vibration of the feelings around the word 'embracing,' for me was pretty high because I finally realized the good that would come to me once I moved beyond my obstacles"

Merriam-Webster uses words like welcome, cherish, and love when defining the word embrace, which is why it felt so good to say it. By sending out love for my challenges, the Universe was sending me back more challenges to love. Challenges to love, are those challenges that help you grow and become the person you want to be and to have the life you want to have. Sometimes, you have to overcome a challenge to realize and achieve what you want.

- Like the baseball player who embraces the challenge of playing in the major leagues.
- The student, who embraces the challenge of furthering her education.
- The doctor, who embraces the challenge of saving a life.
- The entrepreneur, who embraces the challenge of starting a business.

When you learn to embrace your challenges, you learn to appreciate what you gain by overcoming them. By focusing more on that appreciation than on the oppression of the challenge itself, you attract more to appreciate.

And life wouldn't be life without challenges. The First Noble Truth of Buddhism is that "in life, there is suffering," which means, "In life there are challenges." Too many of us don't accept this. We think challenges are something to be avoided. But challenges can't be avoided because there is no life without challenges. Therefore, if challenges are part of life, then how we view our challenges is of utmost importance in keeping our vibration high and manifesting our desires.

What you resist, persists.
~C. G. Jung

Typically, we either fight, resent, or resist our challenges. By doing so, without our realizing it, our energy is totally focused on our challenges, on what we don't want. It's that energy that not only keeps us from overcoming our challenges but keeps more unwanted challenges coming at us.

The Law of Attraction is not a sometimes law; it's a constant law. And the Universe does not differentiate between good and bad. It just sends you back more of whatever you send out.

By embracing our challenges, we change our vibration around them. When we have a difficulty that we work hard to avoid, our hard work (struggle) has a vibration. And that vibration is one of fear, lack, and insecurity at being able to overcome that difficulty. The Universe then sends us more difficulties to be fearful of. By embracing our challenges, we send out a vibration of love, confidence, and competence. And so the Universe sends us back more challenges to love, to enjoy, and to feel confident about.

Years ago, when I felt like I was victimized, I allowed myself to become a victim. And I refused to deal with it for a very long time. But by refusing to deal with it, the energy I was emanating continued to be that of a victim, and the Universe sent me back more reasons to feel like a victim. And the more I felt like a victim, the stronger the chains holding me in that vibrational place continued to grow.

This concept is so important, I want to emphasize it here: What we focus on expands. When we focus on our problems, the Universe gives us more problems. When we focus on our well-being, the Universe sends us more reasons to feel well.

At some of my workshops, I hold up a white sheet of paper with a big black dot on it and ask, "What am I holding up?"

People often call out, "A black dot."

I answer, "No, I'm holding a white sheet of paper with a black dot on it."

Just like in life, we can focus on the dot, our problems, or we can focus on the sheet of paper, the areas of our life that are going well.

And again, this is not just some woo-woo spiritual law of the Universe. This is also a law of science and comes directly from physics. Remember Sir Isaac Newton's first law of motion? "An object at rest remains at rest, an object in motion remains in motion unless acted on by an external force."

It's a simple matter of momentum. When you, your thoughts, and your energy are moving in a positive direction, they build momentum and will continue to move in a positive direction unless acted upon by an external force with equal or stronger momentum.

Unfortunately, the same is true when you, your thoughts, and your energy are moving in a negative direction. I've found, at least in my life, what this means is that when things are going lousy, they will continue to go lousy unless I do something to change it. I have to provide the *external force.*

And that external force is my thoughts, my vibration. By embracing my challenges, I am energetically releasing the command my challenges have over me. The frequency I'm emitting is one of confidence in my ability to handle whatever life throws at me. I feel empowered, and the Universe replies in kind.

By embracing my challenges, I learn to love them, which brings me to the second practice I developed.

When I was a child, my favorite television show was "Get Smart," with Don Adams playing bungling secret agent Maxwell Smart, also known as Agent 86. Maxwell Smart was the absolute best at not letting situations dictate his vibration.

A recurring theme in the series would have Max in trouble. Maybe he would be handcuffed and surrounded by 300 enemies with machine guns in a submarine off the coast of someplace with no apparent help in sight. Every time, when his adversary would point out how hopeless his situation was, Max always replied, "And loving it!" Whatever trouble he found himself in, he would always say, "And loving it!"

I thought of Max as I was driving home from Rita's that night. As I turned onto Route 130, I concentrated on my current physical and financial troubles, and loudly proclaimed, "AND LOVING IT!"

"And Loving it! And Loving it! And Loving it!" I decided to turn this fun memory into a one-minute practice, and so I continued to repeat it over and over. "And Loving it! And Loving it! And Loving it! And Loving it!"

As I consciously practiced saying the phrase, I actually started "loving it." By the time I pulled into my driveway, I was laughing, and, even better, I thought of two different potential solutions, one for each of my "challenges." The Wingman's Path had taught me the importance of repetition, of practicing a thought until it becomes a belief; walking into my house that night, I was loving the fact that I believed everything would work out for me.

When I was young, I would just laugh at the show and Max's comedic behavior. But when I woke up the next morning, I was still smiling, thinking of the show. I recognized the real genius of Max. By embracing his challenges, and "loving it," he was able to change the energy of his dire circumstances and extricate himself from whatever predicament he happened to be in, in that episode. What a great role model!

How about you?

- Do you ever find yourself surrounded by 300 enemies?
- Or late on your mortgage payment?
- Or sitting with an angry boss?
- Or an unsatisfied client?
- Or in a difficult relationship?
- Or receiving some bad news from a doctor?

What would happen if you started "loving it"?

History is rampant with people who failed over and over, or overcame great odds, on their road to becoming wildly successful. Oprah Winfrey, Jim Carrey, Albert Einstein, Franklin Roosevelt, Frederick Douglass, Henry Ford, R.H. Macy, Thomas Edison, the Wright brothers, Winston Churchill, Steven Spielberg, Stephen King, Jay Z, JK Rowling, Michael Jordan, Walt Disney, Colonel Sanders, Abraham Lincoln…The list goes on and on. If they could do it, it means you and I can as well.

A Wingman Practice:

Embracing Challenges and Loving it!

Today we have two practices to help you change your vibration around a challenge you're currently facing. Say for one minute, out loud or to yourself, either, "I'm embracing my challenges," or "And loving it!"

As you say the words, think of your challenge. I've found as you do this, it's best to have a smile on your face, or even better, to start laughing. Your mind will begin coming up with potential solutions. If not, don't worry, practice it again tomorrow. The more you can embrace or love your challenges, the more you will enjoy the process of successfully overcoming them. It's been very rare in the history of our world, that we haven't arrived at a solution to defeat even the most stubborn challenge.

23
The Four Questions

Things started going my way. I hadn't heard back from either doctor, which I took as good news, and a couple of health insurance commission checks came in the first week of the month, so I was only seven days late in paying my mortgage. I was learning more and more about how practicing positivity and raising my vibration could help me move in the direction of creating a life of my choosing. And on top of it, I was having fun.

As I began setting my intentions with more and more trust that the Universe would deliver them to me, I realized I wanted to learn more about why my one-minute practices worked, and to see what else I could do. I knew I was still a novice, but I had unearthed something special, and I wanted to understand it better. So, I decided to further my education by taking a course to become a Certified Law of Attraction Life Coach

I researched different Law of Attraction Coaching schools and decided to sign up for the Quantum Success Coaching Academy. And a funny thing happened when I did. They had me speak with a graduate of their school. It's how they help people decide whether to sign up. It was funny because the gentleman they had me speak to said he didn't think it would be worth it for me. I was firmly on The Wingman's Path by this time, and he thought I knew as much about the Law of Attraction as anyone.

I knew I didn't.

The Wingman's Path is now a path of one-minute practices based on the Law of Attraction, Buddhism, Business Acumen, the Bible, and Old-School common sense. But at that time, it was still being uncovered by me. That gentleman may have seen my future, but at the time, I felt I needed more direction and discipline. Definitely more discipline.

It was really no different than when I started my Meetup group or my working with Rita. It was another opportunity to broaden my schooling, my coaching abilities, and my self-discipline. Have I mentioned I thought I could use some help with discipline?

I saw the course as a way to form a Sanha, the third jewel of Buddhism, which is a community of others on the path. Buddhists participate in and interact with the Sangha in order to grow; it is an integral part of a healthy practice. And I was looking to expand my Sangha.

And expand it I did. I was put into a Pod Group that expanded my Sangha to include two women, one from Michigan and one from Atlanta. To this day, we still hold our pod-group talks, which I continue to find inspirational and integral to the Wingman's Path. They are definitely Wingmates, who have helped light my path and helped me on my journey.

During one of our Pod Group sessions, they reminded me of one of the coaching practices from our class. It's an easy practice, one where you ask yourself three questions:
1. What do I want?
2. Why do I want it?
3. How do I want to feel?

Seems pretty simple, right? Some might even say it's downright obvious, although I've found sometimes that what's obvious to others is not always so obvious to me. And so, I practice.

Since my time in the coaching class, I use this practice often. It's not only fantastic when setting big objectives, like what I desire to manifest in my life, it's wonderful for daily or weekly goals, as well as immediate situational-type intentions. I can't tell you how often I've been standing in a line at the supermarket or Post Office and utilized this practice.
1. What do I want? *I want this line to move quicker.*
2. Why do I want it? *Because I have other chores to do and want to get out of here.*
3. How do I want to feel? *I want to feel relaxed and calm, that I'm not rushing to my next meeting or appointment.*

As I said, simple, right?

Now you may have noticed that this chapter is called "The Four Questions." That's because I'm a big advocate that behavior must follow thought, so I've added a fourth step to QSCA's three-question practice:
4. What one action step can I take to move me closer to realizing my intention?

In the example above, you may think there is no actionable step to helping move the line along more quickly. However, because I'm such a huge believer that my vibration creates my reality, the action step in the above scenario was simply to change my vibration from one of worry and irritation that the line wasn't moving, to relaxing into the situation, seeing everyone doing the best they can, and visualizing the logjam breaking up.

Sometimes that's difficult to do, but that doesn't mean we don't continue to practice raising our vibration. I will tell you that the more I practice not letting these normal, everyday inconveniences, such as lines, traffic, and dealing with others affect me, I have found these normal, everyday types of inconveniences rarely get me worked up. It doesn't mean I don't get stuck in traffic: it means that when I do, I don't let it turn an otherwise good day, bad. Like when standing in line: by focusing on how I want to feel, my body relaxes, and then standing in line transforms from an uncomfortable challenge to a relaxing respite before whatever comes next for me that day.

As for the Four Questions practice, I always, always, always use it in determining any goal.

1. What do I want? *I want to write a book that helps people.*
2. Why do I want to write it? *Because I believe that in discovering The Wingman's Path, I've happened upon a corridor to a better life. I'm certain it can help others to do the same. I feel if I'm able to help others, I have a responsibility to do so. Also, I've always held the limiting belief that I could never write a book. Knowing I have something important to convey inspires me to break through that limiting belief.*
3. How do I want to feel? *I want to feel helpful. I want to feel successful. I want to feel that I can accomplish something of importance. I want to feel that if I set my mind to something, I can achieve it.*
4. What one action step can I take to move me closer to realizing my intention? *The day I did this exercise and wrote this as my goal, the step I wrote down was to call a friend who was in the book business. She helped me plan the many action steps that were necessary for completing the book you are now reading.*

By asking myself these four questions, I immediately begin to change my vibration around my desire. Does it always work? No. While the Law of Attraction always works, my being able to change my vibration doesn't always work.

I mention this because the day after being reminded of this practice by

my two Pod-Coaching buddies, I was heading to the doctor for an examination.
1. What do I want? *I want this appointment to go smoothly and for me to receive good news.*
2. Why do I want it? *Because I want to be healthy and not need to have any type of procedure.*
3. How do I want to feel? *Healthy, happy, strong. I want to feel I have a clean bill of health.*
4. What one action step can I take to move me closer to realizing my intention? *I can practice the feeling of being healthy, of hearing good news from the doctor. I can visualize Jan and me celebrating the good news at dinner that night.*

There aren't many more vulnerable times than when you're in a doctor's office wearing a gown. Especially for a mature gentleman (my wife might say that's an oxymoron when applied to me) with a couple of young women sitting in the room taking notes while we discuss my situation.

Things didn't seem to be going swimmingly. While I was splayed out on the table and the doctor was telling the two nurses what was needed, my first thought was *this isn't at all how I pictured the appointment going,* followed by my saying out loud, "And Loving it!"

My words brought me a smile, which helped me decide that this would be a great time to turn this situation from a negative to a positive. I decided to continue with my *And Loving it!* practice. As I considered the situation, I breathed in and said the words "And Loving it," but then I saw the doctor pull out a sizeable needle.

"Wait! Where you puttin' that needle, dude?" I blurted out. I didn't mean any disrespect, but it was a pretty big needle! Needless to say, instead of practicing, I got my ass kicked. I forgot all about conditioning my mind to be positive.

The results? My *no big deal* visit to the doctor turned into a *why-me?* pity party. It wasn't until after getting home and licking my wounds, that I realized how easy it is to let detrimental thoughts totally take over my mind. By five o'clock, it was pretty clear I had let those harmful thoughts develop into a negative vibe, which wrapped around me like a strong body odor. You know what I mean, right? The kind that by the time you get a whiff of it on yourself, others have been smelling it for a while.

Been there, done that. But this time I wouldn't become a victim again, as I did twenty years earlier. I wouldn't go from "Singing in the Rain" to getting soaked in the rain now. I would stop the negative trend of my vibration. As I summed up the situation, I realized what was needed. An emergency Wingman session.

Not just one minute. I decided to go crazy positive for ten minutes. Laughing, clapping, screaming "Who Da Man!" and giving thanks to anything and everything. It was a valuable ten minutes. For as I clapped and laughed, yelled, and gave thanks, I felt that stench slide off me like I was the star of a soap commercial.

And I learned a powerful lesson. Nothing can keep me down if I don't let it. That's right, I'm in control of me. No matter what happens.

> **Everything changes when you start to emit your own frequency rather than absorbing the frequencies around you, when you start imprinting your intent on the Universe rather than receiving an imprint from existence.**
> ~Barbara Marciniak

I can't tell you why things went so awry in the doctor's office. I thought I was sending out a vibration of good health and positive energy but, as is so often the case when dealing with health, money, and relationships, we think we're sending out a positive vibe but, without realizing it, we're very fearful of the opposite. That conflicting vibe is emitting from us, too. Maybe it was simply that some negative energy was flying around the doctor's office, and although I felt like the vibration I was sending out was of good health and positive energy, maybe the unspoken fears matched that negative energy and added to it.

Whatever it was, I got caught absorbing those negative frequencies surrounding me. I do know there have been times that I've been hit with negative energies, but my vibration was strong enough that I "imprinted my intent on the Universe" and was able to withstand the incoming negativity and continued to move forward. So I know it's possible. It just takes practice, and lots of it, to build your vibration to where you're doing the imprinting and not the other way around.

I'm happy to tell you now, I not only overcame that physical challenge, but I finished my year-long course with the Quantum Success Coaching Academy. Finished. Which meant I was a finisher.

You might not think that's such a big deal, but for me, it meant the world. It meant I had set a challenge for myself and had succeeded. I was now a Certified Law of Attraction Life Coach.

What did it mean to me to be a finisher? It meant I now saw life with different eyes. I now saw life as one who finished what he started. Unfortunately, there haven't been many moments in my life when I would call myself a finisher. Fortunately, this was one of them.

It felt good. It was the feeling of satisfaction, of a job well done. I had challenged myself, and I had succeeded. And I knew I would continue to finish and succeed in other adventures.

I keep mentioning Sir Isaac Newton's First Law of Motion (an object in motion stays in motion, an object at rest stays at rest, unless acted upon by an external force). I do so because it applies so well to how we create our lives through our thoughts. If we're in the motion of feeling better, by definition of Newton's first law, it makes sense that we would continue feeling better, right? Unless acted upon by an external force.

Oops!

What might that force be? In my life, that force always came from the darkness of my own mind. Negative thoughts that sabotaged me from finishing things I wanted to complete, from having that wonderful feeling of success. Those thoughts get fewer and weaker each day I'm on the path because my practices are a force to be reckoned with.

And you know what? You can create your own force to stop the negative, unwanted momentum in your life. And a good way to start it is by asking yourself The Four Questions.

A Wingman Practice:

The Four Questions

Ask yourself these four questions and allow the answers to propel you to manifesting your desire.

1. What do I want?
2. Why do I want it?
3. How do I want to feel?
4. What one action step can I take to move me closer to realizing my intention?

24
Lime-Green Cars

With my health challenge behind me, Jan and I drove up to Providence, Rhode Island for a couple of weeks to hang out with my mom. She lived up there with my sister and her husband, and whenever they go on vacation, I drive up and stay with Mom. It's an arrangement that has worked out well for us. My mom didn't drive, and although my sister obviously had the lion's share of taking care of her, the arrangement allowed me to feel like I was pitching in, and I got to spend some quality time with my mom.

As we took off on our five-hour drive, I, unsurprisingly, brought up my latest Wingman practice. Equally unsurprising was the slight eye-roll from my wife.

"I have a perfect practice for us to do on our drive," I said.

The eye-roll became an eye twitch. (If only I could read tells like that at the poker table.)

She stayed true to form though, sweetly and lovingly asking what type of practice it was, and where had I heard of it.

"From the book *E Squared*, I responded, "the author, Pam Grout, comes from a science background. The premise of this practice is that what shows up in our lives is a direct reflection of our thoughts and emotions."

"Really, how does it work?" she replied with interest, or maybe she had just figured out her tell.

"It's simple. We pick something unusual to look for, like one of her suggestions is a green car, and we count how many of them we see."

She thought about it for a few seconds and asked, "Ok, but let's make it unique somehow."

"How?"

"Make it a lime-green car."

I agreed. I knew it was her favorite color, and I was excited for her to try out this new experiment with me. And really, how many lime-green cars do you really see?

I kept the conversation alive, "How many lime-green cars would you have to see, for you to believe?"

"You mean to believe we can set our intention and have the Universe bring it to us? I don't know, it would have to be more than a few. Are you saying to sort of believe, or to know without a shadow of a doubt"?

"Either," I immediately answered, but as she was reflecting on her answer, I said, "Change that. You need to know it without a shadow of a doubt."

"Not sure, let's see what happens."

So began our quest to see lime-green cars, and with it, perhaps a better understanding of our Universe.

It started out slowly. I saw only one by the time we arrived. The next day, as we explored Newport, Jan spotted two lime-green cars.

On the second day of our visit, we were driving with my sister and brother-in-law. I told them of our little hypothesis, and my brother-in-law soon spotted one. No one else saw it, so he actually turned the car around to drive back to where it was. What makes this so surprising is he is more of the academic type. He's the dean of a medical school and doesn't normally go in for these types of "shenanigans." But there he was, being a valued contributor to our study.

From that point on, and for the next two weeks, it seemed like we saw lime-green cars everywhere we went. It was crazy. One day, driving into Boston on I-95, we ended up behind, next to, and in front of three different lime-green cars. We were literally surrounded by them. When we went to the mall one day, in the parking lot right next to us, you guessed it, two different lime-green cars. It even happened when watching a television show: a car commercial came on featuring a lime-green car.

However, my favorite moment of our successful research project happened on our way home from Rhode Island. As we seemed to pass lime-green car after lime-green car, Jan exclaimed, "We have to pick another color; there are just too many lime-green cars!"

Which brings me back to the proposition of the experiment...if I set my intention to look for something (lime-green cars), will I find it?

The answer was an unqualified yes. We had unequivocally proved it without a shadow of a doubt.

I decided to do more research and found myself reading all about quantum physics and something called the observer effect.

The Observer Effect is "the theory that the mere observation of a phenomenon inevitably changes that phenomenon" (*Challenges Surfaced by Complexity Theory by Eric B. Dent Chapter in Managing Organizational Complexity: Philosophy, Theory and Application* edited by Kurt Richardson. Information Age Publishing, 2005) In simple terms it states that by the very act of watching, the observer affects the observed reality.

Wow! No wonder we saw so many lime-green cars. By looking for them, we influenced our reality and saw them. The more we did, the more the cycle continued, and the more we saw them.

> In a study reported in the February 27, 1998 issue of "Nature", researchers at the Weizmann Institute of Science conducted an experiment that demonstrated how electrons are affected just by being observed. "The experiment revealed that the greater the amount of watching, the greater the observer's influence on what actually takes place."(https://www.sciencedaily.com/releases/1998/02/980227055013.htm)

I decided to create a practice based on the Observer Effect. The first thing I did was to set my intention to find money. When I mentioned my new objective to Jan, she wasn't quite ready to believe it. After all, she alleged, cars are material things, something that has been built and could be touched.

"Look," I surmised. "We set a goal to see lime-green cars, and we saw far many more than expected. I want to find money."

What happened over the next month was pretty unbelievable. Three checks, all expected, were delivered to me. However, the values were for far greater than anticipated, each of them being ten times the predicted amount. It was like when playing Monopoly and landing on the space where you received the card *Bank Error in Your Favor*. Instead of a $300 check, I received $3,000. A $600 check came in for $6,000, and then the *piece de resistance* was an unbelievable surprise check for almost $50,000. Yes, you read that correctly. I was expecting a check for $5,000, and instead, it was for $50,000.

Wow!

Do I have your attention now? The observer effect certainly had mine.

As I write this, I'm realizing that for some reason, I stopped looking for money after that. Perhaps I felt flush for the first time in a very long time because instead of looking for money, I started looking for inner peace, happiness, and a path to help others. Maybe. I'm not sure why I stopped looking for money, but I am certain, as I'm writing this now, I will begin this practice again immediately.

How about you? What are you looking for?

How about you start off small and look for something unusual? Prove it to yourself that quantum physics is correct and what you look for, you will find.

A Wingman Practice:

Lime-Green Cars

Set your intention to see something. Pick something unusual; it can be purple feathers, red flowers, or lime-green cars. Just be clear about what you want. Let yourself, and the Universe, know *exactly* what you want to see by stating it clearly out loud. Then, for one minute, think about what you want to see, and say over and over, "What I look for, I find."

Now keep your eyes open with the expectation of seeing it.

25
My Eighth-Grade Self

I wanted to combine some of the processes and lessons I'd been learning and set my intention on finding people to help that week. Of course, two opportunities came about. After all, what I looked for, I find.

The first request for help came from the Center for Family Services, a major non-profit organization in Camden, New Jersey. It was to talk with a group of children. Sounds like fun, right? But these weren't just any kids, these were kids in the Foster Program. And this was Camden, a city consistently ranked at the very top for highest crime, lowest income, and most habitual cities in America.

Yeah, *most habitual*. That is my take on it anyway, because the challenge of breaking the consistent stranglehold of the generational pull of drugs, guns, and violence seems inescapable. It's not a place anyone looks to move to; it's more a place you want to escape from. It's right across the river from Philadelphia, but getting out of Camden, without being in a pine box or going to jail, hadn't proved easy for many.

As Matt Taibbi, wrote in *Rolling Stone* magazine:

> The first thing you notice about Camden, New Jersey, is that pretty much everyone you talk to has just gotten his or her ass kicked. There's no hope in this major metropolitan area run by armed teenagers with no access to jobs. The city is almost completely ungoverned. ("Apocalypse, New Jersey: A Dispatch from America's Most Desperate Town," 11 Dec. 2013.)

Perhaps it's needless to say why, when I got the request to give the workshop, I was both excited and more than a little nervous. And to think I had asked for this! Well, here it was being delivered.

> "I wanted to shoot people because that's what I saw growing up," said Anderson Baker, a Camden native who spent four years in jail after being involved in several shootings. "When I was younger, I would see my boys and cousins going into jail, and when they got out, all the girls wanted them. So, I wanted to go to jail. I wanted to be like America's Most Wanted. I wanted my name to be known on the streets." (Alcindor, Yamiche. "New Jersey gun laws don't curb violence in Camden." USA Today. Jun 4, 2013).

I began by looking up quotes I thought might resonate with the kids but quickly I realized how foolish these quotes might sound coming out of my mouth. The Social Worker who had sent me the request made it very clear that these kids were tough and would know if I wasn't genuine.

Genuine. How could I be genuine in a way that would relate to them? The message came to me loud and clear. I didn't hear it, I felt it. It was a message from my inner Wingman: "If you want to really help them, help your own inner child, and teach what you need to learn. Pay attention to the message."

Excuse me? What I need to learn?

I was taken back by the suggestion. But the message seemed to be delivered from higher myself. I truly felt it. I needed to heed the advice. Yet, as an older gentleman, I was coming from a whole different place than where these boys and girls were. How could what I need to learn mean anything to them? Or rather, what my inner child needed to learn.

While I thought about what my inner child needed to learn, I received the second request for help. It was from a client who was to give the commencement speech to an eighth-grade graduation class in his hometown. He asked me to be his speechwriter. Oh, and could I write it as a message to my eighth-grade self?

How did these dissimilar situations, foster kids from the inner city and an eighth-grade graduating class from a school in a rural area, tie in together? Or did they?

There was definitely a theme connecting the kids in Camden and the graduating class that my client was to speak to. And that theme was about me, my younger me. But what was it that my inner child, specifically my eighth-grade self, needed to learn? And why was the Universe hitting me with two fists to make sure I received the message?

I thought back to that time in my life and quickly recognized the moment I needed to revisit. Tears welled up in my eyes.

I was about twelve years old. My mom was driving my sister to the orthodontist, and I went along for the ride. We neared a busy intersection in Philadelphia and stopped in front of the office just long enough for my sister to jump out of the car for her scheduled appointment. My mom paused to ask if I wanted to stay with her, or go with my sister. I stayed with my mom. But at the next block, when she stopped at a red light, I jumped out for seemingly no reason, with a quick comment: "I will go with Sandy."

Less than one minute later, my mom, who afterward said her brakes had failed, went through a red light, crashed through a picture window, and landed in a bookstore. It was an accident that made the front page of the newspapers.

My life drastically changed at that point. And until receiving these two messages, well three if you include the one from the Universe to help my inner child, I hadn't given it much thought. Oh, I've mentioned it from time to time, but I never really thought about it.

You see, my mom was never the same after that. She grew depressed and despondent and was constantly in and out of hospitals. She became a shell of her former self, and it took years and years for her to recover. As an immature kid, the enormity of the situation was lost on me, though I knew something had definitely changed. My sister, just two years my senior, basically took over as my mom, but from then on, although she was in charge, we took care of each other as best we could. Instead of the normal food my mom used to cook, I ate mostly Cocoa Puffs cereal and Chef Boyardee Mini Raviolis. I basically just listened and did what I was told, which wasn't much, never realizing the depth of the destruction of our family. (Years later I still have a fondness for "meat and noodles.")

You want to really help them, help your own inner child, and teach what you need to learn. Pay attention to the message.

"It's not your fault."

That certainly seemed like a good message to start with for the kids in the foster program. And for me. Although I wasn't sure how to convey that without having a much closer relationship with them. I didn't think it would come out right.

I decided to see if I could come up with the same message to both groups of kids. As I did, I kept coming back to me and realized the best way I could help my client and the kids in Camden was to start with a letter to my younger self at my graduation from middle school (it was called Junior High School back then). So that's what I did. Here is what I came up with. I'm not sure I would have listened back then, but I'm certainly hoping my eighth-grade self hears me now.

Congratulations! You did it! Celebrate this moment. Others may not understand this accomplishment, but you and I do. We both know how you stepped up when circumstances got difficult, when your schoolwork got heavy, and your family life got more challenging. We both know how, when you put your mind to it and focus on what you want, you are able to achieve great things, and that is why today, we celebrate you and your graduation.

Be Happy today.

You've done a great job. Enjoy this feeling of completion, and whenever a challenge arises, remember this happy feeling of success and the work you did to achieve it. It will spur you on to many great accomplishments.

Be Grateful today.

As you're feeling this wonderful feeling of achievement, remember to say thank you to someone who helped you along the way. Be it a friend or family, an older grandparent, or a younger sibling, thank them for contributing to your success. Always take time to say thank you.

Be Helpful today. Make it a daily habit to think of one person you can help today. It can be as simple as helping your Mom by doing chores at home without being asked, or helping a classmate, who's having a difficult time. I've found each and every time I've helped someone else, I've helped myself as well. I always seem to feel great when I do.

Be Healthy today. I'm not telling you to stop eating cheesesteaks, hoagies, and ice cream, but our body will sure thank you if you can cut down on them. As Lady Gaga said, "I do yoga, I do Bikram, and I run, and I eat really healthy." Maybe you could do the same, and we can get in really great shape.

And most importantly...

Focus on the Positive today. I've learned in these past many years, we have control over what we choose to focus on. Choose to focus on the positives, the solutions, and on what's going right today. Always choose to focus on what you can do, never on what you can't. Be sure to practice positivity for one minute each day.

Enjoy today. You've earned it.

I Love You,
Your Older Self

From there, it was easy to write the speech for the graduating class. The kids in the Foster Program were another story. They weren't graduating with all their families around them congratulating them. There was nothing special for them about the day. Other than I was speaking to them. And I was determined to make it a very special day by inspiring them to believe in themselves and to believe they could accomplish whatever they set their minds to.

I took my speech to my younger self, and I went into Camden, prepared to teach what I needed to learn. I spoke about what I do, how I do it, and how it has helped my clients and me. We then did one-minute practices, and we inspired each other. And I paid attention to the message. And when we finished, a young man asked if I could come back. I still get chills when I think of it.

Later that day, I received the following email.

Mike-

I can't thank you enough for coming in to liven up the program with your positive message. Thank you also for not being offended by the kids' acting up. This is a tough crowd, but they really took to you, and that's really saying a lot. Even the director and the other staff commented on how responsive the kids were. Yay, Mike!! Way to go!!

I would love for you to come back the next available time you have. However, the director says she'd prefer you have a bigger audience, by which she means the fall... Either way, just give me a call, and I'll let them know when you're available. Heck, I'd love it if you could make it into a monthly series!! Whatever you can do will be so appreciated...

After you left, we had a discussion about forgiveness...I can't help but think the love you left behind had something to do with them opening up. Each kid at the program has their story and your message of

positive thinking is so, so important for them to hear.
God bless for the work you do, and thank you again from
the bottom of my heart for coming in.

Warmly,
Sara

And I say, "Thank you, Sara" from the bottom of my heart, for allowing me to be their wingman and helping me teach what I needed to learn.

A Wingman Practice:

A Letter to a Younger You

Set a little time aside and write a letter to your younger self. Marinate on it for a bit and allow the age to come to you. The age doesn't matter, what you write does. And pay attention to the message.

26
William and Ronja

I did go back and speak with the kids again. And the more I visited Camden, the more I started seeing the possibilities of Camden's rising. Not that it was easy to see. As Peter Moskovitz reported, when asking if you could gentrify America's poorest and most dangerous city, it was far easier to focus on why its rebirth was near hopeless (Moskowitz, Peter. "Can You Gentrify America's Poorest, Most Dangerous City?" Gawker. November 10, 2014). Camden was that; its poverty rate was high and stagnant, consistently around 40 percent year after year. And the murder rate in Camden was still higher than Detroit's, several times the national average.

> **Success consists of going from failure to failure without loss of enthusiasm.**
> ~Winston Churchill

    I thought about my journey and what I'd been through. Camden was no different than me, or any other Phoenix, rising from the ashes. The path upward required staying focused on what you can do and taking steps in that direction.

    Camden took a big, albeit very unusual step, by eliminating its police force and replacing it with a new one run by the county. Things began to improve. Yes, the murder rate was still crazy high, but shootings were down 43 percent in the last two years before the printing of this book, and violent crime down 22 percent. The little league had grown from 150 kids playing baseball to almost 500. There was also an infusion of cash and high-paying jobs, and more and more people were visiting the city's revitalized waterfront district.

Things were looking up, and most importantly, when speaking with residents, you could feel the trust the new police department had engendered, along with the hope for a better future.

I hadn't been around Camden that long, but I could feel it in speaking with the kids in the foster program. One of them told me I should meet William and Ronja Butler. So, I reached out to them and was glad I did. I had never met anyone who's faith was so strong. It was their faith that lit the path for my next practice.

The Butlers had been doing service work in a variety of places when they learned of Camden through articles speaking about the city being the most impoverished and crime ridden in the US. After praying, they believed they were meant to visit. They didn't know a single person in Camden, or in the region, yet they moved to the city on faith. Ronja told me that on that first visit, they believed God was confirming they should move to Camden by allowing them to meet many of Camden's people and incredible leaders.

William Butler is an artist, and Ronja Butler is the CEO of Thomas Lift, a socially conscious company creating inspired art and design as a brand of love and justice. I met William at his studio, a converted firehouse, and I listened as he told me they had moved from Des Moines to Camden because they had a calling.

I was incredulous. "No one looks to move to Camden, they look to escape it," I said.

"Mike," he answered, "Sometimes doors open to take us out of our comfort zone."

I may not have understood that type of faith, but I was motivated by William's vibration.

They started a Third Thursday Art Crawl where people in the community would come out for a night of art, inspiration, and connectivity. Since then, Third Thursday has grown to an evening of live music, other open local art galleries, and many different restaurant specials.

Jan and I drove to his gallery for their next Third Thursday. As I stood there watching kids from all different backgrounds, I saw a young boy holding a camera, pretending to take pictures. When he "took" my picture, I asked his mother about him, and she broke into tears. He had never before held a real camera, and she had never seen him this happy. It was then I understood the power of William and Ronja's vision.

As we left that night, Jan and I invited William, Ronja, and their two boys over for a Friday night Shabbat dinner. We hadn't had one in years, but I guess faith begets faith. When we sat down to eat, William asked if he could lead us in grace. I was caught by surprise but sputtered out a *yes*. I had never before said grace in my life.

"Bless this food and our new friends who prepared it with love. May our bonds, our faith, and our bodies grow stronger."

There may have been more, but that was what I remembered. As I took my first bite, I felt his thankfulness, and a warm embrace of love. It was a wonderful night, and I was inspired by their vibration, their beliefs, and their commitment.

William and Ronja were true Wingmates, unlike any I had ever met before. They were helping connect the people of Camden. Art may have been their starting point, but it was their smiles and their infectious energy that made it stick.

Ronja mentioned how it seemed like Camden was on the rise, and how living and working in the city, they had witnessed the tremendous healing and restoration that was taking place. I mentioned I just heard that sentiment expressed by Richard Stagliano, the CEO of the previously mentioned Center for Family Services. I was in his office one day after speaking with the kids in the foster program, and we were discussing this latest rebirth of Camden. He said to me, "It feels different, this time."

I love when I can help, especially when I can help connect people. As luck would have it, William mentioned wanting to meet Richard. "Consider it done," I exclaimed. "I'll set up a lunch meeting for us."

As they were traveling for the next 10 days, I called Richard and set up a lunch for the end of the month. After emailing Ronja the details, I received the following email.

> That is so wonderful to hear. We look forward to it.
> I have a wonderful story to share with you. We are traveling for work in TN and VA until the end of the month. Yesterday, as we were leaving NJ (we are driving) and right after I shared with my family about your lime-green car idea, we saw 6 lime-green cars on the back of a truck carrier. How funny is that!
> The boys decided we would look for bright pink or purple cars, which was fun to do, and now that we are in TN, we are looking for men with long beards down to their stomachs. We have seen a few already. How fun. Thanks for the reminder that God has so much for us to see and celebrate if we really truly seek Him and look. :)

Love to you and Janet and all your loved ones. We hope to see you all soon, and our prayers are with you.

"The desert and the parched land will be glad; the wilderness will rejoice and blossom."

Isaiah 35

It was at our lunch at the end of the month that the practice I was to learn from William and Ronja was granted to me. Like all the practices on The Wingman's Path, I say granted, or gifted, or given, but really, it's just me, finally awakening to a new way of raising my vibration through practice, and seeing something, that I may have seen many times before, but didn't notice.

I'm a pretty casual eater, so I was thrilled when we decided to meet for lunch at a little sandwich shop in Camden. As we sat down to cheesesteaks, chicken wings, and pizza, William turned to me and said, "Michael, how about if you lead us in Grace."

I was dumbstruck, but what could I do? As we held hands, we closed our eyes and I said...Nothing.

I was speechless. I didn't know what to say. After we sat there in silence, for what seemed like several minutes but was only a few seconds, William followed with, "Any time now, Michael."

I smiled at the situation and responded, "Thank you for this moment. I feel blessed and honored to share food with such wonderful Wingmates."

I'm sure it was a wonderful lunch, with happy banter, strategies to help further the cause, and promises to stay in touch. But what I remember most was my first time ever leading Grace. As I write these words, I'm smiling at the memory. My eyes were closed, but looking back, I can still see Ronja holding my left hand and Richard holding my right. I can still see the inside of the restaurant, with its four little tables. And I can still smell the food wafting up my nostrils as we sat in silence waiting for me to speak. It is a moment I still feel thankful for.

I wish I could tell you I've since said Grace every time I've sat down to a meal, but that would be untrue. What I have done, however, is made certain to recognize the many different moments in each day by saying, "Thank you for this moment." I have said it before a meal, as well as after a meal. I've said it during a wonderful moment, and I've said it when I'm in a difficult spot. It really helps me to appreciate those great moments, like sitting on a quiet beach, spending time with loved ones, or taking my morning walk, wherever I happen to be in the world.

Surprisingly, I've found it also helps when facing a difficult situation. At those times, I usually follow, "Thank you for this moment," with something like, "I appreciate the opportunity to demonstrate to myself, and to the Universe, that I can overcome any challenge that's put before me." By giving thanks for even my most demanding moments, I'm able to keep my vibration high, and not let the struggle overtake me.

William and Ronja: "Thank you for this moment."

A Wingman Practice:

Thank You for this Moment.

For one minute, say out loud, or quietly to yourself, "Thank you for this moment."

As you repeat the phrase, let the words wash over you. The idea of this practice is to have the words infiltrate your subconscious, so you remember to say them at different moments during the course of your day.

Then, when particular moments do arise during your day, whether spectacular or challenging, make sure to say the words, "Thank you for this moment." As you do, think about what you appreciate in that moment. Obviously, it's much easier to find appreciation in the better moments. What I've found, however, is that this practice has improved my ability to find something to appreciate during my most challenging moments. The improvement has been instrumental in keeping my vibration high and helping me to get back on track sooner, rather than later. The importance of that cannot be overstated. The longer you are in the rabbit hole, the tougher it becomes to bounce back. This practice is fabulous at keeping your momentum moving when things are good, and turning it around when things aren't.

27
Miss New Jersey

You never know when or where the next opportunity will arise. That lesson, which I supposedly had learned with Rita and the *Talk-n-Angels* radio show, clearly did not stick, and I was fortunate to be re-taught it by a good friend.

I had declined an invitation to participate in a health fair for municipal workers, and I mentioned it over the phone to my buddy, Al. He asked, "why?" My answer was so convoluted and made so little sense, I actually hung up with Al mid-sentence so I could call the organization back to accept the invitation. Thankfully, it wasn't too late.

When told Al I decided to do it, he asked the same question, "Why?"

I said, "Al, because of you, you're the one who convinced me."

"Mike," he replied, "I didn't say anything. I just asked *why*."

Funny, isn't it? How the very simple question "why?" can help us recognize our correct answer?

So, there I was at this health fair with a bunch of municipal workers filing by. I decided to have some fun and see if I could help them bring more positive energy into their municipality, and into their lives.

And fun I had. As each person walked by, I had them pull out a slip of paper with a different practice I had written on it. Then, together, we would go back and forth saying the practice for one minute.

"I'm a lucky guy." "I'm a lucky Lady."

"Congratulations." "Congratulations."

"Hocus, Pocus, change my fous." "Hocus, Pocus, change my focus."

"Find the positives." "Find the positives."

Back and forth I was going, practicing, and laughing with each person who walked by. The fair, which was being held in a gymnasium, felt our energy. I was absolutely lighting it up with positivity. And then a nurse, another vendor, came over to see what was happening and why everyone seemed to be smiling and laughing on my side of the room. I had her pull out one of my practices. It was insightful.

"I am open to opportunities coming my way."

We went back and forth, saying it to each other. As soon as we stopped, she offered me my next opportunity.

"I'm a director with the Miss New Jersey Pageant organization. I have a woman I think you could help."

"Of course," I responded, "It would be my honor." It may take me a while to learn my lessons, but eventually, I do. And the fact that the practice we shared was about being open to opportunities was not lost on me.

Later, after the fair had ended, she asked me if I would also consider being a judge. "Are you asking an older gentleman if he would like to judge beautiful women in bathing suits?" I jokingly replied.

That was the beginning of my education in the pageant world. Because while everyone outside of it looking in believes it to be a beauty contest, those associated with the Miss New Jersey and Miss America pageants recognize it as an education or scholarship competition.

And that's exactly what I found it to be: an organization that helps educate and empower young women to become the best versions of themselves. While winning the competition is a great kickstart to a career, I've found just being a pageant girl seems like a recipe for success for the rest of their lives.

Maybe it's the self-discipline they learn, or the experience of public speaking. Maybe it's learning how to get your message out or just getting started at a young age volunteering and helping others. Maybe it's learning how to be poised, confident, and self-possessed. Or maybe it's the work ethic they learn from a young age—while all of these girls go to school full time, they also must spend hours upon hours, volunteering, practicing their talent, keeping up with current events, and working out at the gym.

Whatever it is, so many women who cut their teeth in the pageant world, grow up to be successful, whether it's in acting, journalism, healthcare, or business. And it takes a whole lot more than a pretty face to do that. Who wouldn't want a bright, educated, hard-working, and confident woman as part of your team?

The success of the pageant world is not defined by the close to one hundred Miss Americas, but rather, by the thousands and thousands of women who go on to flourish in productive careers where they utilize the skills they learned from this incredible sisterhood. Think Oprah Winfrey, who won a scholarship to Tennessee State University, where she got her first job in a radio station, or Diane Sawyer, who won a prize that paid for her first year at Wellesley College.

But it's still a competition. Everyone wants to win, and be it business, politics, job hunting, professional sports, and yes, beauty pageants, when the difference between candidates is slim, you need an edge. Often, that edge is simply a more positive attitude. As in every profession, when you're competing against the best, it's not always easy to maintain that positive attitude. And that's where I came in.

> **Many of life's failures are people who did not realize how close they were to success when they gave up.**
> ~Thomas A. Edison

How many of us have given up when we were so close to success? How many of us have allowed some small defeat to get in our head, and quit because of it? How many of us have allowed the pressure of the situation to destroy our dreams?

> **Last year I made third-runner up. I said I made top 5, I'm fine, I don't need to compete again. My parents said they wanted me to give it one more shot, I'm so glad they did.**
> ~Cierra Kaler-Jones,
> Miss New Jersey 2014

After coaching a few pageant women to some increased success, I was honored to receive a request to be part of Miss New Jersey, 2014, Cierra Kaler-Jones' success team as she headed to the Miss America competition. I was to be her confidence coach, although, after reading her extraordinary resume, I wasn't sure what I'd be able to offer this remarkable young lady. After all, she not only had just won the Miss New Jersey pageant but before that had been selected for a fellowship to present at the Women's World Congress in Hyderabad, India. These two successes were just the latest in a long stream of accomplishments.

How could I possibly help? I couldn't imagine having the confidence to achieve all she's done, much less walk around in my bathing suit in front of 5 million people.

I decided to approach it the same way I did every client; after conversing about some of her struggles, we started working on a process I use with successful people to help them stay on top of their game. And this woman is on top of her game. We spoke about my one-minute Wingman practices and how certain words or affirmations can really help keep us focused and positive. Especially those quiet few minutes before the big game.

We did visualizations. I had her imagine winning the Miss America Pageant. Could she see it? Could she feel it? And more importantly, could she believe it? Because when you believe it, you're 90% of the way there. And that's when she came up her own practice that she would take with her to the Miss America Competition. *Others have done it, I can too.*

It's a practice I have since used many times in corporate settings, hospitals, and Wingman's Path live practice sessions because it's not just for those heading into big competitions. Many clients have told me it's helped them overcome a variety of challenges from succeeding at getting a new client, to feeling confident in battling different diseases and feeling strong and healthy.

Others have done it, I can too.

Remember, by saying it over and over again, your mind starts believing it. And it's easier to believe because it's true: others have done it, and you can too. Once you start believing, anything is possible. Even winning the Miss America crown.

> As I was preparing for Miss America, I met with Michael, whose enthusiasm and positive energy created a space for me to believe wholeheartedly in myself and potential. I could not have walked into the Miss America competition with more confidence because Michael instilled such positive thoughts in my mind that allowed me to self-actualize.
> ~Cierra Kaler-Jones

While Cierra didn't win the Miss America competition that year, she was a finalist for the Miss America Quality of Life Award, and she went on to great success in other areas. She is a teaching artist, writer, and rising scholar based in Washington, DC. She had her writing featured in Education Post, Nia Magazine, Midnight and Indigo, and on Ebony.com. She has been recognized internationally for her social justice work with students and was a guest speaker at the White House Initiative on Educational Excellence for African Americans and the United States Department of Education. To say this woman is successful is an understatement.

It was an honor to work with her and the practice that came from our association has helped me, and so many of my clients to move in the direction of their dreams.

A Wingman Practice:

Others Have Done It, I Can Too.

Say, "Others have done it, I can too" over and over to yourself for one minute. While saying it, think about what it is you want to accomplish and think of others who have succeeded at achieving that same goal.

This practice works so well because it is a true statement 99% of the time. Because others have done what you are looking to do, it's easy to believe it. And when you believe, you send out a vibration of believing in yourself and of knowing that others have done it, and you can too.
You've got this.

28
Here Comes Da Judge

After my success working with Cierra and other pageant contestants, I was asked to judge the Miss Eastern Shore, Atlantic Shores, and South Shore Tiny, Little & Pre-Teen Beauty Pageants.

The comments I heard from clients and friends ranged from, *You mean like Toddlers and Tiaras? That's awful!* to *What kind of Mom would have her child in one of those?* Oh yeah, I heard judgments about these girls' moms everywhere I turned. Everyone had an opinion, and none of them were positive.

With those "warm and fuzzy" comments in my mind, I drove to my first competition, not quite knowing what to expect. What I found was exactly the opposite of all the negativity people were spewing. It wasn't young girls being overly made-up and sexualized. Actually, it felt more like young girls joining a team, making new friends, and being mentored by the older girls. It felt like they were joining a sisterhood, where everyone looks out for everyone else. There were no bathing suits, crazy outfits, or backstabbing. And there were no losers.

On the contrary, I was even more impressed with the pageant system than I had been before. What I witnessed seemed very similar to the teams I played on in my youth. Instead of it being soccer or baseball, it was pageant, and instead of older team members giving me advice, some of which I still remember to this day, it was the older girls, all pageant winners, helping their "little sisters."

I still remember watching fellow judges, Miss Ocean City, Devon Vanderslice, and former Miss New Jersey, Ashleigh Fairfield, speaking and coaching some of the younger girls. It was a win-win for everyone, a beautiful thing to see, and I was thrilled to be a small part of it. The more I was around these pageant women, the more impressed I became. They were all team players, all smart, all confident, and all willing to help others. These women were all every parent would want for their child.

Driving home, I couldn't understand why so many people were so judging and so unkind, about something they knew very little about. If they had been with me that day, there is no way they would have felt that way. And who were they to judge, anyway?

And then it hit me. I, too, have judged others harshly whom I knew nothing about.

Why just the day before, I was in my car in a supermarket parking lot while Jan had run in to pick up some groceries. As I waited, I noticed people parked in such a way that they were blocking traffic. I immediately judged them as boorish, rude, and ill-mannered.

Oh yeah, I'm as guilty as the next person. I'm big on *shoulds*. I have a list of rules in my head of how people *should* act, and when they don't, I get incensed and irritated. And don't even get me started on when someone is talking loudly on their cell phone in a public place.

Here Comes Da Judge.

Fortunately, I had a long drive home that day and, while driving, I recognized that when I judge, my vibration always, always, always decreases. Meaning, some person about whom I know nothing, does something that I find inappropriate or wrong, and my vibration takes a hit. How stupid is that?

I decided right then and there, as I was exiting the Atlantic City Expressway onto Route 42, that I would do my best to stop judging others, especially when their behavior had nothing to do with me. Because, really, it's never about them; it's only about me. And if I'm allowing their rudeness to lower my vibration and knock me off my path, then it will take me longer to manifest my desire of creating a life of my choosing.

I realized how often I judged people. It seemed like every day someone would annoy me. Walking slowly, dressing weirdly, speaking loudly, sneezing, coughing...the reasons were endless. And every one of them lowered my vibration.

It's not about them, it's only about you.

As I pulled into my driveway, I decided every time Da Judge came out in me, I would combat it by thinking something positive about that person.

> I remembered a story I had read about being judgmental from Psychologist and meditation teacher Tara Brach... Imagine you are walking through the woods and you see a small dog. It looks cute and friendly. You approach and move to pet the dog. Suddenly it snarls and tries to bite you. The dog no longer seems cute, and you feel fear and possibly anger. Then, as the wind blows, the leaves on the ground are carried away, and you see the dog has one of its legs caught in a trap. Now, you feel compassion for the dog. You know it became aggressive because it is in pain and is suffering.

Jan and I went out to dinner with friends after I got home that night. One of them gave me a saying that I have turned into a favorite practice: *I don't get it, but I don't have to*. It's changed my life. Every time Da Judge starts to rise inside me, I quell it quickly by simply saying, "I don't get it, but I don't have to." I no longer allow people or situations that I know nothing about to get into my head and possibly take me down a rabbit hole I don't want to be in.

It's not about them, it's only about me.

A Wingman Practice:

Here Comes Da Judge!

Think about the times you've judged others harshly. As you do, recognize the feeling that arose in you. Was it one of joy and happiness, or anger and frustration?

Now say the words "Here Comes Da Judge" followed by "I don't get it, but I don't have to" over and over for one minute. Allow those words to permeate your subconscious, so the next time Da Judge starts rising inside you, you eliminate it rapidly before it affects your energy.

29
A Message from the Dalai Lama

It was time for a little getaway. Jan and I decided to drive up to Maine for some natural beauty, a little hiking, and a lot of relaxing. We headed to Acadia National Park but stopped in Belfast, Maine for a couple days on the way up.

The first morning in Belfast was beautiful. I took a walk along the coast and returned to my car around 7:30 am. As I stood on the side of the road, in the driveway of a small business off of Route 1, a Toyota Prius zipped by me, going faster than I thought a Prius could go. It passed me, made a U-turn on the road, then pulled into the driveway, right up next to me.

A woman, an old-school hippie, eating a good-looking ham, egg, and cheese sandwich, opened her window, looked up at me through her sunglasses, and asked, "Are you all right, do you need a ride?"

"No, thank you. I'm fine," I replied. Unsure of why she would think I needed a ride, I decided to risk it and ask. "What made you think I needed a ride?"

"I felt your energy as I passed," she said.

My first thought was that I didn't need a ride, so that couldn't have been the energy I was emitting, so if she felt that, she probably wasn't great at feeling energy. But I could feel my face break into a big smile, and whenever that happens, whenever I'm smiling, I like to allow that vibration to continue. So, I let it go.

For the next 20 minutes, she regaled me with stories. From her days at Antioch College to her 14 years with the Dali Lama. She spoke, laughed, and completely held my interest.

Time passed quickly. When I realized it was time for me to go, she said she had a message for me.

"A message, why didn't you say so?" I exclaimed.

Excitedly she stated, "This comes from the Dali Lama, he wants you to say the mantra to the Green Tara, and pass it on to others."

"Wait!" I was a bit bewildered. "You have a message for me from the Dalai Lama, and you waited 20 minutes to mention it?"

She nodded her head, as if delivering a message from the Dali Lama was a perfectly normal thing. "I was enjoying our conversation."

"The Green Tara. Huh?" I continued. "Is that anything like the Green Lantern? Or the Green Arrow?"

She just stared at me. Clearly, she didn't have my appreciation for DC comic superheroes.

I resumed: "Who is the Green Tara, and what is the mantra?"

She looked around her car and then pulled out an old piece of cardboard from between the passenger side seatback and bottom. From her glovebox, she grabbed a black magic marker and wrote *Om Tare Tuttare Ture Soha* on the cardboard before handing it to me.

Now it was my turn to stare.

"What does it mean"? I eventually asked.

"I don't know, but it comes from the Dalai Lama to you," she answered.

Now you might think I'd turn and run from this woman as quickly as I could. But I do love a good practice. And a mantra delivered to me from the Dalai Lama, or even someone purporting to be his representative, would seem to be a practice worth considering.

I'd been very clear that I would try anything that might help in my stated goal of constantly conditioning my mind to be positive. And although this certainly seemed a bit crazy...well, who I am to judge? I mean really, if it's good enough for the Dalai Lama, it's undoubtedly good enough for me. And even if this woman was crazy, and she certainly seemed to be, how often do you receive messages on the side of a major highway from a woman who "felt your energy" as she sped by?

So, when I got back to my room, I Googled *mantra to green tara,* and I began reading and listening to some of the different versions. I even watched a YouTube video of the Dalai Lama chanting the mantra to the Green Tara. Was it possible that this woman, seemingly transported straight from the 1960s, truly delivered a message to me from the Dalai Lama?

I considered the possibility as I furthered my research.

Turns out, in Tibetan Buddhism, the Tara is very well known and is one of the most popular Buddhist deities. A female Bodhisatva, or Buddha of compassion and action, she's a protector who comes to our aid to relieve us of physical, emotional, and spiritual suffering.

She is often referred to as the grantor of wishes who will bring blessings into our lives. It is said that it is her compassion that allows her to grant our wishes and remove any obstacles that are in our way.

My mind is a bad neighborhood, I try not to go there alone.
~Anne Lamott

By practicing the mantra, you call on the Green Tara to guide and protect you as you journey through your mind. She promotes healing and transformation, shielding us from fear, anxiety, and adversity.

The more I read, the more I believed. Although, I also came across the clip from the movie Caddyshack, where Bill Murray, in the role of Carl Spackler, spoke of caddying for the Dalai Lama. "Hey, Lama, hey, how about a little something, you know, for the effort, you know." And he says, 'Oh, uh, there won't be any money, but when you die, on your deathbed, you will receive total consciousness.' So, I got that goin' for me, which is nice." I couldn't shake the feeling that I was now playing the role of Carl Spackler. Although I love the movie, it wasn't a compliment.

"So I got that going for me, which is nice."

Instead of saying that, I said the mantra, "Om Tare Tutare Ture Soha," and it felt pretty good, which is my first prerequisite for any practice.

After a little more research, I learned the actual meaning of the words are:

Om: Om has no conceptual meaning. It is the sacred sound, believed to represent the entire Universe, past, present, and future.

Tare: The liberation from samsara and the sufferings, feelings, and problems of our lives.

Tutare: Means protection against the internal fears and external dangers.

Ture: Represents the fulfillment of our spiritual path and the cessation of suffering.

Soha: Establishes the foundation of the path and allows this mantra to take root within your heart and mind. *So let it be written, so let it be done.*

Lama Zopa Rinpoche explains that, like many mantras, the Green Tara Mantra is much greater than the sum of its parts, with layers of meaning and benefit that resonate with us beyond what our minds perceive. But by calling on the Green Tara's protection, our body, speech, and mind are transformed into Tara's holy body, holy speech, and holy mind. We will then be relieved of our suffering for the benefits of all beings.

I still wasn't sure if my new friend was a figment of my imagination, but I took it as a message from the Universe, anyway. I saw it as my next step, the newest practice for me on The Wingman's Path.

Back in Maine, as I said goodbye, I reached in to hug her. I mean, how often does one get a special delivery from the Dalai Lama? A few minutes later, after I parked my car and walked back to my motel room, I started questioning my sanity, or if this even happened. But when I walked into our room, my wife said I smelled nice, of patchouli. Old-school hippie indeed.

A Wingman Practice:

The Green Tara Mantra

Chant the words *Om Tare Tutare Ture Soha* for one minute, or 108 times, which is the Buddhist tradition of one mala (think rosary beads). While chanting, envision the Goddess Green Tara sitting with you. Imagine her providing you protection from your challenges and relieving you of all problems, concerns, and suffering. See yourself as totally stress-free.

Reminder...Do not attach yourself to any precise outcome because that will affect your vibration and be self-defeating.

30
Weekend at Bernie's

On the way back from Maine, Jan and I stopped and stayed with my sister at her house, which is near where Dr. Bernie Siegel lived. Bernie, as he prefers to be called, had invited me to join him as he spoke to 150 cancer survivors at the National Cancer Survivor Day at The Veterans Hospital in West Haven, Ct.

I had mentioned Bernie and some of his accomplishments in an earlier chapter. What I didn't mention was his work with cancer patients and how, back in 1978, he originated a group therapy practice called Exceptional Cancer Patients (ECaP). ECaP helped facilitate patients' empowerment, healing, and lifestyle changes utilizing their drawings, dreams, images, and feelings. His belief that everyone is capable of exceptional behavior is what improved participant's curative rates by bringing about benefits in their physical, spiritual, and psychological well-being.

In short, he advised love as a path to healing. Sounds crazy enough now, imagine what they thought back then! But when you don't feel traditional methods are working, crazy becomes ingenious.

The National Cancer Survivor Day event was amazing for me. It was like I got accepted into a graduate program, *Living an Authentic Life* (his term) with Bernie as my chosen professor. It felt even more surreal because when Jan and I first arrived at my sister's, she had a magazine with Bernie on the cover. An article inside discussed his work and mentioned that Watkins Review of London honored him as one of the 20 Top Spiritually Influential Living People on the Planet. And there I was, at his invitation, hanging with him for a very special presentation.

I'd been fortunate to take many walks with Bernie and his dogs, but I'd never seen him "operate." There, speaking in front of so many fighting this dreadful disease, I learned what it means to be a true Wingman: to help, to inspire, to give hope, to give courage, to give support, to give a smack upside the head, to give whatever is needed. Most importantly, to give love.

He spoke more like a poet than a surgeon, mixing statistics and stories that were easily understood by these battle-scarred veterans of the cancer wars. He spoke of waking up when he read the words, *Self-Induced Healing* in Aleksander Solzhenitsyn's book, *Cancer Ward*, and also of his many cancer patients, especially those who had not only survived, but thrived against all odds. How instead of handling it like other doctors of his time, saying it was a spontaneous remission, a miracle, or a mistaken diagnosis, he delved deeper.

"You can't learn anything from 'spontaneous remission,' he said. "But you can learn from 'self-induced healing.'"

He opened his mind to the possibility that his patients might be his teachers. And when he started to learn from them, he learned they all have similar stories. Come from love. Have some fun. Start laughing more. Get a dog. Take some vitamins. Show up. Love yourself. Love your life. Love your fate.

"Love my fate?" a crusty voice rose from the back.

"Yeah," Bernie echoed, "Love your Fate." He went on to quote Joseph Campbell discussing Nietzsche: "Whatever your fate is, whatever the hell happens, you say, *This is what I need.* It may look like a wreck, but go at it as though it were an opportunity, a challenge. If you bring love to that moment, not discouragement, you will find the strength is there."

"How do I do that?" asked the crusty voice.

Bernie summarized, "When you're going through hell, ask yourself...*What am I to learn from this?*"

And learn from it.

Afterward, as Jan and I were driving the four hours home on rain-soaked highways, I began to think about the teachers in my life. Not the obvious ones like Bernie, but the ones I haven't yet opened my mind to. Much like Bernie discovering that his patients could educate him as to how better to heal from disease, it occurred to me that maybe I was too closed off, not from people, but from difficult situations. Maybe by unlocking my mind and asking what I can learn when facing hardship, I can stop being a victim and start taking back control of my life.

Of course, another lesson then presented itself that next week. A friend of the mom of one of the beauty pageant women had heard of my positivity work. She had just been diagnosed with breast cancer and thought I might be helpful.

Me? I wasn't so sure. I had seen the devastation of cancer from up close. Within two years, a few years previously, my brother died from the disease, and Jan had successfully overcame it.

When Big C comes calling, priorities become really clear, really fast. Pageants, businesses, houses, bank accounts, fancy cars no longer mean squat. The only thing that matters is getting healthy and kicking cancer's ass. Talk about your new normal! I've run into too many people who have been visited by Big C: breast cancer, lung cancer, lymphoma. It doesn't matter what they call it. It always brings more questions than answers.

After our first meeting, I wasn't so confident that my simplistic approach and one-minute Wingman practices were up to the task. So I took a drive back up to see Bernie and get his opinions from him.

As we were once again taking a walk with his dogs around his neighborhood, I said, "Bernie, I'm worried my one-minute Wingman practices aren't really the answer for clients with cancer."

His reply emboldened me. He said, "you never know what bringing positive energy into someone's life can do."

Oh yeah!

That was what I needed to hear! I'd been saying, on a pretty constant basis, that bringing more positive energy into any situation can only help. I just didn't want to give false hope. But then I thought, *who gives a f*#k if it's false hope? And how can that even be?* When cancer stains your doorway, hope is all you have. And knowing that what you think about you bring about, then my bringing hope into the cancerous muck, brings more to hope for.

Bernie helped me clarify what my job was: to help my clients change their vibration because when you can change your vibration, you change your situation. Helping businesses increase profits, hell, that's a cakewalk compared to helping people heal. I've seen and heard too many stories about not having hope, and I've seen first-hand how they end. It's not pretty. Those who have hope always have a better experience. I think it has something to do with feeling a little better...*an object in motion stays in motion*...feeling better helps you feel even better...*an object in motion stays in motion*.

I can't tell you how many times I've walked with Bernie and heard the stories of miracle recoveries from people fighting back with just attitude, laughter, and a bit of hope. So back I went, ready to coach my cancer-stricken client, and be the best Wingman I could be.

As we sat down, I began the same way I begin many meetings: by attempting to raise her vibration by asking of any recent successes.

"This could be the best thing that ever happened to me," she said.

"Excuse me?" I questioned.

"My daughter told me this could be the best thing that ever happened to me," she repeated confidently.

"Do you believe her?" Although I had found great relief with that practice, I wasn't so sure it would work with cancer or any health condition.

"I'm starting to."

We went back and forth saying: "This could be the best thing that ever happened to me."

A week ago, she was crying. Today she was laughing. Talk about learning from an unexpected source! It was the greatest session I could ever imagine.

While I worked with the client to help her find hope and stay positive, the Universe gave me more ammo, as if to make certain I learned that lesson of perspective. As my wife mentions often, in order for me to learn something, sometimes I have to have an "ice pick shoved up my backside." I'd say I'm insulted, but I have come to appreciate the additional tutorial. After all, the ice pick makes sure it sticks.

Anyway, the ice pick came in the form of an article on the back cover of my favorite newspaper, the Philadelphia Daily News. The back page, for those of you who are not initiated in the pleasure of sitting with a cup of coffee and this particular tabloid, is the reason I purchase it. It's the sports page, and on this day, its headline was: *Brandon Boykin doesn't want your pity*. (Hayes, Michael. "Eagles' Brandon Boykin's life filled with joy" Daily News. July 15, 2015.)

Brandon Boykin was a professional football player who, at the time, was playing for the Philadelphia Eagles. As I read the article, I learned a broken leg got him dropped from the first round to the fourth round and cost him 5 million dollars. "It might be the best thing that ever happened to me," Boykin said.

Although this time, I noticed the ice pick had a twist. When my client had stated, "This could be the best thing that ever happened to me," she was put it in the present tense, as she was in the midst of the confrontation. She's going through it currently and viewing it in a positive light.

Brandon Boykin's quote was not quite the same, "It might be the best thing that ever happened to me." He was speaking of it in the *past* tense. He was looking back at a negative situation from his past and saying how it was such a positive.

His quote got me thinking of a new experiment. Could I utilize this practice, not only while going through a problematic experience but also to change my vibration from a historical perspective? Could I revise history? By thinking about destructive events from my past, events which at the time felt like catastrophes, and changing my memories of them to "It *might have been* the best thing that ever happened to me," could I change my present reality?

Wow. Revisionist history happens all the time, doesn't it?

Could this simple practice help me to reach into my subconscious and change negative beliefs that may have gotten lodged in there, into more positive patterns and responses? And if it could help me, might it be able to help even the most resistant of us to seek joy in every situation? Even those miserable events from our past?

I mean, when Brandon Boykin got hurt and lost out on being a first-round pick and the money that came with it, he was "devastated."

"For the first time in my life I was seriously down," Boykin said. "Preparing to be a first-round pick was all my life consisted of...." He arrived at rookie camp humiliated. It was then he "realized that, once you're here, nobody cares when you were drafted. It's about how hard you work."

Boykin went to work. He worked harder than everyone else, even going the extra mile by taking Bikram yoga, gymnastics, and stretching classes to strengthen his body and his mind.

If you've ever been beaten down by something or had the rug pulled out from under you, it's easy to allow it to victimize and define you. Boykin didn't, and I think we can all learn from him.

How? By looking back at those "unhappy events" from our past and viewing them in the light of "It might be the best thing that ever happened to me." I thought about my past misfortunes that I allowed to prey on me, my mind, and my vibration.

Losing that $100 million dollar deal..."It might be the best thing that ever happened to me."

Getting terminated from that great job..."It might be the best thing that ever happened to me."

Getting divorced..."It might be the best thing that ever happened to me."

I started looking at some of the ways my seemingly undesirable events have shaped my thoughts and beliefs. How they've helped me grow into the person I now am, with better clarity of what's most important in my life.

As I would say the words, *it might be the best thing that ever happened to me,* I would consciously look for something I might have learned, something good that came from those unwanted experiences, or anything positive I could cull from those miserable memories. At the same time, I realized my mind was trying to make sense of what I was saying. The more I said it, the more it seemed my mind wrapped around it, and my subconscious began to search for ways that *made* it the *best* thing that ever happened to me.

As Boykin now says, "You can't focus on the outside noise, the negative comments. You have to keep your confidence up. Whatever happens, I know I've been blessed."

It might be the best thing that ever happened to me.
It might be the best thing that ever happened to me.
It might be the best thing that ever happened to me.

I practiced by reflecting on each of those unfortunate occurrences in my life while saying, "It might be the best thing that ever happened to me." And then I came up with a reason as to why that statement was true.

Each time the reason was the same. It helped lead me to where I am today. And today, my life is pretty great. I'm on The Wingman's Path to Positivity, helping others, and myself, to bring positive energy into our lives, to raise our vibrations, and to create lives of our choosing. I've never been happier.

I have since revised my own history. I'm no longer a victim of circumstances but a warrior who's successfully overcome an obstacle. To use Joseph Campbell's mythological narration, I've taken my hero's journey, faced my decisive crises, came out victorious, and have been transformed by the experience.

My client, the woman with breast cancer, was also successful at overcoming her obstacle. Last we spoke, she had started a new business and was getting remarried. It might have been the best thing that ever happened to her.

A Wingman Practice:

The Best Thing

This practice is two-fold, depending on where you are on your path.

1. If you are currently in the midst of a crisis, say to yourself for one

minute, "This could be the best thing that ever happened to me." As you say it, think about how this challenge *could actually be* the best thing that ever happened to you. Think about what you can learn from it and how it might transform you into a better version of yourself.

2. If you're still struggling with a past situation, one that has victimized you and kept you from moving forward, then revise your history. Say to yourself for one minute, "It might be the best thing that ever happened to me." As you do, reflect on what you've learned from it and how you've made it through your hero's journey. Allow yourself to feel like a warrior who's made it through the biggest battle of your life. Stronger, wiser, and grateful for making it through.

If you're not "feeling it," i.e., you're practicing but not able to get that "It might be the best thing that ever happened to me" feeling going for you... Utilize Bernie's answer to the crusty voice and start by asking yourself, "What have I learned from this?" or "What am I to learn from this?."

Oh, here's an interesting side note: when Bernie and I were driving back to his place from the VA, I asked him about "What am I to learn from this?" He told me Joseph Campbell said it to him.

31
And Down I Went

As you can tell by now, I love the Law of Attraction and I love Sir Isaac Newton's First Law of Motion, which in his original verbiage, goes like this: "Every object persists in its state of rest of uniform motion in a straight line unless it is compelled to change that state by forces impressed on it." Both have been instrumental in my discovery and following of the Wingman's Path.

However, neither had been able to fully answer the question as to *why*? When things are going fantastically well for me, why can the positive momentum be broken, seemingly without any logical reason?

For example...

Things were going wonderfully. I was helping people, financially things were wonderful ($50,000 can do that for you,) and I was feeling great. I was riding the wave of higher frequencies and enjoying everything coming my way: the challenges, the successes, and the lessons learned.

I was smiling more. I was feeling, "I'm Da Man, Billy Tan." I was on a roll, in the zone, and in the vortex. All wasn't just good. It was amazing. Jan and I even booked a trip to Thailand to visit her daughter, who was teaching English in Bangkok.

According to the Law of Attraction, and Isaac Newton, things should have continued going well. The better it gets, the better it gets, right? I mean, I had all the momentum going in my favor.

So how is it, that without warning, the wave crashes, the positive energy gets sucked out of you, and you fall into a vibrational hell? A friend tried to explain it to me by referencing the story of Icarus from Greek Mythology.

Icarus was the son of Daedalus, who dared to fly too near the sun on wings of feathers and wax. Daedalus had been imprisoned by King Minos of Crete within the walls of his own invention, the Labyrinth, which he had built to imprison the Minotaur. But the great craftsman fashioned two pairs of wings by adhering feathers to a wooden frame with wax. Giving one pair to his son, Daedalus warned Icarus to fly at medium altitude. If he flew too high, the sun could melt the wax of his wings, too low, and the sea could dampen the feathers, making them too heavy. But Icarus became ecstatic with the ability to fly and forgot his father's warning. The feathers came loose, and Icarus plunged to his death in the sea, now called the Icarian sea.

I got the moral of the story, but I didn't think I was flying too high. I know I have a tendency, when I am flying high and everything's going great, to forget to keep practicing, to stop greasing the skids, and to forget what got me here. But that wasn't the case. I was practicing. I even started a Wingman's Path home course, emailing a group of people the practice I was doing each day. Each and every day, I was doing different practices and doing them with more mindfulness than usual, because I was sending them out to others.

And every client who was in the program had written me about how it was helping.

Then down I went!

It happened in a split second. The countdown was on until we were to leave for a two week trip to Thailand, and one moment of carelessness had put the Land of Smiles in jeopardy.

It happened on a Monday morning. I went to salt my front steps after an icy sleet we received Sunday night. I thought I was being careful. I was wrong. I took one step and down I went. Hard. My left leg bent behind me, and my head banged the third step of my wooden staircase so solidly, it broke the wood.

Ouch!

Flat on my back, my first thought was about a good friend who had died by hitting his head from a similar fall. Lying there, I began to assess. *Was I hurt?* I thought I might be. *Was anything broken?* Hmm, I didn't think so. *Could I get up?* Yes.

My head hurt, I could barely walk, and my elbow was bleeding. Needless to say, it wasn't a positive moment. Matter of fact, not only was I unsure of my pain, I felt really stupid. It wasn't a good feeling.

Nothing seemed broken, so I finished salting. But I knew something was wrong. Not with my head thankfully, but I felt a throbbing pain in my leg. Jan was immediately there with Advil and Arnica to reduce the inflammation. After a more complete assessment, we decided to set an appointment with my doctor for later on Tuesday. Jan then provided me with ice and helped me elevate my leg. Which gave me time to think about why. Why, when everything had been going so well, did I get struck down?

Here's what I figured out. Life will continue to happen, which means you will continue to experience contrast for a variety of reasons—including, you might slip on the ice on occasion. That's how you grow. That's how you figure out what your next goal is. Keeping positive will help you find the reason for the fall, reach your goal, and eventually win. If your energy is bad, however, you will always lose, you will get stuck being a victim.

While trying to figure out what I could learn from the fall, I decided to do what I do: a Wingman practice. I did a healing exercise that we had applied years ago in Hawaii. Back then, the night before we were leaving for a big hike, Jan went down with an ankle sprain. We were in the middle of nowhere, without an Urgent Care Center, a doctor, or even a pharmacy to be found. It was so bad, we had to change rooms from the second to the first floor at the little guest house where we were staying because Jan couldn't possibly get upstairs, even with me and another man helping her. Jan was in a lot of pain and upset to be missing the amazing hike we had planned for the next day. After a few tears, she remembered a healing practice she had read about. We jumped in. Amazingly, the next morning Jan and I were able to go on our breathtaking hike.

With my tumble on the ice that morning, I knew I needed to bring out the big guns we'd used in Hawaii. It was actually a favorite Wingman's Path process I call *My Body Can Heal Itself*. I use it with clients who are ill or injured. It's based on the belief that by thinking positively about our bodies, we can mend ourselves. By flooding our body and our psyches with positive, loving, kind, healing thoughts we can activate our cells to do what they do best: heal.

It comes from a combination of the books, *Mutant Message Down Under*, by Marlo Morgan (HarperCollins 1994) and *Ask and It is Given, Learning to Manifest Your Desires* by Abraham Hicks (Hay House, Inc. 2004). And it involves practicing feeling better by reminding yourself that your body knows how to heal itself. My practice went something like this.

"My leg's been great to me."
"You've (talking to my leg now) served me well."
"You helped me run a marathon."
"You helped me run and play with my children when they were small."
"You helped me take walks all over the world."
"You helped me take morning walks with Monte these last 15 years."
"You helped me hike up Observation Point in Zion National Park."

"You helped me climb Mt. Masada in Israel."
"You helped me ski some wonderful mountains..
"Thank you for being such a great leg to me, I look forward to many more adventures."
And then I went on to my body's wisdom.
"It's natural for my body to be well."
"Even if I don't know what to do in order to get better, my body does."
"I have trillions of cells with individual consciousness, they know what needs to be done."
"I don't need to know how to heal my leg quickly, my body knows."
"Let go of the Pain."
"It doesn't matter that I caused this, I can heal it as well."
"It's natural that it will take a little time for my body to align with my thoughts of well-being."
"There's no rush, I'm not going away until Saturday."
"Well-Being is natural to me."
"My wiser self is very aware of my physical body."
"My cells are asking for what they need to heal me, and my source is answering those requests."
"I'm in very good hands."
"I will relax now, and allow my body and my wiser self to work it's magic."
"My only work is to relax and breathe."
"I can do that."
"I can do that easily."
"The sensation of pain is an indicator that my Source is responding to my cellular request for energy."
"I will relax into this sensation of pain because I understand that help is on the way."

Unfortunately, my practice didn't seem to work. And my subsequent visit to the doctor didn't go as well as expected. My GP sent me instantly to an orthopedist, who immediately put me in a full leg/knee splint and sent me for an MRI.

My positive vibes took a beating. When I mentioned to the orthopedist that I was soon leaving for Thailand, he said surgery was more likely where I'd go. But we wouldn't know for sure until after he saw the results from my MRI the next day.

"Doc," I asked, "Have you ever seen this type of thing heal by itself?"
His answer was right up my alley: "It would be a miracle."

"Awesome," I responded. "I'm a big believer in miracles."

As I lay in the MRI scanner, I began my healing practice again. I knew of too many stories of people healing themselves, from every imaginable disease and injury, to lose faith now.

The result: I ended up having a torn quad tendon. I was able to travel and walk all around Thailand, but I needed to have surgery immediately upon my return.

While I still needed the surgery, the fact that the doctor agreed to postpone the operation until my return leads me to believe that the practice I did helped my healing process. Who knows what might have happened had I had a few more days to practice?

And, what's more, after reading the next chapter, you might agree it was "meant to be" and that there were other forces at work. I will tell you though, Jan and I have had much success with this practice at other times. We are big believers and have used it to help us heal from sprains and other non-breaks, as well as after medical operations to aid in our recoveries.

A Wingman Practice:

My Body Can Heal Itself

Remind yourself that your body can heal itself by saying, "My body can heal itself" over and over. While saying those words, also give your injured body part some love. It will love you back.

32
Zen Master Jung Bong Mu Mu

Thailand! We were on our way; me with a giant rubber leg brace to help me when my leg got tired. I didn't need to wear it for protection. I had torn my quad tendon about 70% of the way and was to be operated on when I returned. Whether I tore it a little more didn't matter, the operation would be the same.

After five days in Bangkok, we arrived in Chiang Mai, the second-largest city in Thailand, for the second half of our trip. It was there, by sheer coincidence, if you still believe in that sort of thing, that I would receive my next practice. After receiving it, I assure you I no longer believed in coincidences. Here's what happened...

Early one morning, Jan and I were out exploring when we came upon the impressive ruined Temple, Wat Chedi Luang. After meditating in the inner temple, we walked around the impressive grounds, but with my torn quad tendon I decided a rest would be wise. Imagine my surprise as a Zen Master and his two disciples traveling from South Korea, decided to rest at that time as well.

A Zen Master is a term used to describe a Buddhist Monk, who through years of meditation and research has attained a higher-level vibration. A Zen Master hasn't actually reached enlightenment yet, they would then be a Buddha, but it is someone far closer to enlightenment than you or I. It is an individual who has been authorized to teach the tradition of Zen Buddhist meditation.

How fortunate that one of his disciples could speak English well enough that she was able to be the translator. You could feel their energy. I was in Wingman Heaven. They asked what I did, and when I said I'm a positive energy coach, the Zen Master spoke English for the first time. I'll never forget his words:

Truth is Positive Energy.

I swear the world stopped in that moment for me. I no longer felt my leg. Change that, I felt weirdly pleased that I had injured my leg. As if the Universe had a plan for me. If I had not injured it, I probably wouldn't have been in that place at that time to get that message from the Zen Master. I felt like Cain in the old television series, "Kung Fu." I was Grasshopper.

Truth is positive energy. The words have remained with me ever since.

Upon returning home, I had a great deal of time on my hands. I had the operation to repair my quad tendon and was laid up for six weeks as my leg healed. As I lay on my couch, unable to move with a metal wrap around my leg, I thought about my synchronistic meeting with Zen Master Jung Bong Mu Mu and his words to me that day.

A friend stopped who, after seeing how "up" I was, said, "it's OK to be down about being laid up for so long." I agreed and told her so. But I wasn't down. I was seeing my accident as a fortuitous event.

When Jan came home from work that day, I told her about my friend's comment and how I was viewing my accident and subsequent operation. "I believe this was supposed to happen. Perhaps I'm supposed to slow down," Her reply, "How much slower can you get?" was not exactly the answer I was expecting.

But slow down I did. I didn't have much choice. I kept repeating the words, "Truth is positive energy." I became obsessed with "truth." There, laying on the couch day after day, I practiced it. I repeated *Truth is positive energy*. I turned it into an emotion and meditated on it. I lived it, loved it, and learned about it. I lost it, found it, and lost it again. I Googled it, read quotes on it, and looked up different definitions of it. I talked about it with everyone and anyone who came to visit.

As time passed, I coached about it, and spoke about it on the radio.
Truth.

In some of my coaching sessions, it resonated immediately, and people "saw" their truths clearly. Me, I had to keep practicing the word, just saying it over and over again, as I searched for my truth.

I practiced it in many different ways.
- I meditated on it by breathing in *truth* and breathing out *truth*.
- I practiced emoting it by saying, "I feel my truth" while practicing feeling it.
- I said: "When I live my truth, I feel better" over and over.

- I kept it really simple by just saying the word "truth" over and over, and over again.
- And I constantly came back to simply saying, "truth is positive energy."

The more I practiced it, the more I learned of my truth. The practice seemed to bring me more clarity about myself, my past and my present. I was no longer just practicing *It might be the best thing that ever happened to me* as I thought of my financial and personal losses, I was believing it. I stopped being embarrassed by my failures and saw them as lessons learned on the path to successfully creating a life of my choosing. I had made it through my struggles. I was now the Wingman on the Wingman's Path to Positivity, and you don't get there without overcoming your share of obstacles.

I had overcome my share and was now able to appreciate the painful occurrences of my life for the learning experiences they were. I started seeing life as a process. You have a desire, you create a plan, overcome challenges, and succeed at manifesting your desire. And then you do it again. And again. And again. I still valued the momentary sensation of satisfaction when my goal was achieved, but the happiness I now sought wasn't one of temporary euphoria. My truth was that I now wanted more. I wanted the feeling of confidence, clarity, and calmness in knowing I could handle anything that came my way. I wanted to feel secure that everything would always work out for me. And I wanted to keep learning about my vibration, and how always to be in control of the energy I was emitting. And tearing my quad tendon is what happened for me to realize this completely.

I was feeling my truth, and it felt very good to me.

A Wingman Practice:

Truth is Positive Energy

Practice your truth in any of the following ways...

- Meditate on it by breathing in *truth* and breathing out *truth*.
- While saying, "I feel my truth," practice feeling it.
- Say, "When I live my truth, I feel better" over and over.

- Keep it simple by just repeating the word *truth* while thinking about what the word means to you.
- Say "Truth is positive energy" and, while saying it, allow the words to wash over you.

33
Bidding War

One truth became very clear to me during the time I was healing: with the health insurance business changing, my income was decreasing, and our house was becoming too expensive. So, we decided to sell.

Having a big old house took a great deal of work to get ready to sell. Not only did we have to improve its curb appeal, we had to get rid of tons of stuff.

Another truth I learned when we were cleaning out the house was that my wife was a hoarder. I would go in every room with the intent to clean it up by throwing things out, and in every room, everything was Janet's. We even had full boxes of her stuff that had not been unpacked in the 20 years since we had moved in.

The funny thing is, once you get your house cleaned and ready to be sold, you fall in love with it again. Not that I didn't love our house beforehand, it's just that seeing it sale-ready took my love to a new level.

Regardless, once we actually listed the house, we began to settle in to a new normal. A new normal? Most certainly! As anyone who has ever sold a house they were living in knows: there's a new normal.

In setting our intention to attract the perfect buyer, part of that included being ready for the stream of people who are constantly coming through our house. And that meant every dish, spoon, fork, can of dog food, piece of paper, T-shirt, coffee mug, pair of shoes, etc., must be put away immediately and consistently. I was even drying out the kitchen sink after I rinsed a bowl!

Nothing inspires cleanliness more than an unexpected guest.
~Radhika Mundra

My office was in my home, but I rarely met clients there. So having people come by on a moment's notice was quite the challenge for me. It required a complete change of behavior, which got me thinking: achieving any goal always requires a change of behavior. Whether your goal is to enhance your relationship or begin a new one, improve your health, increase your finances, find a better job, upgrade your vibration, or create a life of your choosing, you will have to change your behavior.

And if we were going to sell our house, I had to change my behavior. Let's face it, a buyer would be more inclined to buy our house if it was clean and tidy rather than messy. Staying neat and organized just became another practice for me. Like all my practices, once I got some momentum going, it became easier. And as with all my practices, I loved the vibration I was creating. I certainly enjoyed how spotless the house always was.

As Jan remarked one day, "It's easy to keep the house so clean because it's already so clean. And the fact that the house never gets messy is so calming."

No question about it. I don't know if the saying is true that cleanliness is next to Godliness, but it definitely was a vibration raiser.

For me the challenge isn't to be different but to be consistent.
~Joan Jett

By the time we were ready to list, I was proud by my consistency. Each day, as I would finish my breakfast and clean up, I was reminded of how methodical I could be. After all, any time a potential buyer was coming by, I not only had to leave, but everything had to be extremely tidy. It felt great to rise to the challenge.

A couple days later, Jan came home from work and said, "It's amazing, all I see are houses with *Sold* or *Under Contract* in front of them. I wonder how they did it?"

"That's funny," I replied, "I only see houses with *For Sale* in front of them."

It was the Law of Attraction at work: when you are selling your house you start seeing all different houses for sale or recently sold. And soon, I noticed the sign on our neighbor's house had gone from *For Sale*, to *Under Contract*. We rushed over to hear the details. Turns out, she not only sold it quickly, but there was a bidding war to boot!

Bidding war! The words brought me a smile.

As Jan and I walked back to our house, I said, "We're not only going to sell our house, we're going to have a bidding war!"

"Oh?" she replied. "How are we going to do that?"

"Same way we'd get to Carnegie Hall: we practice."

And practice we did. Although Jan focused her practice on getting the house sold quickly, *Bidding War* became my new mantra. I silently thanked my neighbor for providing the inspiration. *Bidding War.* The words flowed from me with joy and happiness.

I was surprised by how powerfully I felt the elation of those words.

"Bidding war," I started saying over and over, out loud and to myself.

"Bidding war." I smiled into it as I repeated the words and practiced the feeling. By the end of one minute, I couldn't contain my smile.

I kept speaking the words out loud: "Bidding war, bidding war, bidding war."

As the next minute ended and another began, the practice changed to "Thank you for the bidding war," and I was now singing it out loud with passion and emotion.

My vibe was joyous. "Bidding war" had become an instant classic while I sang, danced, and laughed in the middle of the woods as Monte and I took our morning walks.

Shoot for the moon. Even if you miss, you'll land among the stars.
~Norman Vincent Peale

We didn't get my bidding war, but we did sell our house quickly and for full price. Jan later told me that the thought of a bidding war made her agitated and stressed and that she was only envisioning a quick, simple, and easy sale. Doesn't the Universe always know best!

We were surprised by how many neighbors would stop by and ask, "How did you sell it so quickly?" Jan told them we priced it right and kept it immaculately clean. I told them of our positivity practices. They listened to her and looked at me like I was crazy.

Oh Yeah! Crazy like a fox with a *Sold* sign out front.

A Wingman Practice:

Bidding War

Think of a desire you want to manifest. Now close your eyes and think of the best possible solution. Got it? Great, now push it up a notch and think of an even better result.

    Similar to us selling our house, the desire I wanted was to sell it for full price. It was when I thought of an even better outcome, and I changed my vibration to that of "shooting for the moon" and selling it for even more than we were asking, that we "landed among the stars" and sold our house for full price.

    Think of the words that will help you create the "shooting for the moon" vibration. In our case, it was "Bidding War." Say the words over and over for one full minute. As you do, think it, feel it and see it happening. Close your eyes and believe it as if it were already true.

35
One Amazing Year

When we decided to sell our house, it was about downsizing. Downsizing the space, downsizing our mortgage, and downsizing the upkeep that comes with a big old house. The financial obligations were draining me. Yes, I had received that big check, but I did not want to squander it on the increasing upkeep of the house. I was doing my best to remain consistent with my Wingman's Path practices, but when real life is hitting you in the face in the form of more and more bills to be paid, it makes it that much more difficult to keep your vibration high.

Yes, just because I knew how to keep my vibration high, did not mean I was able to hold it at a high level all the time. We often believe we are thinking about money, love, or happiness in a positive way. That is definitely not the case. I could practice saying, "I'm a millionaire," but with the house in need of repairs along with the money needed to pay the monthly mortgage, I recognized that my focus was, unfortunately, more on my *lack* of finances than on my abundance of such.

So, I practiced to maintain my consistency and to keep building momentum in the direction I wanted to go. By doing so, I would prevent myself from falling down a negative rabbit hole. I've found, that when in the face of struggles, be they financial, business, or personal, if I can keep my vibration vibrant, or at least keep it from tanking, when a bit of good news comes my way, it can provide a real bounce to my vibe. And that is what happened to me when we obtained an offer for our house. I received an energy boost.

However, our house sold so quickly, we didn't have a plan as to what to do next. It was a Friday afternoon. Jan had just returned home from work, and we were reading over the offer. We were elated, we were giddy, we were excited. We did a happy dance.

And then Jan uttered the words that shone a light on my next practice: "What do we do now?"

I didn't have an answer right away, but I did remember some advice I'd received about thirty years earlier when a friend had said seven words to me that I have never forgotten. Fantasy Baseball was in its infancy back then, and I was joining him and his friends as the last team in their league. They were interviewing me as we sat around a large circular table at a bar in the center of Philadelphia to see if I would be a good fit. After they decided I would, someone suggested that they should go around the table and take turns giving a piece of advice.

My friend's words: "Good plan, bad plan, have a plan," stuck with me ever since. Whether you're playing games, building a business, or creating a life of your choosing, "Good plan, bad plan, have a plan."

We didn't have a plan for what to do when we didn't have a house or mortgage holding us down. It was at that moment I heard my inner Wingman's words, "Practice what you preach, do a practice."

"Janney," I turned to her and said, "we need a plan. Let's do a practice to figure it out."

I gave her a brief description, and here's what we did. It was the fulcrum point that catapulted our lives in a whole new direction. Perhaps it can help you too. We closed our eyes and envisioned it being exactly one year from that day. And we imagined all the fun, inspiring, beautiful, exciting things that had just happened to us during that most amazing year.

You begin by saying to yourself, *What an amazing year I've had!* and see where your attention goes. What made it such a great year? Allow your imagination to take your mind wherever it wants to go. Amazing can come in many forms.

If you are ill, you might picture your amazing healing process, health evolution, and being healthy one year from today. Same as if you're currently lonely and wanting to be in a loving relationship, or having some financial difficulties and desire financial security. Or want to be in a different job. Or living somewhere new. Or...Or...Or...This exercise allows you to stretch your beliefs as far as they will go.

If you do this practice and you don't find your year amazing, do it again. And again. And again. As you'll see, it took me a few extra practice sessions for complete clarity. Thankfully, it's a fun practice.

Here's what happened when Jan and I did it: my vision immediately went to our having a great apartment, and being free from all the monthly expenses that went with our house. It felt fabulous. I saw myself free of stress, laughing, relaxing, and having the best time building the Wingman's Path to Positivity without any monetary tension weighing down my vibration. Jan imagined traveling the world.

"What?" I asked. "What are you talking about?"

"I want to quit my job and travel the world. You said it was an amazing year, that's what I saw," she countered. "Why? What did you come up with?"

I answered a little apprehensively. "Nothing that great. I had us in a little apartment, happy and free of stress."

We conferred and allowed our concepts to mesh. Then began plotting the possibilities of how we could merge our visions. We came up with the idea of renting an inexpensive apartment in Chiang Mai, Thailand, a city in northern Thailand that we had visited and loved. If I had to pinpoint the moment that I began to truly comprehend my ability to create a life of my choosing, this would be it.

Literally three months earlier, when we had said goodbye to Thailand, I honestly thought I'd never be back. After practicing *One Amazing Year* that first time with Janet, and a few more times on my own, I started seeing the potential of us living there. Yes, it definitely took me a few more practice swings to believe it was possible, which is why I mentioned you may want to try it a few times to see what comes up for you.

One Amazing Year works because it helps you see what you want in your mind's eye without any resistance you may be holding in your subconscious. The more you practice it, the more you break down those limitations you've built up in your mind. Unfortunately, it doesn't affect the minds of your friends and family. Ours called us insane.

"How can you do that?"

"How can you afford that?"

"Are you crazy?"

It sounded crazy to me as well, at first. As I said, initially, I had a difficult time grasping the concept. It took me a few more weeks of practice, and of allowing the idea to marinate in my mind, before I was able to "see" it.

I'm a guy who eats the same meal at the same diner every day for breakfast. It took me a while to get comfortable with the idea of traveling to and living in exotic lands. I surely didn't need my friends and family telling me we couldn't do it. I was already pretty good at identifying the obstacles to our success.

"We can't do this."

"We can't afford this."

"Who are we to do this?"

"We don't have the money."
"We're not the type of people to just take off for an unspecified time."
"I need to work and make money."

However, the more I allowed for the possibility, the more probable it became. "We can't do this" soon turned into "We can do this."

"How could we afford it?" easily became reconciled. We would no longer have a mortgage, and I would still have some health insurance commissions coming in. We could rent a storage space for our stuff until we came back. I could coach people online via Skype and Facetime to make a little more income.

"Who are we to do this?" and "We're not the type of people to just take off for an unspecified time," transformed into "Others have done it, we can too."

Whatever the mind can conceive and believe, the mind can achieve.
~Napoleon Hill

It took a little while, but I soon recognized my energy changing. I acknowledged the frequency I was emitting was much higher. I became a "let's do it" kind of guy. I developed a new mantra when anyone questioned our brainstorm: "I'm just practicing what I preach."

What I preach is practicing positivity, raising your vibration, and creating a life of your choosing. That was exactly what I had been advocating: do something that raises your vibration. Thinking about traveling the world and following the Wingman's Path wherever it took us felt different, exciting, and just so cool. I could feel my vibration escalating and gaining momentum as it did.

**If you want to be happy, set a goal
that commands your thoughts, liberates your energy,
and inspires your hopes.**
~Andrew Carnegie

We most definitely had a goal that commanded my thoughts, liberated my energy, and inspired my hopes. Even better: I felt happy. Change that, I was happy. They say *the magic begins just outside your comfort zone*. Well, I was outside my comfort zone, and I felt the magic. I was joyous.

And from our goal grew our plan. Our plan was to explore this earth and expand my brand of positivity. *One Amazing Year* soon became a three-step formula for conceiving, believing, and achieving. And Jan and I are living proof that it works. Give it a try for yourself.

By the way...Those friends and family members who were calling us insane and telling us we can't do it, are now asking us how they might be able to do it as well.

A Wingman Practice:

One Amazing Year

1. raise your energy. This part is too often ignored when setting a goal. Do a practice to improve your vibration and get yourself in a better feeling place. By raising your energy, you will set better goals for yourself and see more clearly a path to achieving them. Makes sense, doesn't it? If you're in a lousy mood, you're going to set lousy goals.

2. Second, once you've raised your vibration a bit, close your eyes and imagine it is precisely one year from today, and say to yourself, "What an amazing year I've had." See yourself one year from today having experienced an amazing year. Even better, feel it. If you like, see the actions and the events in each month of the year. Or you can just see where you are at the end of it. Whatever comes up for you.

   Now, how did you arrive there? Allow yourself to release your inhibitions and expand the possibilities. If nothing amazing develops, i.e., you don't get excited by what you envision, that's OK.

   Let it go, then try it again tomorrow. Do this practice once each day until you "see" something amazing, something that energizes you. Doing *One Amazing Year* reduces whatever restrictions you have built up in your subconscious. And if you're like me, you've definitely constructed some walls in your subconscious. This practice enables you to stretch your aspirations without those restrictive constraints.

3. Achieve a vibrational match with your desire. What does it mean to achieve a vibrational match with your desire? It means seeing it, feeling it, and believing it. It means knowing it is so.

Too many people assume that wishing for their desire will help them attain it. Nothing is further from the truth. As stated previously, the Universe will always send you back exactly what you are sending out, and when you wish for something, hope for something, or pray for something, you are affirming to the Universe that you do not have it. Your vibration is one of lack, so the Universe will send you back more absence of that which you want.

"Therefore I tell you, whatever you ask for in prayer, believe that you have received it, and it will be yours." Jesus Christ, Mark 11:24

So how do you emit a frequency of "having" what you want when you don't have it? The same way you get to Carnegie Hall. You practice. And as you practice seeing yourself having an amazing year, take notice of how you are feeling. It's that feeling of success I want you to practice.

People have asked me why this 3-step formula doesn't include the traditional steps of writing your goal down on paper and creating a plan well. Those are both valuable and necessary steps to achieve a goal, but for this exercise, you will be coming from a place of already having achieved your goal. You will know it to be true. It will be with you at all times, and you will be emitting a frequency of achieving it. And once you've "seen" your desire manifested, you already know the necessary actions you need to perform because you've already "done" them.

As you'll see later, Jan and I definitely wrote down the many different steps that had to be completed for us to make our amazing year happen. It helped keep us organized, focused, and on task. But we did it after we were able to believe in making the trip a reality.

35
My Buddy Coop

As I was working on my vibration to get in alignment with traveling and living abroad for the next year, I got a call from my buddy Coop. Not the kind of call you want. His illness had progressed, and the doctors were only giving him a few more months to live.

I became his caregiver that summer. It was a summer I'll never forget. The news of his situation spread, and friends from far and wide came to pay their respects and hang with Coop. Everyone loved Coop.

We had met when we were in seventh grade when Coop invited me to play poker with him and some other buddies. Back then, we would play almost every weekend. As we aged, Coop's Poker Game became a monthly affair that lasted until his death almost 50 years later.

He always introduced me as "Grossy, from the card game." It was a name I wore with love and pride.

In a lifetime of memories, the card games forever stand out. As I said, it started back when we were kids. Coop had just made it through an illness that many had not survived. In fact, he may have been one of the first to survive Non-Hodgkins Lymphoma.

He once told me he realized the depth of his challenge when, as a kid, he was watching the 1960's TV show "Ben Casey." Dr. Ben Casey was a brilliant doctor who cured everyone, but when faced with Coop's particular brand of cancer said, "No one's ever survived this."

Imagine that! Learning the severity of your struggle by watching a television show. But Coop pulled through. Not only pulled through, but lived another half-century.

It was during that last summer with him, through the many conversations Coop and I had, that I genuinely reached my decision that I was going to travel and live abroad for the next year. Coop had made me promise him I would do it.

"Grossy," he said, "You owe it to me to make sure you do. I can't anymore, so I want you to promise me you'll live your life, not live but LIVE. You never know how long you have."

We both became quiet as we thought about how many from our card game had already passed. Coop's brother, my brother, and another good friend named Michael. Our card game buddies were dropping like flies. And now Coop was joining them.

Coop's brother and my brother may not have been a big surprise, but Michael was another story. He was always the picture of health. He was a bigger-than-life guy who loved life and life loved him back. He was one of those guys who, when you were with him, you saw your world as a better place.

When Coop mentioned Michael, we both teared up. He talked about the card games and how Michael and I would break out in loud, boisterous laughter at the silliest times. I still smile when I reminisce about those games. I reminded him of the time, many years before, when Michael and I met up at Coop's house late one night. We both just happened to stop by to see if Coop was home. He wasn't, so we decided to go to the Pancake house. Michael loved to eat, no matter what time it was.

As we got out of the car, there in the parking lot, five drunk and angry guys started screaming at us while they parked their car. As I felt fear rising within me, Michael had a different response.

"Can you hold my coat?" he asked.

"Can I hold your coat?" I objected. "What are you f#*@ing talking about? Let's get out of here!"

"Just relax," he calmly replied. "It will be OK. I've got this."

And he did. I only had to hold his coat for what seemed like seconds, as Michael dispersed them powerfully and efficiently. Turns out, he was a black belt in karate. As I returned his coat to him, I actually felt like I had assisted. Crazy, right? That was the essence of Michael; he would always carry the load but make you feel indispensable. I will always remember that feeling.

Coop replied with a similar story about when they were in college. We were soon laughing and talking about all the good times we had had together. It felt good to be laughing with Coop again, and I told him so. I also promised him I would take the leap and do the travel thing for one year.

That day with Coop is when I honestly reached the decision to do it. I made him that promise.

A few weeks later, I somehow ended up at a dinner with some people of the cloth. Coop was only a few days from passing at that point, the end was imminently near. It was very much on my mind, so perhaps it's not surprising that I brought up that I had a good friend about to die. A pastor mentioned something about the cycle of life and how Coop was going to a better place. The conversation turned to death and dying, and I was reminded of my promise.

I told everyone there I had given Coop my assurances that I would take this next year to travel and live abroad, and how I would LIVE my life from there on out.

A Rabbi sitting across the table from me said: "We all have two lives; the second one begins when you realize you only have one." It's actually a quote from Confucius, I think.

I thanked her and respectfully responded, "Rabbi, my buddy Coop has been teaching me that for a long time, only he calls it, 'playing with house money.'"

The Pastor looked up from his meal and asked, "What does that mean"?

Not surprisingly, there weren't too many gamblers at the table that night, so I explained to everyone how, after winning a bet, you pocket your original stake and only play with your winnings. There were a few quizzical looks, so I described the feeling, or rather the energy, of what it meant when you were *playing with house money*. It is unquestionably one of the most extraordinary mindsets to have in the casino, or even better, in life.

Playing with house money is an I-can't-lose-I-can-only-win mentality. I didn't have to expound further as everyone at that dinner could feel the vibration of playing with house money. It's pretty much the same as the Confucius quote, but because of Coop, it felt even more powerful for me.

I actually laughed as I appreciated how Coop had just furnished me with my next practice. Even as he lay dying, he shone a light on my path. Because of all the casinos, poker rooms, and home poker games I'd been in with Coop, no one, *no one*, NO ONE, was ever better at playing with house money, then he. When he got on a winning streak, he could parlay it with the best of them.

I was lost in thought as the waiters brought out dessert and coffee. There was a variety of cookies, pastries, and rugelach. Rugelach is a Jewish delicacy filled with chocolate or jam, and coincidentally, it was something we always had at poker night. One of the guys would always stop at a Jewish delicatessen on his way to the game and pick up two pounds of it. There was never any left. I could feel myself beaming as I bit into one. And in that instant, it hit me: no matter how often Coop would talk about winning money, the poker game was never about the money. The poker game was about Coop's second life.

Coop learned earlier than most of us that we only have one life. He cherished it by living it to the fullest, and for him, that meant staying connected with his friends by playing poker. He did it better than anyone. He was the glue that held us together. In a time when most of us don't have the same friends we had a year ago, Coop kept a group of guys together for 47 years. Yes, the card game and Coop are intertwined in my mind and in my heart. Without him, there was no possibility of all of us staying friends and adding new friends to "the game."

The card game saw us through some wonderful times: weddings, business successes, children, and two months before Coop's passing, the wedding of a daughter of a card game member. We all were there—the card-game players had their own table right by the dance floor at the wedding. Only Coop wasn't there. That's when we all knew his time was short. Because there was nothing Coop liked more than a celebration with friends. But celebrations are easy.

The card game also saw us through business failures, divorces, illnesses, and deaths. That's when you learn about true friendship. And that's what Coop brought to everyone he knew. True friendship.

There were about 300 people at Coop's funeral. He was loved. And in accordance with his wishes, we had a Quaker-style service. A Quaker service is a non-denominational service, where people sit in reflective and meditative thoughts about the deceased, and when so moved, they stand up and share a memory. The idea is that the stories will help everyone begin the healing process.

Of course, everyone had a story to share, which made for a beautiful and emotional day. And I loved them all, especially those from Coop's daughter and her friends as they spoke about how he was such an amazing Dad.

But then, one of his daughter's friends asked me: "Why? Why Coop? Why now?"

I had no answer. Other than one thing I knew with absolute certainty: somewhere in heaven, a great card game got started on the day Coop passed. And he was right in the middle of it, along with his brother, my brother, and Michael.

As I sit here writing about Coop, I'm looking at a picture from thirteen years ago. It was taken in Las Vegas, the week a group of us went out to celebrate a milestone birthday. Of course, Coop was the one who put it together. Ten of us went. It was one of the greatest weekends of my life. The picture is of Coop, Michael, and me. I've carried it with me on all my travels. And everywhere I go, I have it with me to remind me of my promise to Coop, to always LIVE life as if I'm playing with house money.

A Wingman Practice:
Playing with House Money

Repeat for one minute, "I'm playing with house money." As you do, practice the vibration of winning so much that you've pocketed your original investment and are only playing with your winnings. Practice emitting the frequency of knowing you cannot lose, you can only win.

If that practice doesn't feel right for you, you can practice the same vibration by repeating the quote from Confucius, "We all have two lives, the second one begins when you realize you only have one."

With either saying, practice the feeling of LIVING your life, of loving your life, and, beginning right now, of moving in the direction of creating a life of your choosing.

36
Wing Dog Down

Two weeks after my buddy Coop passed away, we had to put my dog, Monte, down. It was a tough month for me. The vet came out on a Monday and said, "It's a hard decision, but it's what's best for him."

Actually, it wasn't a hard decision at all. Monte had led a long and wonderful life. We had rescued Monte from the pound when he was just a puppy of one, and Jan and I had decided to move in together. My children were eleven and nine at the time; Jan's daughter was ten.

When I talk of rescuing Monte, the better statement may be that he rescued us. We needed him more than he needed us, as his affection helped bring our two families together. Being a newly blended household, with all the typical challenges that brings, Monte quickly united us into a caring, cohesive family like nothing else could. He brought a level of connectedness and unconditional love that we would not have had without him.

Monte taught me many treasured lessons during our sixteen years together. The first was the value of a good walk. Our walks are what helped me find my way to a large wooded area near our house that not only was filled with wildlife, but is was where I found a community of fellow dog lovers and friends. The walks also connected me to the daily ebb and flow of nature in a way I never experienced before. All because of Monte.

My walks will never be the same.

I'll always remember our first trip there. My son came with us. As he, Monte, and I were walking in, a woman started telling me how great these woods were for dogs. How safe they are because they can't get lost and how the only way out was the same way we were walking in.

Five minutes later, Monte had snuck under a fence and was sitting on a train track that ran by the side of the woods. I couldn't get through the fencing, and I was panicked as I heard a train coming. I called, screamed, and begged him to come back. Eventually, he calmly stood up and slid back through the fence. He then came over to us as if nothing had happened. Monte had been a street dog before we found him, and from that point on, I knew he was very able to take care of himself.

I'm having a hard time writing this right now. Instead of focusing on all the wonderful memories, I'm typing through tears. Monte had that effect on me. Through all the deaths of my friends and family, Monte's death is the one that always brings me to tears. Maybe my emotions are compounded because of Coop's passing just weeks before, but I felt a real sense of loss and didn't want to invite any more in.

"What am I to learn from this?" is what my dog-walking buddy and mentor, Dr. Bernie Siegel, would tell me to ask myself.

What am I to learn from this?

Maybe that it's time for my second life to begin, and this cloud of death that surrounds me is more like a snake shedding his skin. I like that. I always like a positive spin.

> **We must be willing to get rid of the life we've planned,**
> **so as to have the life that is waiting for us.**
> **The old skin has to be shed before the new one can come.**
> ~Joseph Campbell

Maybe that was it. Maybe Monte was just freeing Jan and me up to embark on the life that was waiting for us, with no worries or feelings of guilt. It didn't surprise me. His timing was always perfect, and his love for us, and ours for him, was unconditional.

The day after putting Monte down, I went to the woods for my morning walk. Everywhere I looked, I saw a place where Monte did this, or Monte did that. As I made it to the creek in the way back of the woods, I was reminded of the time Monte taught me always to live in the moment. It became a favorite practice that I do almost every day of my life. I call it *Be Here Now* because it reminds me to be in the moment.

That was a day like any other. As we walked, Monte bolted. There was nothing unusual about that, he often would catch the scent of an animal and take off. After a little while that time, though, I started getting concerned. I couldn't see him. I called out for him, assuming he was fine, just off having fun doing whatever. But I wanted to make sure he was OK, so I called and looked until I finally found him. Although he didn't want to stop what he was doing, when he heard me so close, he looked up and came over. But the thing was, as soon as I saw him, and realized he was safe and happy, I didn't care if he stayed playing where he was. He, however, was already onto the next moment. That fun was over. I, unfortunately, had ended it.

He, on the other hand, was ready for the next moment. He had already forgotten about how much fun he'd been having and was on to the next adventure. I still remember him looking at me like, "Oh, OK. I don't know why you want me to stop having fun over here, but I'll come over and have fun there with you."

I tried to tell him to go back to having the fun he had been having, but to him, that moment was over. It was time to move on.

That moment made me realize how often I live in the past, trying to relive my fun moments, or in the future, worrying about those moments that haven't happened yet. Monte unquestionably lived in the moment, having the best time he could, and from that day on, I made it a practice to do the same. I can't tell you how many times I'd be walking through the woods with my thoughts on work or on whatever I was worried about at the time. Not just when walking through the woods, but anytime I wasn't being in the moment. Maybe I was at work and thinking of a disagreement with Janet or one of my kids. Or maybe I was with one of them and thinking about work.

After that day with Monte, however, I always tried to catch myself when I got caught up in my thoughts, instead of being in the moment. When I would catch myself, I'd stop, and for one minute, I'd get quiet, take some deep breaths, look around wherever I was, and say, "Be here, now."

If I was with someone, I would just quietly breathe in those words. Either way, I stopped allowing my worries of the past, or my concerns for the future, to control my thoughts and emotions of the present moment.

Eckhart Tolle, in his wonderful book, *The Power of Now: A Guide to Spiritual Enlightenment* (New World Library, 2004), explains how the present moment holds the key to liberation and enlightenment. He further clarifies that you cannot find the present moment as long as you allow your mind to control you, instead of you controlling it.

Monte demonstrated that to me every day of his life. Thankfully I caught on sooner rather than later.

A Wingman Practice:

Be Here, Now

Repeat the words "Be here, now," either out loud or to yourself, for one minute. Allow the words to permeate your subconscious, so when you find yourself mentally somewhere else, either in the past or in the future, it's easier for your subconscious to help bring you back.

As you practice, recognize that where you are is where you are with no judgment regarding whether it's a good or bad place. Focus your awareness on the present moment. Let everything else go. Let go of your past, and your story of what was, and let go of any thoughts of the future and what might be.

If just for the moment.

37
It Happened One Morning

One day, the week after Monte died, I entered the woods by myself. It was a cold, gray morning, not unlike hundreds of other days. It seemed so real. Nothing seemed unusual until I came upon two trees in a grouping of trees. I noticed them immediately because they stood together, like two lovers standing side by side. What caught my eye was the white birch tree, it was the only one amongst a group of maples.

Perhaps it was because my daughter had moved from New Jersey to Alabama and was dating a young man from Birmingham. Perhaps it was my concern for her, a stranger in a strange land, but I felt a connection to the birch tree, as if that was her, interconnected with the maple tree right next to her, in this grouping of maples. It brought me a sense of peace and contentment. Or maybe I just wanted to feel, as the birch tree had become a part of these maples, that my daughter was accepted and loved by her new community.

I walked over, extended my arms, and stretched my body to touch both the birch and the maple, with me being the bridge between them. I felt the love, the melding of the old customs and new ideas. New families being formed and brought together in love. And as my skin tingled from the love I felt, I closed my eyes with notions of my daughter smiling, laughing, and being in love.

I'm not sure how much time passed, it seemed like only minutes, but it had grown darker. As I looked up, I saw someone walking by me on the path, maybe 20 feet away. Something seemed a bit off, I wasn't exactly sure of what it was, but I was intrigued. He didn't see me because I was off the path, mingled in the mix of all those trees.

I walked after him. When I caught up, I was surprised by how handsomely he was dressed. An older gentleman, nattily attired in what looked like a dark retro suit, with a Burberry raincoat and hat, and a very smart-looking walking stick. Now I'm in these woods a lot, but I don't think I'd ever seen someone so well-dressed walking these paths, and I'd certainly never seen this particular gentleman.

"Gets pretty icy up ahead," I mentioned. "You may want to stay on this side."

"Thank you," he answered calmly.

We continued along the path together in silence, until I interrupted the quiet and asked him what brought him to these woods on this dreary morning.

His words took me by surprise. "Why, I believe you did, sir."

"Excuse me?" I wasn't sure I had heard correctly. And as I stood there, in my morning woods clothes, looking into the eyes of this elegant man, I felt my skin quiver again. Have you ever seen something that couldn't be? That was the flash of recognition that I felt. But when Monte ran up and joined us, I knew I was in for a different kind of morning walk.

I went with it. "Mr. Hill?" I inquired cautiously, not certain of who, or what, I was now walking with.

"At your service," he replied. "How can I help you"?

As I write these words, I obviously appreciate that it was a dream. But I can see it so clearly: it was a somber, overcast morning. And although it seemed like my very standard morning, it was anything but. For on that morning, I recognized my next practice would be delivered to me by none other than Napoleon Hill, the brilliant author of *Think and Grow Rich*, one of the best selling self-help books of all time.

"I'm glad to make your acquaintance," I said with an uneasy smile.

Thus began my morning walk with Napoleon Hill. I so wanted to believe it was real, especially because Monte was there with us. I mean, how often do you walk with your dog that you just had to put down and an author who'd been dead for almost 50 years?

It felt so normal, yet so surreal.

I'd been listening to his lectures on YouTube and reading his books. I told him so, as well as how what he'd said and wrote really resonated with me.

"How so?" he inquired.

"Well, I have a web site, a business called The Wingman's Path to Positivity, where I espouse many of your philosophies and help individuals and businesses bring more positive energy into their offices and into their lives. I actually break everything down into one minute practices."

"Sir," he responded, "if you have a business, then you need to have a definiteness of purpose."

"Can I ask you what you mean by 'definiteness of purpose'?"

"It means you've got to have a desire, you've got to have a goal, something you want, even if you just make it up. Don't worry about it being the end-all-be-all, or your life's work. It can be a simple goal. But if you can get some enthusiasm behind it, and commit to achieving it, you'll be well on your way to doing so."

It occurred to me that I didn't have a definiteness of purpose for my business. The first thing that popped into my head was how much I loved walking these woods every day. I valued these walks and rarely skipped a day. I wondered if that would be considered a definiteness of purpose? But wasn't sure—I mean, I didn't do business in the woods.

"Mr. Hill, I've been walking these woods every day for the last 16 years, that's certainly been a definiteness of purpose of mine for my life, to get here every day," I replied. "Is that what you mean"?

He countered kindly, without a hint of judgment. "Now sir, we're taking a nice walk here, and I'm glad you've been able to do this every day. And yes, that would be considered a definiteness of purpose for some, but for business? I don't think that's why you invited me here; to talk about walking the woods. I think you may have something more that you want to accomplish, so let's get to it."

As I contemplated his words, he asked, "What'd you say your name was? Mr. Wingman?" Then he continued without me answering. "The only wingmen I know of, unless you're talking angels, are pilots in the Air Force, which help protect and serve their lead pilot to be successful on their chosen mission."

"Well, Mr. Hill," I smiled, "you'd be surprised to hear how that definition has changed in the modern vernacular, but it has kept the same meaning. The mission may have changed, but a Wingman still helps another to be successful."

Happily, at that moment, I remembered my new idea, which could be my definiteness of purpose, and appreciated that it must be the reason I had "invited" him here. It was to accomplish the goal of Jan and me traveling and living abroad for a year. While Jan was growing excited, and I had promised Coop I would do it, I was more nervous about the prospect of it.

I told Mr. Hill of our desire.

"Now we're getting somewhere," he replied with resolve. "Sounds like a wonderful ambition."

I smiled.

"Do you have a plan?" he asked hopefully.

"Not exactly." My apprehension was obvious in my voice. "I'm working on it. Right now, the one thing I do every day is practice believing it to be true. I practice seeing my wife and me living in Thailand. I practice the feeling of us being there. I practice thinking about what it will be like. It's a relatively new goal, so I'm still getting used to the idea."

"That's a fantastic start. What do you see as your next move?"

"I think I should probably write down why I believe I can make this happen, why I want this to happen, and everything I need to do to make this happen."

"A great idea. I find when you write down your goal and your plan, you take it from intangible to more concrete. It makes it easier to see."

"Here's the thing Mr. Hill, I've never done anything like this before."

He responded, "Of course you haven't. If you had, you probably would be setting a bigger goal. You have a desire, and that is a perfect place to start."

"But I'm not certain I can do it. And I'd be crushed if I let my wife down. I've found in my past, that many times I get close to succeeding, I somehow sabotage my success. Every time I practice thinking, seeing, feeling, and believing we can accomplish this goal, I get worried about even just getting on the plane. I've never been a real traveler."

"I had a friend a long time ago," he reminisced. "His name was Henry Ford. He would always say, 'Whether you think you can, or you think you can't—you're right.'"

"I want to believe I can, but sometimes I worry that I might fall back on old habits, and not be able to."

"You've got to give your subconscious a thrashing," he stated emphatically.

"A thrashing. What? How do I give my subconscious a thrashing? What does that even mean?" Although I recognized the line from a book I'd read (*Your Right to Be Rich: Napoleon Hill's Proven Program for Prosperity and Happiness.* Tarcher Success Classics, 2015), I wasn't sure how to do that.

"It means you've got to make sure you're in control of it, and it's not in control of you."

He must have noticed the confused look on my face because he continued. "Let me give you an example. Say some time ago, it could be last week, it could be 10 years ago, heck, it might even have happened back when you were a child. Someone said something negative to you, and it slipped into your subconscious. Now those negative words could be sabotaging your success ever since. And you may not even realize it. When you give your subconscious a thrashing, you take back control of your life, of your business, and of your destiny. You've got to make sure you're in control of your life."

"You mean like a virus might get into a computer, somehow I let something slip into my subconscious that stops me from doing what I want. Maybe it was something someone said when they were just upset, like 'you're no good at that,' or "you can't.' Are you saying that somehow that may have gotten into my head to where I might now say, 'I can't,' or 'I'm no good at that'?"

"Exactly!"

"I get that, but you haven't explained how I give my subconscious a thrashing."

"Now son, I'm known as a business professor, but here's a little bit of psychology for you. The subconscious mind will believe whatever you tell it, especially if you tell it and retell it over and over and over. Why... You can even get it to believe something that you don't even believe. That's right, just by repetition alone you can do that." He grew excited as he spoke. "And when I say to tell your subconscious, over and over, exactly what you want it to know and believe, I mean I want you to say it out loud. I want you to make sure your subconscious hears you. Scream it if you have to. Sure, you can just think it over and over, and I suspect that the Creator can know your thoughts, but I'm a big believer in articulating your thoughts out loud, with enthusiasm. I want you to make certain you awaken your subconscious, and it knows what you want from it."

"I do similar work now. I repeat phrases until I get them lodged into my subconsciousness."

"But do you do them to give your subconscious a thrashing? I can't tell you how many people I've seen who didn't believe in themselves. And just by telling themselves over and over, 'I believe in me,' they began to believe in themselves. Seen it many times over."

We came to a huge tree that had fallen right in the middle of the path. As I circled left and he circled right, I began to consider what he had just said. My subconscious definitely had a mind of its own, sometimes. Despite all the work I'd been doing on the Wingman's Path, It would take over and present itself in the worst ways, and at the worst times. And when it did, it was like I wasn't even there, and I certainly couldn't stop it.

I thought back to my most recent birthday. Janet had thrown a small celebration with a few friends for me, and right in the middle of it, she made a little toast professing her love to me. It was beautiful. And I felt so loved.

And I slimed her.

That's right. I slimed her. Somehow, I don't know how, I became a total asshole. And I knew I had really hurt her. Unfortunately, it wasn't the first time this had happened, either.

Thinking about that, I immediately understood what Mr. Hill meant about it being my subconscious. I seemed to have no control over it. I'd gotten better at it. It didn't happen as often as it used to. But it still happened. After discovering the Wingman's Path and consistently practicing positivity, I had evolved. But then those situations would sometimes occur, and I would behave like my old self. I embarrassed Janet, and I embarrassed myself.

The strangest part of it was when it would happen, too. It seemed to only happen when Jan was being really loving and kind. As if my subconscious wouldn't allow me to accept that kind of heartfelt love. Hearing Mr. Hill's words made me consider my childhood. My parents may not have been the most loving, but they did their best. There was something from my childhood though, that wasn't letting me receive the feeling of absolute love.

Meanwhile, Jan was a font of love, and I felt her love was helping me to break down those walls in my subconscious. Whenever I'd behave like that, I would be so ashamed and so regretful of hurting her. My remorse over my behavior helped me to pull away from my old reactivity, but something was still in there, somewhere deep in my subconscious. I felt my eyes tearing up. It was time to give my subconscious a thrashing.

As I made it back around to the path, I was again, all alone. No Monte. No Mr. Hill. I circled around to look for Mr. Hill but knew he was no longer there. His task had been completed. I made my way back to the parking lot and called for Monte.

Groggily, and from a deep sleep, I felt Janet shaking me awake. "Are you OK?" she whispered. "You were calling for Monte."

Tears welled up in my eyes as I remembered Monte was no longer with us. Gathering myself quickly, I answered, "Better than OK, honey. I'm giving my subconscious a thrashing. And I'm so excited for us to go traveling for the next year. And by the way, I love you, and I promise you I'll never slime you again."

And I haven't.

A Wingman Practice:

Give your subconscious a thrashing

Make certain you let your subconscious know *exactly* what you want, in no uncertain terms. Say it out loud, scream it if you can. But let your subconscious know you are back in charge.

If at this moment, you're uncertain as to exactly what you want, don't worry. Do this practice by repeating out loud, "I'm giving my subconscious a thrashing. I believe in Me!" for one minute.

I've done this practice by saying those exact words more than any others. Saying those words always brings me a smile.

38
My Dearest, Jan

I couldn't fall back to sleep as my dream kept running through my mind. As soon as the sun started coming up, I got out of bed and left for the woods for my morning walk. I wanted to find the path I had just walked with Mr. Hill and Monte.

As I came to the area where I met up with Mr. Hill, a ray of sun, coming through the trees, shone upon my face. Content, I smiled. I saw the area where Monte had joined us, and my smile broadened, but my face became wet with tears. It was an emotional morning for me.

Adding to the sensations, I thought of the promise I had just made to Jan upon waking. My sliming her certainly wasn't a conscious thing, so how could I be sure it wouldn't come out ever again?

By giving my subconscious a thrashing, that's how. That morning in the woods was the first time I ever implemented that practice. I knew I was early, so with no one else near, I began.

"I'm giving my subconscious a thrashing. For now on, I'm coming from love."

"I'm a font of love."

"Subconscious, I love you. You've helped protect me forever, but I no longer need to be protected from receiving love."

I was screaming now.

"I'm able to receive love."

"I'm able to receive love."

"Do you hear me Subconscious? I'm giving you a thrashing. I believe in me and my ability to receive love."

"I'm a receptor of love."

"I'm coming from love."

I feel your love and I'm sending it back."

"Love. Love. Love."

I just kept screaming the word love.

Until I took the turn on the path and there, 20 feet in front of me, was a woman I'd never seen before. She clearly wasn't feeling the love and, leash in hand, quickly turned off the path onto another.

I wanted to apologize to her, but I thought it best to just turn around and walk away. Jan and I had just been talking about feeling safe as a woman walking by herself in the woods. I didn't want her to feel scared, but really what could I say at that moment that she might believe? That's why I just continued my thrashing quietly and went in the opposite direction. I hoped it wasn't her first time in "my" woods, and she wouldn't let my seemingly insane behavior dissuade her from returning.

The thrashing did me good. It made me realize I had something important to do. After continuing my thrashing for what seemed like another ten minutes, I drove home, sat down, and wrote a letter to Jan.

My Dearest, Jan,

I still have a great deal to learn.

Please accept my apology for my period of assholism last week. I'm not certain why I have these moments, but I am certain that I am working to eliminate them.

The good news is... since meeting you, I've learned what it means to come from love. You are a true font of love, and I am fortunate to have you in my life for the last 18 years. Living with love is a wonderful way to learn love.

I now think I discovered The Wingman's Path just so I could practice living with love. You seem to live it naturally, with a grace and elegance born from your early years. My thought must have been, if I could give myself some structure, if I could practice it every day, I would soon be able to master it.

However, my past training certainly has not included that type of love.

Coming from love is a habit that must be lived or a feeling that must be demonstrated. Like anything, though, it can be learned.

Like all lessons, it takes time. Time to erase the trenches of hate and sarcasm, or even worse, apathy.

But change them I have. These moments of sliming, of assholism, of not being the person I want to be, have surely come with much less frequency.

One thing I have learned, is when I do something wrong, when I get into a down feeling, I must not allow it to ferment. As I walked the woods this morning, I relived the words coming out of my mouth. And as I continued to focus on it, those feelings of shame and remorse persisted, adding salt to the wound. Again and again.

So I practiced what I preach, and I set my intention to right this wrong. I thought, what can I learn from this latest episode that hasn't been learned before? Who can help me with this most important lesson? I mean, really, how difficult is it to get the message that I'm able to receive and give love?

I know you know I'm sorry, but I'm writing this to formally apologize. Your love has helped me evolve, it has helped me break down my caustic defenses, along with my feelings of depression and numbness.

Somehow, someway, I've had something in my subconscious that has sabotaged every good thing in my life. From love, to business, to family.

Like Viola Davis said to Bryce Dallas Howard in the movie, 'The Help,' "Ain't you tired Miss Hilly?" I am tired. Tired of losing everything I care about, tired of pushing people I love away, tired of sabotaging my success, and tired of being such a sarcastic jerk.

You've shown me what life can be like when you allow love in. How can I even begin to say thank you? Maybe if I could somehow show my 'before' and 'after' picture. You know, like those pictures of people before they've lost like 100 pounds, and then you see their 'after' picture. In the after picture they're always smiling and shining so brightly. Only I'm not speaking of the physical. I'm speaking of the vibrational. If you could see the before and after pictures of my vibration, I know you would understand how thankful I am for your love. My vibration is now a much happier, confident, kinder, wiser, loving, compassionate, and successful vibration. Like those after pictures one sees, my vibration is shining so very brightly. And I'm thankful for you, for helping that become my reality.

How do you thank someone who opened up your world, who opened you up to a world of possibilities? How do you thank someone who's shown you how to love, how to be open?

By being the best version of yourself. By helping others to be the best version of themselves. By living in joy and helping others do the same. By never falling back from whence you came.

And by demonstrating you've learned the lesson. By living the lesson. By being an ambassador of love. Every single day. By feeling the love and sending it out. By living in a vibration of love. You've taught me about love, and I have learned the lesson.

You've opened me up to living a life of my choosing, to seeing the possibilities, to helping others

I'm able to receive love, and that makes me a pretty lucky guy. Thank you for your love.

Your Loving husband, Michael

By the way...if you're reading this and thinking *coming from love* means being soft, means always bending to the will of your loved one, or always doing more for them than they do for themselves, please don't. When I speak of *coming from love* in this practice, I'm speaking of the love between two people for relationship purposes, i.e., between spouses, partners, couples, or however you describe a loving, romantic relationship between two people.

However, I think this practice is even more valuable for someone who is single and looking for a partner. When you practice coming from love, you become a more loving person. When you're a more loving person, your energy is one of love, and you will attract more love into your life. Coming from love means seeing things and experiences through the eyes of one who is loving, caring, compassionate, accepting, and tender.

- When you come from love, you see yourself as a person who...
- Sees the best in yourself and your loved ones.
- Helps yourself and helps your loved ones to help themselves.
- Treats yourself, and your loved ones, considerately.
- Is open and honest in your communication.
- Is loyal to yourself, and your loved ones.
- Feels secure with who you are and in your relationship.
- Makes sure your loved ones feels the same.

- Respects yourself, and your loved ones.

It is easy to hate, and it is difficult to love. This is how the whole scheme of things works. All good things are difficult to achieve; bad things are very easy to get.
~attributed to Confucius

Difficult, but not impossible. All it takes is a little practice.

A Wingman Practice:

Come From Love

For one minute, repeat out loud or to yourself, "I come from love." As you do, practice the feeling of being a loving, caring, and compassionate person. See yourself loving yourself, feel yourself being surrounded in love, and believe yourself to be worthy of receiving love.

39
Swan Lake

From the moment I'd woken, both literally and figuratively, from my morning "walk" with Napoleon Hill, my vibration kept rising. I found myself smiling constantly. I was about to begin living my second life, and things were progressing pretty quickly.

Have you ever suffered the unfortunate emotion of feeling like a fraud? Not that you were, but ever have the voices in your head nag you with questions? Maybe not just your internal voices, but your friends and family as well? A couple weeks after I started my meetup group, a good friend who was helping me, questioned, "Who are we to lead these discussions? We're not experts on the Law of Attraction." My answer was as honest then as it is today: "Don't pretend to be an expert. Be who you are. I look at it as we're just two guys facilitating a meeting and learning along with everyone."

As my knowledge and practice grew, there were times I was called upon to be "the expert." I played the role to the best of my ability, but those niggling fears would come up from time to time. But no more. I was now stepping into the realization I was practicing what I preached and truly demonstrating everything I had been teaching. My declaration that anyone could create a life of their choosing was becoming a self-fulfilled prophecy. I now not only spoke it, I was validating it. I was creating my new life. Doubts could no longer creep in...or so I thought.

Before we could take off on our great adventure, there were some responsibilities that needed to be tended to. One of those was to visit with my mom in Providence, Rhode Island. The plan was for me to hang out for one month with her, then four months in Thailand, come back and spend some more time with her, then take off again.

On the last morning of that first stay in Providence, I was up and out for my morning walk well before the sun. The streetlights were still on as I made my way along the Seekonk River. There was almost zero visibility, and a thick mist eclipsed the river.

I smiled as I walked, sensing how my vision was mirroring the goings-on in my mind. Yes, it was a bit muddled inside my own head, too, as my personal demons were having a bit of fun with me. They were throwing doubt, questions, and other negative energies into my expectations of my Thailand pilgrimage.

Thankfully, my personal demons also took me back to my first experience with SARK. We were about to interview her for the first time on the *Talk-N-Angels* radio show. Jan had sent me a blog post from someone she followed. It was a re-post from SARK about how, while on a recent book tour, she took off at lunchtime as her inner demons were filling her with self-doubt. Sitting in her car, she noticed a police officer parked nearby. She introduced herself and explained how she was having a crisis of self-doubt brought about by her inner critics. When he asked how he could help, she requested that he arrest them. So he did. Put them all in the back seat of his police van and drove them to the station.

I loved her process and thought it would be a fun way to start our interview with her. Our mayor always allowed two hours of public availability on Wednesday afternoons, so before our show, I went to the Municipal building in my hometown. It was quiet that day, and she was sitting in the municipal court by herself when I entered. I marched in, introduced myself as a resident of the town, and asked her to have my inner critics arrested. The mayor was quick to respond: "We don't have enough jail space for all your inner critics." I couldn't stop laughing at her response. After that, I became a big supporter of our mayor.

Anyway, the exchange with the Mayor brought me right back to the morning fog, and those difficult little devils dancing around my mind. I couldn't seem to shake them. But then, out of the mist, appeared these two beautiful swans at the edge of the water, not more than ten feet from me. It's like they swam straight to me. I considered my Napoleon Hill episode and gave myself a little pinch to make certain I was actually seeing this.

My Wingman sense was tingling. Were these swans real? Their appearance was almost angel-like. I stood there, mesmerized. The background was pure fog, I couldn't see anything behind them. In that morning mist there was only them and me. Knowing my sense of reality had been debatable as of late, and with no one there to confirm this encounter, I decided to check my reality and further confirm this experience.

"Do you have a message for me?" I asked.

They didn't say anything, so I laughed and thought how silly of me. As if! They're swans, of course, they didn't have a message for me.

Then it hit me. THEY WERE the message.

Yes, my Universal Wingmen had outdone themselves. Showing me such grace, strength, and beauty, not to mention a great pair of wings. They were striking.

They snapped me right out of my funk, and then, as if that had been their purpose, they disappeared back into the dense fog.

The message seemed clear enough. *Look for beauty, wherever you are.* Even when the air is so thick it seems like you're looking through pea soup, look for beauty. More importantly, find your own internal strength, grace, and beauty as you set out on your adventure.

I hadn't walked more than another 100 feet when the sun started to rise and the fog lifted, on the river and in my head. It was clear as could be. It didn't seem possible for that much murkiness to have evaporated that quickly.

I surveyed the river, but it was totally empty. No kayakers, no ducks, and not a swan to be seen. I'm not sure I'd ever seen the water so quiet. And how could the swans have disappeared so quickly?

The sun danced on the river. As I watched the water shimmering and reflecting the light, a young student in a Brown University sweatshirt passed by me.

"Hello." I said. "Did you see how foggy it was a few minutes ago?"

Her voice brimmed with excitement, "Yes, Isn't it sensational? It's the dawn of a new day."

"What?" I asked, not certain I had heard her correctly. But she was gone, walking quickly by me.

She certainly seems eager for this new day, I supposed. I then turned and continued my walk.

I repeated her words, but it was really her face that stayed in my mind. I only caught a glimpse of her face, it was shining so brightly. It was like the light from the sun was reflected in her face.

"It's the dawn of a new day," I quietly stated to myself. But it wasn't the words she said, it was how she said them. Sensing more meaning, and a possible new practice, I began reciting her words as a mantra.

As I walked, I said them louder and louder. I was soon under the Henderson Bridge, and I shouted up to the skies, "It's the dawn of a new day."

"It's the DAWN of a NEW DAY," echoed back to me, louder and deeper then I would have thought possible.

The words enveloped me. I could feel them. It wasn't just a new day, it was a NEW DAY. A new life. And for me, I was taking off the next day for a great adventure. It was a new reality. It was the dawn of a new day where I was creating a life of my choosing, where I could manifest whatever I desired. A new life where my universal Wingmen have swans swim up to me to remind me of my beauty, strength, and gracefulness. A new day, where I felt a connection with the Universe, where I understood my power and my ability to change my vibration to match the energy of that which I want.

I could feel the beginning of an amazing new chapter.

"It's the dawn of a new day!"

As I repeated the words, I thought of spring training in baseball. Spring training is awesome. It's when every team is still undefeated. Every team, and every person, from the star player to the bat boy, has the optimism of winning the season, and the hope of winning the World Series, of being the world champions. Every team is full of confidence, believing it's their year to win. One year, my older brother and I drove to Clearwater, Florida for the Phillies Spring Training. The optimism was palpable.

Can you imagine that? Being on a team where everyone is optimistic. Every one of your teammates believes this is *your* year.

Oh Yeah, baby! It's the dawn of a new day.

And for me, it literally was. I was taking off for Thailand, the Land of Smiles, of Zen Masters, and of yet to be lived discoveries.

It was my spring training, and I felt the optimism of my teammates, my Universal Wingmen. The more I said, "It's the dawn of a new day," the more I believed it was going to be my year.

When I returned to my sister's house, I Googled what it meant when swans come across your path. According to spirit-animals.com, they're:

"…heralding in the development of your intuitive abilities and altered states of awareness. You are going to be shown new ways of thinking, breathing and going with the flow of life. You are being asked to accept your ability of knowing what lies ahead. Pay attention to your hunches and gut instincts and honor your feminine intuitive side. Alternatively you are being reminded of your own inner grace and beauty and to allow it to shine forth for others to see."

The dawn of a new day, indeed!

My vibration was flying. My inner demons, beaten down by my enthusiasm, were no longer in my head. I was ready for my new chapter to begin.

As I reflected on my trip to spring training with my brother, I found more clarity. It wasn't just the player's optimism. Yes, they were enjoying spring training, but they were also getting ready for the upcoming season. They were working on their hitting, their pitching, and their fielding. They were visualizing themselves winning their season, getting to the playoffs, and making it to the World Series. They were seeing themselves hitting home runs and making great catches, pitching great games, and striking out the other team.

I realized I had to ready myself for my new season.

I sat down, closed my eyes, and again began repeating the words from the fast-walking girl in the Brown University garb.

"It's the dawn of a new day." As I said the words, I practiced seeing my exciting new year. I envisioned how I wanted it to play out. The words became a mantra for me. I sang them out loud, and quietly whispered them to myself, all the while visualizing and imagining it even better.

I was ready for my new life. You best believe it!

A Wingman Practice:

It's the Dawn of a New Day

This practice became an instant classic for me. Perhaps it's because I'm an early riser and on those days I'm out before the sun, as I see it rise, I always practice "It's the dawn of a new day."

You don't have to be leaving on a great adventure for you to believe it's the dawn of a new day; you just have to get it in your own mind. And the best way to do that is by repetition.

The dawn of a new day implies the sun is coming out, and the storms in your life are clearing. Let this become your mantra for the day. As you practice it, allow yourself to feel the sunshine beaming down on you. Feel the light. It's going to be your season.

Start right now, wherever you are, whether you're in a house that is draining you, a demanding relationship, or you have an illness that's exhausting you. Start right now and allow this new beginning, this dawn of a new day, to start you on the path to creating a life of your choosing.

As you say the words, start seeing yourself creating it. It's the dawn of a new day, where anything you want to do, be or have, is possible. You can make it happen. How? By thinking it, seeing it, feeling it and believing it's going to be a great new chapter in your life.

Can you feel the vibration of all the good things happening for you? Of better relationships and improved health? Of money flowing in and the feeling of abundance all around?

It's the dawn of a new day. It's your time to shine.

40
The Monk's Trail

After a couple weeks exploring Bangkok, we flew up to Chiang Mai, where we had rented an apartment for the next two months. On our first night there, Jan surprised me with the story of the Monk's Trail. She knew how excited I'd be.

She had learned about it from Pinterest: a concealed trek through the forest to Wat Pha Lat, a temple rarely visited by tourists. Perhaps that's because it's hidden, but more likely, the rarity of visitors is probably because it's halfway up the mountain to its much more famous sibling, Wat Doi Suthep, the most well-known, most visited, and (considered) most beautiful of all of Chiang Mai's temples. When driving up to Doi Suthep, Wat Pha Lat is more of a footnote. You wouldn't even notice it as you pass by. Nothing would lead you to believe it was even worth visiting unless you heard about it from someone else.

Our new bed was hard and uncomfortable, but with thoughts of hiking an unknown trail to a seldom-seen little temple where monks lived dancing in my head, I slipped into a restful slumber. The following morning, we were up and out early, totally prepared with water, fruit, bug spray, suntan lotion, and Jan even had taken screenshots of the Pinterest directions, complete with photos to help us find our way.

We found a songthaew, a red pick-up truck-like communal taxi where you sit in the back, going to the Chiang Mai University/Zoo area, just as the directions told us to do. But as soon as we got out of it, all of those exacting directions and pictures made no sense. We walked and walked, asked person after person, but everyone just shook their head. No one had ever heard of the Monk's Trail. Up and down the mountain road we walked, sweating and confused. Finally, almost ready to give up, we trekked back down about a mile from where we had just walked up, and met an older woman, who was sweeping the sidewalk. She told us that we needed to be at the back entrance of the zoo.

Finally! Only the Zoo wasn't open yet, so we couldn't cut through. Instead, we walked past the zoo to the university on the other side. We thought we could take a parallel trail through the university to get to the rear entrance of the zoo. This idea proved to be more challenging than expected. We asked students, grounds workers, security guards, and the receptionist at the Chiang Mai University bookstore, but no one knew, nor could they understand, what we meant by getting to the rear of the zoo.

At long last, a student seemed to comprehend what we were asking and gave us directions in broken English. Maybe it was the broken English, or we just couldn't understand, but once again, we got lost. More walking, more sweating, more confusion. It had now been about three hours since we'd arrived in town, and our energy was waning. It was about a zillion degrees, the sun was beating down on us, we were soaked through with sweat, and we were running low on water.

Another student suggested we get on one of the university jitneys that traverse the grounds. We did, if for no other reason than to stop walking and take a rest. After looping around the school twice, we were then told to get on the Number Five jitney.

It was while we were resting at the student jitney stop that Jan delivered my new practice. I was hot, tired, and perhaps even a bit angry when Janet, smiling, told me of a Facebook conversation she had had with her sister that morning. My sister-in-law had jokingly responded to one of Janet's posts, "Enough already, get back here and get a job!" to which Janet replied, tongue firmly in cheek, "My job is to appreciate the world."

OMG! I love it!

Of course, we joked about our appreciation right then—sweating, tired, lost, and about to give up—but I couldn't stop saying the words: *My job is to appreciate the world.*

The phrase energized us. Suddenly we were laughing. When your job is to appreciate the world, you don't allow yourself to get upset. Instead, we were ready, once again, to embrace the challenge

At just that moment, a Honda pulled over and out popped the young man who had helped us thirty minutes earlier. Jan laughed and told him, "We messed up your directions."

He said, "I will drive you."

It might sound strange that we would jump into his car, but when you appreciate the world, you start with its people. And we were very appreciative. Plus, it was air-conditioned. He and his girlfriend drove us up a long road, twisting and turning until Jan finally shouted, "Here it is!" The Pinterest picture was before us in real life. After thanking him profusely we were finally there.

"The directions say it's just an easy three- to five-minute walk up a slight incline in the road," Jan stated excitedly. "Then we will be at the start of the trail."

Slight incline my ass. This was a heart-pounding, catch-my-breath-every-few-moments, stop-and-rest-again-and-again, you-appreciating-the-world-now? mountainous hill. But that's just it, as I trudged up the steep road, I kept repeating, "My job is to appreciate the world" out loud and to myself. Whereas I normally would get angry and pissy, I was almost laughing at my situation.

"It's a good thing we didn't have them drive us the rest of the way," I chuckled. In a challenging situation, the more you can laugh about it, the better your vibration. The better your vibration, the quicker it gets resolved. And that idea proved true once again as we finally saw the beginning of the trail.

We were ecstatic. And like so many marvels in life, once we stepped upon the trail, we felt the magic. Yes, we were still tired, hot, and a bit dehydrated, but the change in scenery, the green forest, and the magical orange ties wrapped around the trees, put everything in a different perspective. We walked and climbed and breathed in the lush surroundings. Finally, yes, finally, from out of the forest, emerged the sound of monks chanting, then the site of carved white dragons, and an entrance to the enchanting secret Temple.

Everything else from earlier just melted away. We sat on a huge stone mountaintop, overlooking a massive forest with a stunning view of Chiang Mai out in the distance. We meditated with friendly monks and were invited to share some sweet potatoes, juice, and conversation with a monk named Jin. And when we left it, got even better.

For as we began our long trek back down, we met up with a novice monk who spoke enough English that we struck up a conversation. We spoke about his journey to be a monk, his teachers, family, and the village he left behind. We were having such a nice time; I thought introductions were in order. I pointed to myself and said, "I'm Michael, what is your name?" He said his name was Prin, and then said, "You Nakbin."

Thinking he misunderstood, I said, "No, my name is Michael."

He then stated, "Michael, You Nakbin, Wingman."

Whaaaaattttt?
I almost fell down! You can imagine the size of my smile.
"Nakbin, Wingman," he reiterated.

I was laughing, unsure why he said it, when he pointed to my now favorite T-shirt. It features Thai writing above a pair of wings, then the word *Wingman*, in English, on the bottom. I knew it had said *Wingman* in Thai, but didn't know how it was pronounced. It was the first time I had heard the pronunciation. I couldn't stop laughing and smiling as he repeated "Nakbin, Wingman" a few more times.

As we got to the bottom of the steps and said goodbye, he said, "Thank you, Nakbin, for helping me with my English."

I felt honored and was so touched. It made me realize how easy it is to help others. How, when we help others, we help ourselves. How, when we help others, we expand our village by recognizing that we are all connected. How a rising tide lifts all boats and the happier our village is, the easier it is for us, and for each person in our village, to be happier.

The day didn't happen the way Jan had planned. It was hard, and we had moments of doubt. We couldn't have done it without the help of others. And we most certainly might have quit had it not been for the "appreciating the world" comment from Jan. As we sat on a bench, waiting quietly for a songthaew to take us back, we held hands and vowed to each other: Our job is to appreciate the world.

A Wingman Practice:

Appreciate the World

Repeat the words, "My job is to appreciate the world" out loud and quietly to yourself for one minute.

As you do, acknowledge to yourself that appreciating the world is your primary job. You may do something else to earn money, but if you think of that as your secondary job, and appreciating the world as your first job, you'll be amazed by how much more productive and creative you will be.

You see, it's tough to get pissed off when your job is to appreciate the world. When you're appreciating the world, you don't get upset, or hassled, or stressed. You remain calmer, and therefore more focused on achieving your goals and desires.

Rest assured, you will get tested. But if you start repeating "My job is to appreciate the world" as a mantra, you'll find yourself appreciating the world—even when you're lost and walking a mile back down a mountain road you've just walked a mile up; even when things are not going the way you had planned, and you're hot, tired and irritable.

My job is to appreciate the world.

And I love my job. Give it a try. It only takes one minute.

41
Wingman on a Motor Scooter

After that first day in Chiang Mai, I thought my Universal Wingmen would be bringing me brand new practices every other day. After all, I had begun an exciting new chapter in my life, and I was in one of the most spiritual places I'd ever been. I was ready for them, and I was ready for a deeper connection. But it was not to be.

Looking back, I realized that some of the practices I receive remail with me longer than others before. At first, it seemed as if sometimes I'd receive a new one almost immediately, and at other times I'd stay on one practice for a long while before another came along. But then I became conscious that my Universal Wingmen actually sent me many different practices every day, but it was on *my* timetable when I was ready to accept them. I would often need more time with a specific practice before I was ready to move on.

> Keep this in mind: Some of these practices will resonate with you deeper, and be far more meaningful to you on your path, than others. For me, many of my practices became "instant classics," exercises I would do for months at a time. *My Job is to Appreciate the World* became my main practice for that next month. I guess I just needed a bit more time with it to allow it to permeate my subconscious.

In Chiang Mai, there were so many different Buddhist wats (temples) that every morning I'd take a walk and find a new one to walk in and meditate. I'd never been one who meditates. Actually, I'd probably "meditated" a thousand times in my life—and fallen asleep 998 of those times. Yes, almost every time I'd ever meditated, I'd fallen asleep. I believe my discovery of the Wingman's Path came about because I once heard Abraham Hicks say it was easier to get your mind thinking positively, then it was to shut your mind down in meditation.

When the student is ready, the teacher will appear.

Chiang Mai was different. I'd sit and talk with monks. I'd read everything I could on Buddhism. I'd spend time in the many wats. When in the wats, I was able to meditate, at least for about five to ten minutes. I initially thought it was just being surrounded by all this Buddhist spirituality. I now realize that I, the student, was ready, and the Buddhist spirituality and Chiang Mai was the teacher. I had traveled far enough on The Wingman's Path that I could now quiet my mind. I had reached a new level of positivity. My vibration had improved enough that I could now meditate.

But while I was loving Chiang Mai, Jan wanted a change of scenery and some new areas to explore. We decided to head north to Chiang Dao for a couple of days, so we caught an 8:00 a.m. local bus and were on our way.

Ninety minutes later, we arrived at the small Chiang Dao bus station and quickly caught a songthaew to the place Jan had reserved. Traveling takes on new meaning when your taxi is a pickup truck, and you're sitting on a bench seat in the back as you speed along increasingly remote and bumpy dirt roads. We held on tightly the entire way. And finally, we saw a sign for our place:.28 kilometers ahead!

And what a place! All woods and birds and thatched bungalows overlooking green forest. It also had a small pool sitting at the base of the mountain and an outdoor restaurant surrounded by flowering bushes and twinkling lights. It was the kind of place I always wondered how people found or afforded. I gave Jan a look, which said, "Really? We're staying here?"

"How much is this?" I asked in a whisper.

"It's $25.00," Jan whispered back. I was in heaven.

We had planned on staying only one night, but it was so beautiful we extended our visit. And, as promised, the place was only about 200 meters from Wat Tham Pha Plang, the temple of 510 steps built into the side of the Chiang Dao Mountain.

Every day, we would wake up and walk the 200 meters to the mountain and the 510 steps up the mountain. It was perfect. Not only did it give us our physical exercise, but with inspirational, thought-provoking signs all the way up, it worked our minds as well. And spiritually, it was as magnificent a place to meditate as I've ever found.

On the third afternoon, after our 510-step walk up the mountain and a little exploring of the village, we relaxed by the swimming pool in the shadow of the mountain. Our lovely host asked us if we wanted to dine in their restaurant on western food or walk the 700 meters (which is not quite a half mile) to their sister property down the road for Thai food.

"Thai food!" we said in unison. It wasn't just the Thai food, but we were curious to see their other property. Could it possibly be any more heavenly than where we were staying?

At 6:30, showered and dressed in our only semi-decent clothes, we left the bungalow ready for our walk. No sooner did we step out but turned around and headed back. It was dark out, with only tiny lights to illuminate the path, and the temperature had dropped by what felt like 20 degrees. Jan took off her sandals and flowy pants, and returned to her hiking pants, sneakers, and hoodie. It was that kind of night, pitch black and so quiet that by the time we got to the reception area to leave, we were having second thoughts about venturing forth.

I remarked to our host that perhaps we should stay and eat in the western restaurant after all. She laughed and said, "Oh no! It's a very short walk and very safe. No problems. Just take your torch." Jan clicked on the flashlight.

As we started down the dirt service road to get to the main road, we giggled and squealed the way you do when very excited and very nervous. It was the blackness. Not a light, save for the glow that our flashlight, the "torch" cast. We reached the main road, took a breath, and stepped out. Suddenly, from behind us, from down our service road, a songthaew came bellowing out onto the main road. The driver looked out, "Nest 2?" she asked.

We nodded. "OK, in!" she yelled. She didn't need to ask twice. Those 700 meters flew by in the back of that truck, and before we could even ask how much, she had dropped us off, waved goodbye, and drove off into the darkness.

"Now if we're really lucky, the same thing will happen on our way back," I quipped.

Dinner was lovely. We sat overlooking a koi pond, feasting on delectable Thai food, listening to the wind rustling through the trees. We finished dinner, played a couple games of Rummy 500, contemplated dessert, but decided, since it was late and dark, to start the walk back and perhaps have dessert at our place when we returned.

The road back was magical at first as it started out being illuminated by the light of another restaurant and a small guest house a bit further down the road. There wasn't a car or scooter or songthaew anywhere. We passed a small open-air bar and saw two people playing pool and heard a Johnny Cash song wafting out the windows. It seemed so strange. "Where are we?" Jan asked, and we both laughed at the question.

From there, it became darker. There were no more lights or sounds. "Where's that songthaew now?" Jan queried. As I was about to respond, she suddenly sucked in her breath and whispered, "Oh my God, oh my God!"

Nervous and suddenly on high alert, I yelled, "What is it?"

"Look up!" she said.

I did, and there under the blackest sky, stars were dripping down and enveloping us in their lights. It made me think of the painting, "Starry Night." As we stood there, arms akimbo, twirling, laughing and taking it all in, I wondered if this is what the sky looked like on the night Vincent Van Gogh painted his most famous picture.

Jan remarked, "This may be the closest I've ever been to heaven, I think." It was a moment of unexpected joy.

We reached the bend in the road, took a left-hand turn, and then only had about 200 meters to go. In the distance, we could hear roosters and the unmistakable sound of the wild dogs, howling and barking that you hear at night all over South East Asia. Called street dogs, or soi dogs here in Thailand, most are generally placid during the day, but at night they roam in packs and can be extremely intimidating and sometimes dangerous.

We stopped to take it all in, and Jan shared a story. "Thirty years ago, when I was traveling in Bali, in a village now made famous by Elizabeth Gilbert and Julia Roberts, an older Balinese man I met asked me how I was enjoying Bali."

"Oh, I love it here!"she had exclaimed, "if only there were no wild dogs roaming around, it would be paradise." He chuckled. "There can only be paradise in heaven, he smiled, and so, we have the dogs."

We laughed as we continued our walk. While we couldn't see our dirt road turnoff, we knew it was not too far ahead. But soon enough, out of the darkness two dogs appeared, growling and barking at us. We couldn't really see them, but they sounded about 50 meters ahead. We froze, panicked, and then sank back into the trees.

My thoughts raced. Should we keep walking? Should we turn around and head back to the restaurant and see if someone could drive us or find us a songthaew? The walk back seemed very far now. With my mind racing, I stated, "They know we're afraid of them now."

"They're right," Jan confirmed.

If there's one thing I knew about vibration, even before finding the Wingman's Path, it was that dogs can sense fear. And we were emitting a pretty strong frequency of it. I'm not sure how long we stood there, but the dogs continued to growl and seemed to be inching closer.

"Let's keep calm," I whispered. "Let's keep our cool."

"OK," Jan said. "How do you propose we do that?"

"Let's pretend Monte is walking with us. You know we'd feel protected then. C'mon. We need to get going." But we couldn't move. We were glued to our spot.

For some reason, at that moment, Jan remembered a scene from one of our favorite television shows, "Lost." It was when Jack, a spinal surgeon, described an operation he was performing when something went wrong.

"And the fear was so real. And I knew I had to deal with it. So I just made a choice. I'd let the fear in, let it take over, let it do it's thing. But only for 5 seconds, that's all I was going to give it. So I started to count. One, two, three, four, five. And it was gone. I went back to work, sewed her up, and she was fine."

It gave us a shot of courage and together we counted. "5, 4, 3, 2, 1."

Holding hands so tightly that Jan's nails felt like they were drawing blood, we stepped into the street. I heard my voice say, more to myself then to Jan, "Keep your calm, keep your cool. Like we're taking a pleasant stroll. Don't look at them, but don't show fear either."

Just then a sound came up from behind us. A lone scooter on this dark road. It stopped next to us, and an old Thai man lifted off his helmet. I can't imagine where he was going as we were the last property on the road before the temple, but there he was. Jan blathered on about the dogs and the growling and asked if he would drive slowly around them as we walked next to him in an attempt to avoid them. There was no way he spoke English, but somehow, he understood.

He revved his engine a little, and we began our walk. It was only about a two-minute walk, but it felt much longer. As we got to our road, we turned off quickly, knowing we were safe. We turned to say thank you, but no one was there. No dogs, no man, no scooter. There was no more barking, nor could we hear his engine. We heard nothing, and we saw nothing. Like it didn't even happen. One moment he was by our side, the next he had vanished, like a Wingman from the heavens. Just quiet. As if he appeared and then disappeared solely for us.

Breathing rapidly, we reached our place. A few people remained at the restaurant, the lights were still twinkling, there was the sound of an owl in the distance. A pot of hot tea was placed before us. If we looked just right between the tree branches, we could still make out the stars. We gripped hands tightly. It was still paradise. Well, almost.

Something I've always believed about that night was that by keeping (somewhat) calm while facing our fears, the Universe matched our vibration and sent us back more of the same, i.e. the Wingman on the motor scooter, which gave us more reasons to feel calm.

A Wingman Practice:

Keep Your Calm. Keep Your Cool.

Breathe in the above words quietly for one minute.

As you do, see yourself remaining calm and cool in the face of adversity. Practice the feeling of being in a tense situation and keeping your calm and keeping your cool. If it helps, you can think of movie superheroes like Christian Bale as Batman or Gal Gadot as Wonder Woman or real-life heroes in very stressful situations, like Jackie Robinson or Rosa Parks who kept their cool and changed history.

As I now know, even in the midst of walking through paradise, unexpected or unwanted things can jump out at you. But if you keep your calm, and not let it derail you, you can be back on your path quicker than a Wingman on a motor scooter.

42
The Destiny Café

After Chiang Dao, we journeyed to an out-of-the-way little village called ThaTon. We went there because Jan read you can take a public boat along the Kok River to our next destination of Chiang Rai. It's a very scenic route where you pass through hill tribe villages and an elephant camp called Ban Ruam Mit.

Only the water was too low, so the boats weren't running that day. So, we decided to extend our stay a little to see if the water levels would rise. Late in the morning on our second day, I broke my glasses. Little did I know that would be the basis for our next adventure and would lead me to the next practice on the Wingman's Path.

When I asked the hostess at our hotel, the only woman in this entire village who seemed to speak any English at all, where I might get my glasses fixed, she pointed to a road and said the words, "Green House."

We walked down the road, laughing as it went from a gravel road to a dirt one, making it seem rather unpromising that we'd find an optician. Thankfully, I had a spare pair of glasses, so we weren't in dire need. But after about 300 meters, and five or six houses, we saw a green house. We walked around it and came to an open barn where a man worked on a computer circuit board. When he looked up, I showed him my glasses. All he said was, "Chiang Rai," and went back to his work.

Seeing as it was a lovely evening, and we were in this beautiful rural setting, we decided to continue our very picturesque walk. We passed rice fields and dairy farms, and before we knew it, the sun began to set. It was time to turn around and go back to our hotel. But once again, we found ourselves in the presence of some street dogs.,

What is it with the dogs?

Maybe it's just that there are so many street dogs in Thailand? Me, I'm more of a believer that we, and Jan in particular, were still focused on the dogs. Perhaps it was a bit of residue thoughts from our night the Wingman on a scooter came to our rescue, but vibrationally, we were still attracting street dogs into our experience.

It was still a little light out, so we weren't all that worried, but I did pick up a long stick just in case we needed to keep the dogs away. What really saved us though, was a black and white mutt who seemed to relish being in the role of our protector. He was so sweet to us, and so shielding. He stayed by Jan's side, barking at the other dogs and making sure they didn't get too close. While his intentions were good, it seemed the dogs didn't necessarily like him, which meant they didn't like us much, either. I felt sort of safe but wanted to get back to the village and our little hotel. The stick I had picked up gave me some confidence, but really it became more of a walking stick as "our dog" did a wonderful job of safeguarding us.

As we got to our hotel, I bent down to pet him and thank him, but it was Jan he really loved. He jumped up, kissed her on the arm, and then went on his way. Janet was surprised by his jumping up, and soon felt her arm itching. That's when she noticed it was scratched, the skin broken. Whether she broke it by scratching, or the dog had broken it, was indeterminate.

I mentioned earlier how I thought Jan was somehow attracting these dogs into our experience. If it wasn't true then, it certainly was now. For from that moment on, the only discussions we had involved the possibility, or rather the probability, of her having rabies. It was a long sleepless night.

The next day, the water was still too low for a public boat, but Jan was not to be denied our getting to Chiang Rai that day, and to a doctor or hospital there. Our hostess arranged for a private boat. There was one caveat, though, with the water so low, the private boat could not make it the whole way. We would have to get out, walk about a mile on a jungle trail, and catch a boat on the other side, which would be waiting for us. As stated, nothing was stopping Jan from our reaching Chiang Rai, as her concern that she was now rabid was growing.

Everything went smoothly, and soon after arriving at our guesthouse in Chiang Rai, we took off by foot for the hospital. We met with a doctor and Jan began the five-needle process of getting vaccinated against rabies.

I believe, if you're reading this, you fall into one of two categories. Either you're like my wife and believe she was wise to get vaccinated, or you're like me, and think she was crazy.

Whatever your thoughts are, the one thought I always have is to be a good husband. That means, no matter how crazy you think your wife is at times, you always support her decisions.

From the hospital, we walked through the city where we found an optical shop that could fix my glasses. Things were looking good (literally). As we walked back toward our hotel, I said to Jan, "Well, everything happens for a reason, I wonder what this one is."

She's not a big believer in that statement, and quipped back, "Well, I believe my reason is to head into that café and get myself a much needed and deserved watermelon smoothie."

Her smoothie led us to the reason. As we enjoy iced coffee for me, watermelon smoothie for Jan, I looked over the walls that were covered with inspiring pictures and quotes in English. One, on the far side from where we were sitting, declared in bright pink, calligraphic letters:

Everything happens for a reason. Find the reason.

I was pointing it out to Jan when the manager, a young man named Dang, came over to say *hi* and tell us about the café. Turns out, the café wasn't just *any* coffee bar. It was the Destiny Café, a restaurant that is a training and rescue center for young Thai women who are victims of sex trafficking. It houses them and teaches them life and job skills, like being a barista, chef, waitress, and restaurant manager, along with other life lessons.

As Dang was telling me about the place, he asked what we did, and I told him about the Wingman's Path to Positivity and Jan being a psychotherapist. As we finished our drinks, Dang introduced us to a couple of the girls.

I constantly mention how a big part of doing these practices is to get the words, and the vibration, into your subconscious. And that the only way I know how to do that is with repetition. How, by doing these practices consistently, they will help you remember them with perfect timing. I'm happy to say this was demonstrated impeccably that afternoon.

Prior to us leaving on the boat for Chiang Rai, the practice I did during my early morning walk that day, was, "How can I help you?" the practice that started with the Macy's Lady.

Well, that afternoon, as I was paying our bill and Dang was explaining more and more about what they do, I blurted out, "How can I help?" With my wallet already out, I assumed the answer was to give a donation.

But instead, Dang asked if Jan and I would come back and do a Wingman Practice session with all the girls. And so, twenty-four hours later, Jan and I found ourselves sitting around a table at that same restaurant, doing Wingman's Path practices with four teenage Thai girls, and Dang, doing the translating.

Now, I don't know a whole lot about the world of sex-trafficking, but I do know about suffering, about getting beaten down, and about how hard it is to get back up. I also know how consistently practicing positivity can help you raise your vibration and launch you on a path to happiness, success, and creating a life of your choosing. Also, I know true Wingmen when I see them. And Dang, the manager of the Destiny cafe, is one of those special individuals.

It was surreal and crazy as he translated my Wingman's Path practices into Thai. Watching the faces of these young women light up, as they understood and participated in the practices, is something I could never have imagined. Yet there Jan and I were, sitting with these girls, speaking about self-esteem, overcoming challenges, and the vibration you send out into the Universe. Talking, laughing, and joining together in different Wingman's Path practices, I was taken to a new level of gratefulness.

As we went around the room, despite our language barriers, cultural, life, and age differences, I was reminded that we can all find things to value and appreciate...if we're just prompted to do so.

I'm not sure if these young ladies will ever do another Wingman's Path practice again. But for that moment, I experienced a spark of positive energy and felt like I had a small part in helping bring some hope and happiness to this little corner of the world that is the Destiny Café in Chiang Rai, Thailand. It's my belief that when I said to Jan that "everything happens for a reason," that the Universe showed me the reason. My glasses breaking led to the dog "kissing" Jan, which led to us going to Chiang Rai that day, which led to us walking to that specific hospital, which led to us finding that specific optical center to fix my glasses, which led to me saying at that precise moment, "Everything happens for a reason," which led to Jan turning and walking into the nearest café, which happened to be the Destiny café.

The "reason," brought Jan and I a fabulous feeling of being of service. It helped young girls, who had gone through some unbelievable life challenges, to bring more joy into their lives and help them understand how they could live a life of their choosing. It also changed our entire energy and the way we experienced Chiang Rai.

Thank you, Dang, for the opportunity to help,

As we left the restaurant and walked back to our hotel, Jan, in what must have been the emotion of the moment, even conceded, "well, maybe some things do happen for a reason."

A Wingman Practice:

Find the Reason

Repeat for one minute, "Everything happens for a reason. Find the reason."

Even if you don't believe it, say it to yourself for one minute. As you do, think about things in your life that didn't make sense at first, but you later found out "the reason."

What you look for you find, and when you look for the "reason," you'll find it, no matter how well it's hidden.

43
Perfect Emptiness

When I realized we would be in Chiang Mai, the first thing I did was email the Zen Master and his disciples whom we had met back when my leg was in a brace. After some back and forth, where it didn't seem that they could be in Chiang Mai at that time, I received the following message:

> How have you been?
> We've decided to go on a pilgrimage to Chiang Mai in March!
> Our master wants to talk with you.
> We'll arrive on 4th March and leave 11th March.
> You can choose the place where we meet again.
> Let's keep in touch!
> Bye!"

"Jan!" I exclaimed. "He's coming to Chiang Mai on a pilgrimage to see me."

"I'm sure, honey," she replied.

I set the meeting up for Saturday, March 5th at Wat Chedi Luang, the same place we had initially met. If everything happens for a reason, it was now easy for me to see 'the reason for our travels. Our year of travel was for my spiritual growth. I was ecstatic about seeing them.

When I saw him, I could feel myself glowing. I still get chills thinking about it. I mean, who was I to be meeting with a Zen Master? As we sat down, Jan started the conversation by asking him why he was in Chiang Mai.

"To meet Michael," he answered.

I was at a loss for words but uttered, "Thank you. I'm honored."

"You wanted this, didn't you?"

"Yes," I affirmed. "I most certainly did. Is it really that easy, that whatever I want, I can create?"

"Let us sit down," he replied in Korean, with his disciple translating.

Although we had tickets to leave Chiang Mai the following day, we canceled them. "I'm not leaving until he tells us we're done," was my response to Jan's asking, "when we should plan to leave." What followed was four days of laughter, learning, and spiritual bliss. I had planned to meet that afternoon, and we were then taking off for Bangkok the next day. But when he invited us back, again and again and again, I anxiously accepted each time.

We spoke of truth, of perfect emptiness, and of World Peace. He bestowed us with the three jewels of Buddhism: the Buddha (teacher), Dharma (teachings), and the Sangha (Community).

Beyond that, it was surreal being with him. Everywhere we walked people would bow down to him. I always felt as if they were looking at me, wondering *who the heck is this guy*? while they bowed to greet him. One day, as we walked from one Wat to another, some Thai monks bowed to him.

"He's from South Korea, he's just visiting here, why do they bow?" I asked his disciple, Sunim, which means teacher or Buddhist monk or nun in Korean.

"They feel his energy," she answered very matter of factly.

I totally understood. I felt his energy. While I had been trekking the Wingman's Path, and teaching what I was learning about raising your vibration, they lived it. While I had to practice it constantly, it seemed to be a very natural way of life for them. They lived on a higher plane, and you could feel it.

The whole time was a dreamlike experience. One that took me to a new level of awareness. I remember thinking, as I sat there with my new friends and teachers, *I'm discussing Buddha's teachings with a Buddhist Zen Master. Thank you for this moment.*

He taught of the Four Noble Truths, the Five Precepts, and the Noble Eightfold Path. In everything he spoke about, he emphasized practicing. Especially practicing Perfect Emptiness, which he said was the first step of Buddhist studies.

We would ask about having a desire or a goal, and he would answer to practice perfect emptiness. "Everyone can reach enlightenment, but you will not reach it until you understand perfect emptiness."

Jan and I both said we understand the concept, but we didn't understand "it."

"If you understand the concept, you can practice the feeling. Everything's an illusion. Even though we have this body, it's not attaching so much meaning to the body. If you want to let go of those types of attachments and desires, it cannot be through thinking. No matter what you are doing, walking, eating, sleeping, et cetera... never lose the understanding of perfect emptiness. By holding on to the concept of perfect emptiness, we can reach true freedom."

And so I practiced perfect emptiness. And practiced it. If there's one thing I've mastered since discovering the Wingman's Path, it's my ability to practice. Every day, as I would take my morning walk, I would take one minute and say the words, *perfect emptiness*, over and over. I would constantly think of what it means to be perfectly empty, to have nothing, no body, no mind, no attachment to anything. I practiced being the sky and just observing everything, with no attachment to it. I practiced being the ocean and feeling the waves roll on. I meditated on it, I read about it, and I spoke about it. I had said I understood the concept, but in trying to practice it, the less I think I understood it.

I decided I should find a baby step and ended up switching the practice to *let it go*. Letting go, I understood. It quickly became a favorite practice of mine. Anytime I had a negative vibration, I would practice by saying over and over, "Let it go." And I would. Someone got into my head, I'd practice letting them go until I did. Same if I'd made a mistake, I'd practice letting it go until I was able to.

Don Miguel Ruiz, in his wonderful book, *The Four Agreements: A Practical Guide to Personal Freedom* (Amber-Allen Publishing, Incorporated, 1997), says that humans are the only species on earth who pay for a mistake a thousand times. Every other species moves on, but not us. We beat ourselves up, feel guilty, and keep replaying it in our minds.

While *perfect emptiness* didn't stick for me, *let it go* most certainly did. Perhaps because I learned the importance of letting go as a young boy. I learned what happens when you hold onto your mistakes. As stated in an earlier chapter, every child who's ever played Little League baseball has heard it. When you're at bat and you strike out, before you go back out into the field, your coach will say, "forget about it." Every coach says that because he or she knows that if you don't forget about it, you'll then make an error in the field.

I was great at holding onto my mistakes. I was a decent baseball player and a very good gloveman, but I still remember making three errors right in a row. Practicing *let it go*, became a Godsend for me.

As we get older, we get even better at holding onto our mistakes. We not only continue to beat ourselves up, we actually make the same mistake again. And again. And again.

How about you? Do you ever make a mistake and hold onto it by replaying it in your mind? Or even worse, by making it again? I think for so many of us, we make the same mistake over and over because we hold onto it vibrationally.

The definition of insanity is doing the same thing over and over again and expecting a different result.

While I still practice many of the lessons I learned from the Zen Master, *let it go*, which was born from *perfect emptiness*, has become my go-to practice for emptying my thoughts, feelings, and energy leftover from any errors I am guilty of, any people who have done me wrong, or any negative vibrations that are stuck in my subconscious. I still practice *perfect emptiness* from time to time, and hopefully, one day soon, I will not only grasp the concept, but I'll also understand it.

A Wingman Practice:

Let It Go.

Repeat "let it go" for one minute.

As you do, think about the person, place, or thing that you want to release. It's helped me to think, "They should be paying me rent, for how long I've enabled some of those negative vibrations to remain in my head."

For you, maybe it will help to imagine what your life would look and feel like without that negative energy. Sometimes it feels like it's a part of our life, a part of our story, that without it or them, we wouldn't be us. But we can't move forward without shedding the unwanted parts of our pasts.

44
The Miracle of Cha Am

After leaving Chiang Mai and the Zen Master, we returned to Bangkok. I was excited to go back because a yoga studio there had contacted me about doing a Wingman's Path workshop. After meeting with them, we set up the workshop for three weeks from then. How cool was that? I was going international.

Bangkok was crazy hot though, and after a week, I wanted a break from the city. Think New York on the hottest of summers, only hotter, more congested, and more street food everywhere. Jan loves it. Me? It's a little too hot, crowded, and smelly for me.

We decided to take a bus to a beach town called Cha Am about two hours away. As we were waiting in the bus station, I noticed a couple of young monks with beautiful Monk's bags. I'd been wanting one of those bags but could never find one, so I decided to ask them where I could get one. As I walked over to them, I was stopped by a man selling newspapers in English. I didn't really care for one but thought it would be good karma, so I purchased one. With the newspaper in my hand, I went up to the monks and said, "That's a beautiful bag. Do you know where I could get one?"

They were seated, and as they looked up at me, I immediately realized they didn't speak any English, nor had a clue as to what I was saying. I started laughing at my foolishness, thinking they would understand me. They probably had never heard a word of English, and here's this fast-talking guy from New Jersey asking them a question.

It wasn't long, though, before the three of us were laughing and "communicating" about how nice the bag was. At least I think that's what we were laughing about. After about five minutes, Jan called out that our bus was coming. As I stood up and said goodbye, the older of the two monks reached into his bag and pulled out a brand-new bag, still in the wrapping, exactly like his, and gave it to me. I was stunned and so very grateful. "*Khup Kun Krap*," I exclaimed over and over, which means thank you in Thai.

We had a couple of minutes before we could board the bus, so I ran over and bought them some snacks for their bus ride, still thanking them profusely. Jan and I took our seats. I was overjoyed.

"That was a nice surprise," Jan said as we took our seats.

"Considering they didn't speak any English," I answered. "I'd say it was a small miracle."

"All right. Let's not get carried away," she grinned.

And without thinking, I spoke the words that were to be the next step on the Path. "You know me, hon, I believe in miracles."

I fell asleep for the ride with a smile on my face, thoughts of miracles in my head, and a sweet, contented feeling in my heart.

We arrived in Cha Am and walked a couple blocks to a cheap, but clean and welcoming guesthouse. It was right off the main drag and across from the beach. We threw our suitcases in our room and took a walk on the street that ran along the beach.

Cha Am was not Janet's cup of tea. But I was like a fish in water. Every other store was a bar, a T-shirt shop, or a cheap souvenir stand. I felt as if I'd gone back in time by 40 years, when I worked at my brother's bookstore on the Boardwalk in Ocean City, only it's much schlockier.

There were stray dogs everywhere. They all reminded me of Monte, so I stopped and bought a few hot dogs at a 7-11 to feed to them. (Yes, there are 7-11s all over Thailand.) Afterward, we sat on the beach for about an hour, when I think we had about ten people come up to us hawking trinkets. It seemed like every 60 seconds, I was offered something I couldn't imagine buying. And while most people turn their heads to try to avoid them, I love talking with everyone. I'd ask each person who stopped to sell me their wares, how business was, where they were from, etc. Only they didn't speak a word of English, and I can only say *hello* (*sawadee kap*) and *thank you* (*khup kun krap*) in Thai. It made for a lot of laughing.

I had my new Monk's bag with me, and while sitting on the beach, mentioned to Janet again, about how receiving it was a small miracle. Them gifting me this bag gave me such a warm feeling. One of love, of connectivity, and of wanting to pay it forward.

I reached into my bag and pulled out the newspaper I had purchased at the bus station. Suddenly, that wonderful feeling of us all being connected dissolved. The headlines screamed of a shooting in Thailand and another mass killing in America. At that moment, the world seemed very divided.

> **I am saddened by how people treat one another and how we are so shut off from one another and how we judge one another, when the truth is, we are all one connected thing. We are all from the same exact molecules.**
> ~Ellen DeGeneres

I felt awful. There I was having such a wonderful time traveling and feeling connected to others so diverse from me that we don't even speak the same language, yet others are killing people because they're different.

"Our world is hurting," I moaned.

"How can it not be, with so much violence and so many innocent victims?" Jan sighed.

"It doesn't even cause a stir when another mass shooting occurs," I responded.

"World Peace, now that would be a miracle," Jan chided, having a little fun with me and my comments.

Being American, I thought we had more violence than most. Turns out, there's unimaginable violence in almost every country in the world. Even in Thailand, the Land of Smiles.

What in God's name is going on?

Being away from home, and seeing so much seemingly random violence, I thought about the safety of my children. Maybe it hasn't hit someone from my immediate group of friends or family, but sooner or later it will. How can it not?

Yikes! *Cancel, cancel. Delete, delete.* I certainly did not want to let that thought expand. Being human, it seems that something can always happen to reignite negative thoughts in our minds, at least it felt that way to me. But it's our job to make certain we don't let those negative thoughts attract other similar thoughts. Otherwise, before we know it, we're allowing a destructive vibration to overtake us.

In today's society, it happens often. Right now, we're having many protests. People are protesting that black lives matter, blue lives matter, and gay lives matter. And history keeps repeating itself as we continue to form more divisions and create more sadness. Unfortunately, it seems the only color that stays constant is red. Blood red.

And it's staining the fabric of our world. How can we be so connected, yet so hateful of others?

If you're reading this, my hope is that you're most likely someone who treats others as they would like to be treated. And the idea of killing someone because of his or her religious beliefs, skin color, or sexual preference is as foreign to you as the idea of purchasing an AK47 assault rifle. So how do we, you and I, help our community, our nation, and our world, begin to heal when we don't even know these people, or understand their hate?

More importantly, how do we stop this heartbreaking cycle before it hits closer to home? Because the odds are, it will. Maybe your son, cousin, or nephew goes out for a night of partying in a gay bar? Or your daughter, sister, or niece is at an airport leaving on a vacation, or your husband or wife is at their place of work and violence erupts?

For some reason, Martin Luther King's quote popped into my mind as I sat next to Jan trying to get control of my thoughts.

Martin Luther King said:

Darkness cannot drive out darkness, only light can do that.
Hate cannot drive out hate; only love can do that.

But how do we feel love for people who seem so crazed with hate? And why are they so hateful?

"It seems impossible," I groaned in answer to Jan's world-peace challenge. But then I thought about the Wingman's Path and where I was before discovering it. I was hurt and I was angry. I was miserable in my life, and from there, it's not a big leap to being hateful.

I mentioned in the first chapter about how bringing more positivity into your life changes everything. How it brings more love and happiness into your life. And how I've seen many miracles that have happened in people's lives when they've discovered the Wingman's Path. It may be far-fetched, but I believe if each and every person found their way to the Path, World Peace could conceivably be brought about.

The world as we have created it
is a process of our thinking.
It cannot be changed without changing our thinking.
~attributed to Albert Einstein.

What would changing our thinking look like?

For me, I began to think about the small miracle of one person bringing more positive energy into their life, and consequently being happier and less hateful. How that could then become a huge miracle of every person in this world doing the same. And maybe, just maybe, our connectivity is what could make it happen, with each person on earth becoming just a little happier, and their lives becoming just a little better, with a little more love, opportunity, and abundance. If it could happen with me, and I could share that vibration with you, and you could share it with someone else, and so-on and so-on.

It was there, on a beach in Cha Am, reading a Thai newspaper for English speaking tourists, with a green Monk's bag on my shoulder that was gifted to me, and Jan mentioning the seemingly impossible miracle of world peace, that I began a new practice.

"I believe in Miracles," I prayed. But it sounded like a prayer of desperation. And desperation is never the frequency I want to be emitting. So, I said it again. And again. And soon, I was practicing speaking it in an expectant sort of way. Like I believe in miracles because I see them happen every single day. Maybe not on the scale of world peace, but it was a start. I could feel it in my vibration.

And I visualized everyone living on our planet, realizing the diversity of our world is what makes it so great. And we start appreciating our differences, rather than disparaging them.

I practiced holding onto that thought for 60 seconds as I repeated the words, "I believe in miracles."

The next day, I was out early for my morning walk. I just thought I'd walk the beach and do my new Wingman's Path practice since I hadn't seen any wats, or temples. So far, this town seemed more about drinking than it was about spirituality.

You can imagine my surprise, then, when I heard some monks chanting. It seemed so out of place. I had to check it out. Soon, I joined six or seven people praying along with about ten monks as they recited their mantras. At first, I stood in the street, but then a woman brought me a chair, so I sat. It was a wonderful moment. I was so happy to be there.

After about 20 minutes, they stopped, and the woman who'd given me the chair started serving the monks food. I felt a bit out of place and left, excited to tell Jan of my morning adventure. Only I didn't get very far. The woman came after me and asked me to join them. I had no money on me, but she insisted it was free. Talk about miracles! She was serving up Tom Yum soup, but for me, it was manna from heaven.

I'm not sure what it is about someone offering me free food that warms my heart so. Jan thinks I must have starved to death in a past life. I can't really explain it, but every time it happens, it feels like falling in love. And in that setting...well, I was in Wingman heaven.

After eating, the Monks chanted for a few more minutes, and then the celebration seemed to be breaking up. I thanked my hostess and hurried back to my room. I couldn't wait to show Janet this little mecca, sandwiched between two bars.

That's when things got a bit crazy, or I thought they did. When we got back down to that spot on the street, maybe just ten or fifteen minutes later, the wat had disappeared. In its place was a T-shirt shop. Was this another dream? Jan was looking at me as if I had lost my mind, and I couldn't blame her.

I was walking back and forth, muttering to myself and to Jan, that "IT WAS RIGHT HERE!" when, thankfully, the woman who had brought me the chair and the food walked from out of the back. She noted my surprise and informed Jan and me that they had transformed the shop for the ceremony. It was only a one-day celebration for good luck, and it wouldn't happen again until the next year.

I believe in miracles became an instant favorite practice right then and there.

A Wingman Practice:

I Believe in Miracles

For one minute, say out loud or quietly to yourself, "I believe in miracles."

As you do, imagine seeing, feeling, and believing the world is at peace. Visualize everyone emanating a vibration of World Peace, the Universe sending us back World Peace.

Whether we receive world peace in our lifetime or not, I'm certain the more you practice this vibration, the more likely you'll see miracles happen in your life. Who knows, you might even find them in a T-shirt store.

45
The Brimfield Flea Market

We'd been back home in New Jersey for a couple of weeks. My discipline had been wonderful and I'd been a constant on the Wingman's Path by practicing daily. Miracles, I'd seen a few. One happened even before we arrived "home." I put home in quotes because although we were back on our home turf, we didn't have a home. All our stuff was still in a storage unit, and we needed a place to hang our hats while we were there.

The plan was to pay for a hotel for a couple of nights and try and find an inexpensive, furnished apartment for the three months before we took off again for parts unknown. New Jersey is much more expensive than Thailand, so I wasn't certain what would happen. My vibration, which had been fantastic, was developing a "twang" as my concern over money creeped in.

"Everything's been working out for us," Jan declared. "No reason it shouldn't continue."

I loved the sound of her words. "Everything's been working out for us. No reason it shouldn't continue," I repeated again and again.

Two days before we boarded the plane for home, we received the following message from a friend:

(Husband's name) just left me, when are you guys coming home and can you please stay with me?

To which Jan replied:

OMG! So sorry to hear, be home in two days. And yes, we can.

Everything's been working out for us. No reason it shouldn't continue. Not that this was a good situation we were walking into. Our friend, as expected, was in an awful place. But having us, Jan being a therapist, and me being a Wingman, be able to stay with her through this difficult time was so helpful for her. I actually said to Janet at one time, "I'm so glad we're able to help. I can't imagine two better people to help her through this difficult time than you and I."

And us having a place to stay, was great for us. Even though we weren't paying rent with money, we were certainly earning our keep. It was a win-win. And I love a win-win.

After spending some time with our newly separated friend, catching up with old friends, and visiting Jan's mom and sisters, it was time to drive up to Providence to see my sister and mother. The plan was to drive up to Providence for five days, fly from there down to Alabama to see my daughter, fly back to Providence for a few more days, and then drive back home. Yikes, in catching up with family, we were traveling more now than when we were on our adventure.

Fortunately, that Saturday was the Brimfield Flea Market, in Brimfield, Massachusetts. It was only an hour and small change from Providence, and it was one of our bucket list items. It's been described as a cross between the ultimate antique treasure hunt and a three-ring circus. It's not that we were looking to purchase anything. We didn't even have a home. It's just that we love walking around these types of markets. And we've always wanted to make it to this one.

When I woke up the morning of the flea market, I thought to myself, "It's going to be a great day." As I did, I remembered saying those words about three years earlier. When I said it back then, I thought it would be a great practice, but I guess I hadn't fully embraced the Wingman's Path, so it didn't stick. That day I realized it was one of the well-lit steps on the Path, and even though I missed it back then, it circled back around to make sure I got it. Things seem to do that on the Path.

While it seems easy to practice *having a great day* when you're about to do a bucket-list item, and it is, the practice isn't just for those days you're really looking forward to. Actually, since then, I've found it works best on normal, everyday days. It's a great practice to do each day because it raises your vibration and gets you looking for the best your day has to offer.

I had developed the *having a great* day *practice* back when Jan and I were still working the regular nine-to-five. It was a rainy Monday morning, and we were getting ready for work. I was making my breakfast when she came down to the kitchen. "What's your day look like?" she'd asked.

Without thinking, I answered, "I'm having a great day." She held her hand up like a police officer saying "stop." She just didn't want to hear it as she was not looking forward to her day and was running late for the train.

After she left, as I took a bite of my chicken and roasted peppers, (sometimes I'm a dinner-for-breakfast kind of guy) and I thought about my day. I *was* anticipating a great day. I was coaching a businesswoman in the morning, having lunch with a friend, and then doing a corporate presentation in the afternoon.

I was looking forward to it, as well as expecting to make some decent money. I started thinking of Jan's day and wondered what would happen if she had the same belief as I did, that it would be a great day. If she did, would her day then be better?

That question led to, what if I could paint every day with that expectation? Would I then begin to see each of my days through the filter of it being a great day?

And more importantly, would my days be better because of it?

I decided to try it out the following day, which was not a day I was looking forward to, as I had a lot of grunt work I didn't care for, to do.

I woke before the sun and immediately spoke the words, "I'm having a great day," although I didn't really believe it. But as I said it over and over again, I thought through the details of my day ahead and practiced the feeling of them being enjoyable. A slight shift in my outlook occurred and realized I was on to something.

As I experimented with it further, I noticed the more I said it, the more I became a bit more enthusiastic about my day's schedule. Then it became its own self-fulfilling prophecy.

If you think that's preposterous, think again. I started researching it and saw that it happens every day in every walk of life. Athletes visualize winning the game, and do; salespeople picture themselves making the sale, and do; students see themselves successfully taking a test, and do; and actors "become" the person they are portraying.

I googled "self-fulfilling prophecy." What I learned validated my assumption that by saying, *I'm having a great day*, the odds would increase of me having a great day.

But let's get back to the day of the Brimfield Flea Market. As I took my morning walk, I did the practice by repeating "I'm having a great day." The more I said it, the more enthusiastic I became. Again, it's much easier to practice on a day you're expecting a great day.

Jan and I got out early. I always love getting to the markets when they're opening, finding the food trucks, and starting my day checking out the breakfast. We got on I-95N and were making great time until we took exit 23 to merge on RI-146N. Boom! We suddenly hit some monster traffic and were basically in a parking lot on 146.

"What?" I exclaimed. "This can't be!"

Jan, still half asleep, yawned, "It's just traffic, why can't it be"?

"Because I did my, *I'm having a great day* practice. And hitting traffic wasn't in the plan."

She chuckled. Yes, she literally chuckled. "It is now."

As she dozed, I grew frustrated. But then I laughed thinking about how quickly I was on the verge of annoyance. How could this be? "I'm having a great day," I said sarcastically to myself.

Sociologist Robert Merton is credited with coining the term "self-fulfilling prophecy" in 1948, and defining it as: "A false definition of the situation evoking a new behavior which makes the originally false conception come true."

In other words, he noticed that sometimes a belief brings about consequences that cause the reality to match the belief. If I believe I'm having a great day, my belief will bring about a great day.

The best proof of this comes from the medical field with what is known as the Placebo Effect. when someone believes they are receiving a treatment that will cure them, even if they are given a fake, or "placebo" treatment, they often feel cured. As stated in Harvard Medical School's Men's Health Watch, "Your mind can be a powerful healing tool when given the chance...science has found that under the right circumstances, a placebo can be just as effective as traditional treatments."

Experiments on the placebo effect have proven that belief is a very powerful thing! Looking back now, I find it interesting that even though it worked for me, and it was verified by my research, it didn't become a practice for me at that time. Sometimes things have to come up for me, and maybe for you, more than once.

It's been so interesting seeing my transformation. In my past, when I would get irritated, I could stay in that mode for a while. That anger would stick with me for days, if not weeks. I would almost always end up in an angry rabbit hole whenever I was triggered. Now I'm able to recognize my energy going south much more quickly. And when I notice it, I make certain to alter the vibration that I'm sending out into the Universe. ASAP. So, before I allowed myself to get pulled down into the emotional mud, I started repeating quietly to myself my mantra for the day

"I'm having a great day."

"I'm having a great day."

"What are you doing?" Jan asked when she woke again. In the last 30 minutes, we'd maybe moved a half-mile.

"I'm doing my practice from this morning."

"Try something different," she advised.

"Any thoughts?"

After a few more minutes of still sitting there, we decided to "come from love."

"Come from love," we each said to ourselves for one minute.

"Come from love," we then said to each other for another minute.

It certainly broke up the monotony. And it definitely made the drive a lot more palatable.

The traffic soon broke, and it wasn't long before I was enjoying a lobster roll and a walnut-maple glazed donut from Faddy's donuts. The morning traffic was easily forgotten as we walked among some wonderful, and not so wonderful, antiques. And the people watching was a blast. It really was a great day.

But even better was what happened later that night. We ran out for some Thai food, and it was then that the higher vibration of our *come from love* exercise really kicked in.

Instead of it just being dinner, it became a date night. We laughed, talked, reconnected, and even kept the night going by taking a late-night walk. But it wasn't just us, it was everyone around us. From our young Cambodian waitress, with whom we discussed Cambodia, delicious recipes, and the Law of Attraction, to a "hippie" couple sitting near us who not only wanted to "bask in our vibe," but added to it tremendously. It was just a wonderful evening.

"How was your day?" my sister asked when we returned from our late-night walk.

Tired, but happy, I smiled. "I had a great day."

A Wingman Practice:

I'm Having a Great Day

For one minute, repeat "I'm having a great day."

While saying it, think of each segment of your day and what would make it great.

And then go about having a great day.

46
I Forgive You, and I Forgive Me

Back in New Jersey, my cell phone rang as soon as we pulled into our friend's condo parking lot. It was my ex-wife calling.

After checking in on how our daughter was doing in Alabama, she told me about this wonderful teacher she'd been following. He was speaking the next day on the Power of Positivity, and she thought I would love it and should go. Well, actually, she thought I should go and take our son with me.

"Are you going?" I asked.

"Yes," she replied.

"Why aren't you taking him?" I dug a little deeper.

"Because I'm going with friends, and we're making a day of it."

Seemed legit, I thought. She's having a fun day and wants our son to be there, just doesn't want to hear him complaining about it.

"Ok, I'm in. I'll take him."

It was Wednesday. Although I was pretty tired from our recent travels to Providence, Alabama, and back to Providence and was looking forward to a little quiet, alone time, I had the radio show that night. I really wanted to rest, but followed through on my commitment to Rita.

"You're on the *Talk-N-Angels* radio show. How can we help?"

"I'm looking for forgiveness," the caller responded. She spoke about wrongs done against God, and wrongs done against other human beings. She went on to tell us it was Yom Kippur later this week, the Jewish New Year. She said she wanted to be absolved by God for all her sins on that "Day of Atonement."

I smiled as my mind started racing. After speaking with my ex, I realized I had some thoughts about forgiveness, too: about forgiving her, and more importantly, about forgiving myself for the failure of our marriage. Forgiving her. And forgiving me. And then, out of the blue, someone calls the show about forgiveness.

Maybe it wasn't "out of the blue." Maybe I attracted that call because it was time to take notice. Since discovering the Wingman's Path, I'd become very observant when something presented itself to me at two different times. And forgiveness just did.

I asked her how certain she was that God would forgive her of all her sins.

She explained how, according to tradition, God judges all creatures during the ten Days of Awe between Rosh Hashanah and Yom Kippur. It is the deciding time, when God decrees who will live, and who will die this next year. The righteous, they get inscribed in the Book of Life, the wicked aren't as fortunate. If you fall somewhere in between, you repent for your sins, by praying, reflecting, doing good deeds, and making amends. You do that and God forgives you.

I said, "Maybe it's not God's forgiveness you're seeking."

"What do you mean?" she replied.

I thought about my conversation with my ex and how I believe God had forgiven me. If God could forgive me, maybe it was now time for me, to forgive myself. I mean, if I create everything in my reality, then I created all the messes, and the craziness, and the homelessness, and the losses. Yeah... the losses really hurt. Maybe it was time to forgive myself?

I repeated to her what I said to myself. "I mean, if God can forgive you, maybe it's time for you to forgive yourself."

In Buddhist law, things are much easier. It's Karmic law. You do good, you get good. You do bad, you get bad. Whether in this lifetime or the next.

As I mentioned earlier, in his book *The Four Agreements*, Don Miguel Ruiz discusses how humans are the only species on earth that pays for a mistake 1000 times. We dwell on it, we stew on it, we just don't let it go. And by the Law of Attraction, it continues to impact our lives in a negative way.

That which is like unto itself is drawn.

If I'm holding onto something on a vibrational level, something for which I cannot forgive myself, it seems to reason that I will attract more of that which I cannot forgive myself. But, if God is able to forgive me, shouldn't I be able to as well?

"How do I do that?" Her question brought me right back to the radio show.

I had been thinking the same thing. How do I forgive myself? I mentioned a favorite movie of mine, "House of Games." The ending scene has Lilia Skala, as Dr. Maria Littauer saying to Lindsay Crouse, playing psychiatrist Margaret Ford, "When you have done something unforgivable, I'll tell you exactly what to do. You forgive yourself."

I felt the practice rising up inside me.

"I forgive you, and I forgive me. That's how we do it," I declared excitedly. "We practice forgiveness, for others, as well as for ourselves. As soon as I said it, the caller was screaming, "Yes! Let's do it!" I knew I had another instant classic.

"I forgive you, and I forgive me."

"I forgive you, and I forgive me."

"I forgive you, and I forgive me."

I said it, the caller said it, Rita said it. Back and forth we went for what seemed like ten minutes. The feeling of forgiveness was awesome.

"I forgive me."

"I forgive me."

"I forgive me."

The next morning, I woke up with just the second half of the practice swimming around my mind. Maybe it's only me I have to forgive, no one else, just me. I picked up my son, and we drove down to Atlantic City to see my ex's teacher, a rabbi she found inspiring.

He spoke of forgiveness (surprise!), and how the Bible teaches that because humans have been given free will, they are responsible for their own actions. If they commit an action that is wrong, then they must seek forgiveness.

Again, with forgiveness. Like what's up with that? Was I still missing something? Was I not getting the right message?

I had done the practice that morning. Saying, "I forgive you, and I forgive me," and it had felt very freeing, but it didn't feel easy. I recognized this practice would take some time for me to truly vibrate pure forgiveness. But I could feel myself greasing the skids, or priming the pump, as they say in the corporate world. Halfway through, the words "I forgive me" were the only words I was saying. It would take far more time to forgive myself, than it would take to forgive others.

**Don't judge each day by the harvest you reap,
but by the seeds you plant.**
~Robert Louis Stevenson

I was planting seeds of forgiveness. It was a good day.

Driving home with my son, I pointed out how the message was very similar to Karmic Law, or natural law. Some call it the Law of Nature or the Law of Cause and Effect. I told him my beliefs, that what you put out, you receive back. No different than nature. What you plant, you will harvest. You reap what you sow. You can say it however you like, I call it Karmic law.

"Are you saying Karma is like currency?" my son probed. "You create all your life experiences, the good, the bad, the happiness or sadness, and then get repaid by the Universe for your actions?"

"That is exactly what I'm saying," I replied. "Like putting money in a savings account at the bank, you can put Karma in the bank."

As I said it, I realized my Karma might not currently be earning too much interest. I recognized the possibility that without my even realizing it, things might happen that give me negative Karma.

"OMG!" I exclaimed. "We need to clean up our Karma."

"What are you talking about Dad? You're sounding crazy."

"No. I'm not crazy, or at least I don't think I am."

I went on to explain how often we might have a negative interaction or thought about someone or something. I'm certain those experiences slip into our subconscious and create a negative vibration. If we don't clean them up frequently, they can grow into larger, undesirable, and more unwelcomed energy.

With all this talk about forgivenesss, I realized the newest Wingman's Path practice was the perfect "Karma Cleaner."

What a revelation!! Clean up your Karma. Much like cleaning your bathroom. It doesn't seem dirty and then, two weeks later you clean it, and you can't believe how filthy it had become.

I have to clean up my Karma. If not daily, at least weekly. You don't want to allow any negative energy to slip into your subconscious. If you do, it might grow.

That night, as I fell asleep, I repeated the words, "I forgive you and I forgive me." I wasn't thinking of anyone in particular, more the Universe as a whole. And I was clear that this was a perfect way to clean up my Karma. With forgiveness for myself and for others.

The next morning after my walk in the woods, I called my ex. After a brief conversation about her day, my day, our son, and the class, I said, "I want you to know how sorry I am for our failed marriage. I realize how immature I was, and how unready I was to handle things when they went downhill. I apologize for the pain I put you through."

"I apologize to you. We were both too immature. I panicked. You got depressed. We weren't ready," she responded.

I wanted to say how Jan's love had helped transform me and help me grow, but I thought it might be wiser to leave that unsaid.

But we did speak the truth. I was immature. I was unready. And I did fall into a depression.

After we hung up, I realized what I sought was forgiveness, and my ex most definitely forgave me. I also realized it wasn't her forgiveness I longed for. It was mine.

How about you? Can you give yourself a pardon? Can you forgive and forget the things you've done? Or at least forgive? Or will you continue to hold onto your mistakes and carry them around with you for another year?

I'd like to tell you I forgave myself that day for everything I ever did that was off. What I really did was begin the process of consciously practicing self-forgiveness. It took longer than any other practice in this book to penetrate my subconscious. The walls of my own culpability were clearly well built from decades of self-blame.

So, I practiced. Every morning, for about six months, I would say, "I forgive you, and I forgive me," for one minute. And every day I said it, it seemed that after about 30 seconds, I was no longer focusing on forgiving anyone else, and strictly concentrating on forgiving myself. I may have started every morning with, "I forgive you, and I forgive me," but each practice always ended with "I forgive me."

It wasn't until a few months later, at dinner with old friends, that I comprehended how far I had traveled. It was a simple question, "How are you?" that brought me clarity.

My answer, "I'm doing the best I can, with the cards I've been dealt," slipped out easily, with a higher vibration then I remembered previously. As I said it, I experienced the warm sensation of self-forgiveness. My energy had reached a new plateau. I'd become well aware of my good fortune at finding the Wingman's Path, and the appreciation of life that I've since enjoyed.

My karma was clean. By forgiving others for their transgressions, and myself for my own misbehaviors, I was able to clear out the negative energy from my past. By no longer condemning myself, my energy became lighter, easier, and more joyful. I can't explain it, but somehow I recognized there would be no more self-sabotaging of my goals. I was creating a life of my choosing with no interference from past experiences.

And it felt good.

A Wingman Practice:

Forgiveness

Repeat either out loud or quietly to yourself, "I forgive you, and I forgive me."

As you say it, think of either someone who has done wrong by you and see yourself forgiving them. Or think of something you did that was wrong, immoral, or "unforgivable." And practice the feeling of forgiving yourself. How would it feel if you forgave yourself? That's the feeling I want you to practice while saying the words.

As stated earlier, I found this practice, and the feeling of self-forgiveness, took longer to permeate my subconscious and saturate my vibration than any other. But when it did, it provided more light on my path to creating a life of my choosing than any other practice.

To forgiveness!

47
A Jammy Bastard

Two months later, we were off to Ireland where Jan had signed us up to house and dog sit. After a Skype interview, we were heading to Howth, Ireland, a little fishing village about 20 minutes outside of Dublin. As we exited the Dublin airport at 6:00 a.m., having been whisked through customs, and given a free Irish breakfast of a shot of Jameson's whiskey, we were already a little bit in love with Ireland.

Standing at the curbside taxi stand, the driver who pulled up looked like he had come straight from an Irish movie. Cap, scarf, charm, and a wonderful accent to boot. As we drove through the deserted, and still dark, streets of Dublin, our conversation floated between Irish history, architecture, and the details of our trip.

As we explained our house and dog sitting opportunity, along with our love of travel, I offhandedly commented, "Plus, I wouldn't mind finding some of that luck of the Irish I've heard so much about." We pulled up to our hotel. As he helped with our luggage, he smiled, looked at me, and said, "You say you've been traveling the world, eh?"

I answered, "Yes."

"And now you're about to stay along the Cliff Walks in Howth, for free?"

"We do have to watch the house and take care of their dogs." I replied.

"But you're staying there without having to pay any money?" He was quizzing me now.

Again, I answered in the affirmative.

"Well then you don't need the luck of the Irish, you're already a Jammy Bastard."

I must have looked confused because he followed up his comment by saying, "we don't say luck of the Irish, we say jammy, which means lucky, and a Jammy Bastard takes luck to a whole new level."

"I'm a Jammy Bastard," I beamed as I paid him and walked into our hotel.

We stayed in the hotel for one night before hopping a train out to Howth. The house and dog owners picked us up, and soon we were off to see our home for the next three weeks as well as meet the dogs we would be taking care of.

It's always a nervous moment when first meeting the dog, or dogs in this case, that you'll be caring for. Since house and dog sitting now for a few years, Jan and I have decided the dog(s) make the house sit. If they're a pain, the house sit won't be fun. If they're good, no matter what the house or area is like, the time spent will usually be successful.

This housesit was a homerun. Not only were the dogs wonderful, we were a five-minute walk from the Cliff Walks of Howth. Each day we would walk them on leash to the Cliff Walks, where we would then let them run as we'd walk for an hour. I don't think I ever walked in a more beautiful setting, and the fact that we could let the dogs off leash, and they would run around, but stay with us, made this one fabulous housesit.

And every day, as we walked those magnificent hills, overlooking the Dublin Bay, I would repeat my now favorite cab drivers' words, "I'm a Jammy Bastard"! It was very comparable to saying, *I'm a Lucky Guy*, but as with many similar practices, we hear them slightly differently; they slip into our subconscious differently. It's like exercising your bicep muscle with two parallel exercises, but they build the muscle in different ways. Same with Jammy Bastard.

Every morning, as I said it, I would think it, and I would feel it. Most definitely, I was also emitting a frequency of being a *Jammy Bastard*. Life was good. One evening, while Skype coaching with a client, I mentioned my *Jammy Bastard* practice. His complaint, and my response, got right to the point of the Wingman's Path and creating a life of your choosing.

He griped, "If I were staying in Ireland for free and hiking the Cliff Walks, I'd be feeling positive too."

"It's not your physical location that creates your vibration," I explained. "It's your vibration that creates your physical reality."

Is it easier to feel and practice positivity when you're in a fantastic location such as the Cliff Walks? Of course, it is.

But that's the game of life, isn't it? To not let your situation dictate your emotions? If you do, then maybe you get lucky, or "jammy," and things go well, and you start feeling better. But to hope for that is to give up all your power to create the success you desire. You become a victim of circumstance, whether those circumstances are good or bad.

But let's face it, if you've read this far, you know that we're guaranteed more jammy days in our lives when we're able to create them, rather than hope and wait for a bit of good luck that may or may not come. And to do that takes practice. So whether I'm in the muck or the money, I make certain to find something positive I can focus on. And that's how you become a Jammy Bastard.

A fantastic example of this was our afternoons in Ireland. I mentioned the mornings when we walked and played with the dogs. It was easy to practice being a Jammy bastard then. But every afternoon, we wanted to get out and explore the Emerald Isle. And to do that, it meant we had to drive.

The good news was the homeowners left us their car. The bad news was I was apprehensive. Everything about driving in Ireland was different than in America. And to make matters worse, the car had a manual transmission. I had to learn to operate the stick shift with my left hand, from the "passenger" side of the car, while driving on the "opposite" side of the road. Oh, and if you've never driven the roads in Ireland, they are narrow, winding, and twisty.

The first day I got nauseous as we were about to leave, so we took a bus instead, then walked a mile to the supermarket. Everything about driving in Ireland nerved me out. Forget the fact that we were driving on the opposite side, I hadn't driven a stick shift in 30 years, and never with my left hand. On our bus ride, Jan said something that would become my new practice, "Nothing exciting ever happens without a little nausea." She said it jokingly, but I loved it. As we walked home from the bus, I told Jan I wasn't going to let my fears stop us from exploring this wonderful area.

So the next day, we got in the car, and drove back to the supermarket. I kept telling Jan to keep saying, "Left, stay left."

On the scale of fear, this is a pretty minor one. But like any fear, no matter how small, it grows larger when we allow it to. And then, it takes over our lives. Yes, the fear of driving may be seemingly insignificant to you, but I assure you there are many who have allowed that fear to keep them stuck in one place.

And that's a "minor" fear.

How about those who have a fear of failure? Or death? Or rejection? Or ridicule? Or loneliness? Or pain? I was even just reading about people who live in fear of the unknown. How about the fear of flying, or public speaking, or heights? Or the fear of intimacy, or commitment?

Are any of these fears hitting a little closer to home for you?

I have a client who wouldn't leave her home, and another who wouldn't let her husband, whom she loves very much, touch her. And don't even get me started on spiders or snakes...So, how about you? Have you ever let your fear stop you from doing something you wanted to do?

What is it about fear, that many of us enable it to run our lives? And more importantly, how do we stop it, and take back our control?

First off, let's make sure we're on the same page as to what fear is. Fear is an emotion. A feeling. It is caused by the perceived threat of danger, pain, or harm. It is a vital response to physical and emotional danger, if we didn't feel it, we couldn't protect ourselves from legitimate threats.

But what is a legitimate threat? And who gets to decide that?

Often, our fears develop over time from our childhood and/or from traumatic experiences. And without even realizing it, we start holding back, playing it safe. We build a wall around ourselves so as to avoid failure, embarrassment, ridicule, pain, death, and even success.

I believe it's at that point when we stop truly living. I further believe it's our responsibility to recognize, confront, and ultimately conquer our fears.

So how do we stop allowing our fears from extorting the joy, happiness, and excitement from our lives? How do we stop existing, and start living? At the risk of being called simplistic, I have a very easy two-step answer.

Which is exactly what I did every afternoon in Ireland.

Step one is we challenge ourselves to overcome our fears.

The brave man is not he who does not feel afraid, but he who conquers that fear. --Nelson Mandela

If you want to change your life, change your energy. And there is no better energy to be sending out into the Universe, than that of conquering your fear.

Step two is to practice. And the way I practice is by repetition. I've been fortunate to discover the Wingman's Path, a path of simple practices, which are hidden in plain sight. These practices enable me to change my belief about any obstacle that is preventing me from achieving that which I want to achieve.

It's the repetition of affirmations that leads to belief. And once that belief becomes a deep conviction, things begin to happen.
~Muhammad Ali

Once I believe I can, I can. I practice the thought I want to turn into a belief. I practice it over and over and over again, every day for at least one minute. Until I believe it.

So every afternoon, before we got in the car, I would practice for one minute, sometimes longer by saying, "Nothing exciting ever happens without a little nausea. Today, I am conquering my fears."

And we would get in the car and take off exploring all Ireland had to offer. I'm not sure what I enjoyed more, the fantastic sites of Ireland, or the fact that I had conquered my fear, which is how you truly become a Jammy Bastard.

A Wingman Practice:

Conquering Fears

Repeat "nothing exciting ever happens without a little nausea. Today, I am conquering my fears."

Allow it to sink into your subconscious so that when fear arises, and you get that nauseous feeling, the words slip out smoothly and easily, and remind you that some excitement is on its way to you. Permit the knowledge that these words helped me to overcome my fear, to give you the courage to move forward and conquer yours.

48
My Vibration Has a Twang

What is going on with my vibration? That was the question I was asking myself. And with good reason.

We had returned from Ireland the prior week. It was the perfect time to take care of some physical issues: dentist appointment, yearly physical, and a couple of specialists to make sure all was well. I especially like taking care of these appointments when my vibration is good. And coming home from Ireland, my vibe was flying. Not only did we get to explore one of the most beautiful countries in the world, but as mentioned in the last chapter, I conquered a fear, lived there free of charge, in a great house near the beach and the Cliff Walks.

Oh yeah, life was good. And then boom! The hammer dropped.

It started at the dentist's office, after my check-up, I had to get a tooth pulled; it was infected and causing me some pain. The dentist who was doing the procedure was new to the dental office where I was a patient. I was soon questioning how new he was to the dental profession. The pain I had been feeling was nothing compared with the pain of him yanking, twisting, and tugging on my poor molar.

When an hour into a 30-minute procedure had passed, and he declared, "If I knew it would have been this difficult, I would have had you go to an oral surgeon," I knew something was amiss with the frequency I was emitting out into the Universe.

The next day I dropped my cell phone, and it totally stopped working. At the cell phone store, they told me the data may be irretrievable.

Now you may think these are no big deal, and they're not. It's not like I came down with a major illness or a loved one died. But after being on the Wingman's Path for some time now, I'd become extremely responsive to even the slightest undesirable turn in my energy. Perhaps you've started noticing it now that you've been on the Path? Have you detected an increased ability to recognize a slight movement of your vibration, be it up or down? For me, whenever I would feel a downward shift in my energy, I would call it a "twang."

There was certainly a twang in my vibration.

And you always want to correct a "twang" before it becomes a "thang."

So, I got back to basics and asked myself, "What's going on with my vibration?"

But my vibration felt fantastic. I was emitting the happiest of energies.

How can that be? According to the Law of Attraction, "the better it gets, the better it gets." I should have continued to feel more and more joyful. Same thing when viewed from a scientific perspective. "An object at rest stays at rest and an object in motion stays in motion with the same speed and in the same direction unless acted upon by an unbalanced force."

What happened? Was there a feeling somewhere deep in my subconscious that I was undeserving of such happiness? And how did I even end up with this particular dentist? I was in pain; my vibration had taken a hit, and I was blaming him. But was it actually my own vibration that was the "unbalanced force" that caused my happiness to come crashing down?

I don't know why I still ask myself this question. I know the answer. I preach the answer. Did I think because I was teaching people the Law of Attraction, I would somehow be exempt from the law? It's a law of the Universe. It doesn't bend for anyone. Everything is energy. Whatever energy you are emitting, is the exact same energy you are receiving. As in nature. If you plant corn, you get ten-times more corn; if you plant lettuce, you get ten-times more lettuce. And if you plant seeds of positive energy, you get ten-times more positive energy.

Somehow, even with all seeds of positive energy I'd been planting, and all the positivity practices I'd been practicing, I must have still had some unresolved feelings of lack, unworthiness and being undeserving of such joy.

It gave me pause. Here I was, preaching about how there are no coincidences, there are no accidents, and each of us is 100% responsible for every experience in our lives. But I was sending out positive energy, I was feeling great, and I could not for the life of me figure out how I could have possibly created this moment, with this dentist whom I had never even met before.

I thought back to my client with breast cancer. Before her saying, "This may be the best thing that ever happened to me," I remember her asking,

"Are you saying I caused this to happen to me? Isn't it possible that there is some random negative energy that just happened to hit me?"

My answer to her was the same answer I was now telling myself. "I believe in the Law of Attraction, and when you believe in the Law of Attraction, you believe you are responsible for every event, interaction, and experience in your life. There are definitely undesirable energies floating around, looking for someone to attach to. However, they will not bother you unless something in your vibration matches their unwanted energy."

Hmmm... so there it was. It was my vibration that attracted a bad dental experience and a broken cell phone. I continued to reflect on it but could not come up with how I was "vibrating" such negativity. My vibe had been so great. It's then I decided it didn't matter. What's done is done, and the more I continue to think about these two unwelcome occurrences, the more unwelcome occurrences I would attract into my life.

It was time to change the frequency I was producing.

I was reminded of my sister-in-law asking me if I ever have a bad day. I answered her with a resounding, "Yes! Why do you think I come up with all these practices?" Well, suddenly bad days were coming at me with a bit too much regularity for this wingman's liking.

What's a wingman to do? Practice, baby, practice.

I know we all have our hero's journeys, and whether they're tests from the Universe, the randomness of life, or me overcoming a defect in my vibration, these challenges have to be handled. Because if they're not, you're going to end up in a similar rabbit hole. And then you have some real work ahead of you to not only get out of that hole, but to get back moving in a positive direction.

The best way to do that is vibrationally. Because if things are going to hell in a handbasket, then something is wrong with your vibration. It doesn't matter what is wrong. What does matter is that you get yourself back moving in a positive direction.

I had to take a stand and stop those bad vibes right then. Before they could overtake my mind and turn me into a victim of circumstance, again.

No F+*&ing Way.

I had a vibrational challenge in front of me, so I went immediately to my, *And loving it!* practice, and echoed it over and over. I love when one of the Wingman's Path practices comes out easily when the situation demands it. So I added another: *I'm embracing my challenges*, I claimed, trying to convince myself. I even laughed when I said it.

It's much easier to shift your vibration back up when it's just a twang you have to deal with. It may seem simplistic, but the practice seemed to work as I heard from the phone store that my data was recovered. Suddenly my tooth was feeling better as well. And at my annual physical, my lab results were so great, my doctor was asking me all about the Wingman's Path.

Things were looking up.

Or maybe not.

The next day I was at a specialist. He was tossing around words like biopsies, catheters, and pain. It was no longer a twang, it was an emotional free-fall. From good, to bad, to worse.

"I didn't expect that," I said. It was like a gut punch and I was reeling. And then..."What a great challenge, I can't wait to see how I succeed."

I had survived the gut punch and was ready to fight back. The words seemed to come from my inner Wingman. They felt good, like I was respecting the challenge, but also letting myself, Jan, and the Universe know that I would succeed, even if I didn't know how. I began repeating them over and over on the drive home.

Two weeks later, after having my kidney biopsied, I'm lying in a hospital room at Fox Chase Cancer Center. It's 2:00 a.m. and I was unable to sleep. Between machines continuously beeping, a loud and deaf roommate, and nurses constantly coming in and sticking needles in me, I'm wondering how anyone ever sleeps in a hospital room.

"What a great challenge, I can't wait to see how I succeed." The words were bouncing around my subconscious, and I again started repeating them. They felt good as I said them, and I began to breathe them in.

As I did, I somehow remembered the Thanksgiving I did the *Find the positive* game. I figured it was as good a time as any to play it. It's such a perfect practice to utilize in any situation, no matter how bad, upsetting, or undesirable it happens to be.

> **Look for something positive each day,
> even if some days you have to look a little harder.**
> ~Unknown

Why is it so important? Because no matter what is going on in your current reality, the only true predictor of your future reality is the vibration you are sending out into the Universe now. You can say "You Reap what You Sow," or call it Karma or cause-and-Effect, or say it's the Law of Attraction.

The bottom line is the Universe will always match your energy and send you back more of the same.

> **Offer a vibration that matches your desire**
> **rather than offering a vibration that keeps matching "what-is."**
> ~Abraham-Hicks

The challenge is that when your present actuality is lousy, it's easy to focus on the lousy. And if you allow yourself to see only the negatives going on in your life, that's exactly what the Universe will return to you: more negatives. The only way to change your current circumstances is to change the frequency you are emitting.

And that takes practice. And there is no better place to practice finding positives than in a hospital room. There's also no better place to see negatives. Such as...

- It was 2:00 a.m. and I could not sleep.
- I had a stent and a catheter and not only felt pain, but also the constant pressure to urinate.
- The maintenance men were fixing the room above mine, and had been hammering, drilling and sawing until midnight.
- I had a roommate. He may have been a nice guy, but he was very hard of hearing and when he's awake, he keeps asking, "Is someone saying something to me."
- That was far preferred to when he was sleeping. His snoring could wake the dead.
- I have an IV in my elbow crease, and every time I bend my arm the machine behind me beeps like crazy.
- The Wi-Fi isn't working.

Like I said, it's easy to see only the negatives, our mind goes there automatically. It takes work to concentrate on positives, but when you do, they too, seem to multiply.

"What you focus on expands."

- I have health insurance.
- I had chosen this hospital, and contrary to what I said above, it was excellent.
- I had chosen my doctor, and he was fantastic.
- The procedure went exactly as expected.
- My nurse and nurse's aide were wonderful, helpful, and caring.

- The TV worked.
- I was going home the next day.
- Most importantly, The results were perfect. I received a clean bill of health. Hallelujah!

That's right, I was healthy, and that was worth repeating over and over and over. It felt great to say it, and the more I did, the better I felt.

It just takes a little practice.

I did not know *the how*. But I did know, and I made certain to let the Universe know I knew, that I would succeed at overcoming my challenge.

A Wingman Practice:

What a Great Challenge

Repeat: "What a great challenge, I can't wait to see how I succeed."

Do you have a great challenge in front of you? Change your vibration around it by declaring, "What a great challenge, I can't wait to see how I succeed." The reason this practice feels so good and works so well is because you are respecting the "greatness" of the challenge, but also emitting a confident frequency, one which lets the Universe, and you, know you expect to best this obstacle.

As you say it, allow yourself to feel the sensation of successfully overcoming your challenge. Don't worry about the how, just practice the feeling and the happiness of your succeeding.

49
An "Out of Buddy" Experience

After making it through my physical challenges, we were back on the road. I should say most of my challenges, since some of them were still with me. I was still getting used to some that were still with me, so I was still adjusting to another new normal.

We were staying at Hosteria Izhcayluma, a small lodge in the mountains surrounding the village of Vilcabamba, Ecuador. It was junglelike and beautiful. The area has been historically referred to as the Playground of the Inca, because it was once used as a retreat for Incan royalty.

We had arrived a day later than expected. For the first time since our nomd adventure began, we had some difficulties with our travel plans. After arriving in Quito, the capital, we were supposed to fly to Loja, but that flight was diverted to Guayaquil, a port city in Ecuador, known as a gateway to the Pacific beaches and the Galapagos Islands. We didn't realize it at first, because even though they announced it, it was only in Spanish. No one spoke English on the plane. As it landed, Jan and I started to get up but soon realized no one else was moving. They had landed because of the weather, and now needed to refuel before returning to Quito.

Once back in Quito our flight was canceled. We, along with everyone on our plane, were trying to get on one of the next two planes to Loja. There were way too many people and not enough seats. I was pretty resigned to the fact we would have to wait until the next day. I did have some fun and kept my vibration high by getting the crowd riled up doing a Wingman's Path practice. I did have a little help. One lady spoke some English, and when I told her of my practices it was really she who got the crowd going. I was the only one chanting in English: "We will be successful!" (in all of us getting our flight rescheduled for later that day), while they did it in Spanish.

I'm not sure how it happened, but 13 hours later, after our flight to nowhere, delays, miscommunications, and many Wingman practices to keep us positive, we finally arrived in Loja. We shared a taxi with another couple and drove about two hours through rain, mist, and twisty dirt roads to Vilcabamba. I sate in the back seat, and Jan sat up front. As I spoke with the couple, Jan never even turned around. She just sat there, gripping the seat, staring out the window, silently in prayer. It was that kind of drive.

The drive turned into the theme for our time in Vilcabamba. Wherever we went we had fun, but were constantly outside of our comfort zone.

The next morning, after a decent night's sleep, we decided some exercise was in order. Our host at the reception desk pointed us on an easy hike, which his "70-year-old mother could do." It had wonderful views of Mandango Mountain, also called the Sleeping Inca, which overlooks the Valley of Longevity, and whose presence is said to protect the area from earthquakes and other natural disasters.

It's called the Valley of Longevity because it is widely believed that its inhabitants grow to a very old age. The reasons for this claimed longevity are debatable, with many researchers arguing between the anti-oxidant rich fruits and vegetables and the mineral-rich water. Either way, the locals are said to live a longer life than most.

Fifteen minutes into our hike, though, found me wondering if I'd live to see the next day. We're trudged through creeks, slogged through mud, and balanced ourselves on trails made for horses. I was definitely a little outside my comfort zone, and the comic relief from my thought that his mother must be a mud-runner was the only thing keeping me going forward.

We finally made it to a dirt road, which seemed to be an easier path, other than the fact it went straight uphill. I'd like to blame the 5,000-foot altitude, but the extra ten pounds I'd gained during the holiday season certainly had as much to do with my huffing, puffing, sitting, cursing, and resting every few minutes.

Not long on the road, a four-wheel-drive truck came cruising up the hill. The driver stopped and asked if we'd like a ride.

"No thank you," we both panted.

"You're going to end up at my house anyway," he smiled. "Everyone does. The map they gave you is wrong."

Visions of us being chopped up in little pieces and never heard from again lost out to the burning sensation in my legs. Outside my comfort zone, you betcha. But at least I could breathe for the moment.

Now here is where it got funny. The guy turns out to be the former monologue writer for Jay Leno and the *Tonight Show*, Buddy Winston. After an uphill drive, a rocky walk with his groceries over his washed-out driveway, and a mini botany lesson, we arrived at his place in the hills. It was a great little house with 360-degree views. He invited us in for tea, made from Guayusa leaves, which tasted great and reminded me more of the T in THC, than any tea I've had in the states.

We hung with Buddy and his dogs as he entertained us with stories of Hollywood, this area of Ecuador, and his travels and misadventures in Malaysia and Thailand.

He had written a book based on his time in the Land of Smiles. Titled, *An Out of Buddy Experience* (Words Of Winston Publications, 2013), in which he recounts his "95% true" adventures of accidentally preventing a rebel bombing and being chased by a contingent of monk assassins. I bought the book on Amazon later that night and thoroughly enjoyed reading it.

Time went by quickly. When we said our goodbyes and embarked on the downhill part of our journey, Buddy gave us perfect directions, which took us down into the village of Villcabamba. It was about an hour hike, which gave me time to reflect on our day. I recall thinking that this is what makes traveling so magical. It's the people you meet, but also, your expanded horizons, new perspectives, and shared adventures. And especially the unexpected experiences that just magically crop up...such as a truck pulling up behind us and driving us to a new place, with a new friend, and a wonderful experience.

As we made our way to the center into the village square, there, graffitied in yellow paint on a red painted cinder block wall, were the words that made up my next step on the Path.

The Magic Begins Just Outside Your Comfort Zone.

How many times have you seen this saying? How often have you said it?

For me, the answer was many, and often. But I'd never thought to practice it, and I'd never lived it. Maybe I had to experience it, and then see it illuminated in yellow paint. As Jan has often told me, I have to have something shoved up my rectum with an ice pick before I get it, but once I get it, I won't forget it. And that day's events certainly had me believing it. Buddy became a friend. Vilcabamba became a favorite place. And I started practicing and consciously stepping outside my comfort zone to understand that magic.

The funny thing is, when you step outside your comfort zone, in time, a new level of security and safety is established. What once may have seemed scary or anxiety-producing is now your new normal. For me, it began a year earlier. I mean, I'm a guy who ate the same meal at the same restaurant every day. When we had boarded our plane to Thailand for our first, four-month adventure, my anxiety was so off the charts that Jan had to keep reassuring me that if I didn't like traveling we could just change our plans and come home. Now, here we are, starting our second year of travel and I'm hiking through jungles and can't wait for more. I pushed through my worries and have found a new comfort zone.

Perhaps this new Wingman practice can be the impetus for you to begin extending yourself. Whether it's travel, starting a new relationship, or ending an old one, public speaking, a new job, or whatever your desire is, this practice is the perfect strategy to start sending out a new vibration, and begin extending your own self-imposed limitations.

A Wingman Practice:

The Magic Begins

Repeat "the magic begins just outside my comfort zone" to yourself for one minute.

Even if you've heard it before, listen to the words with new ears. Think about your comfort zones and the last time you ventured outside of them. Not just physically, although that can be a start. Open yourself up to someone or try doing something that makes you nervous or uncomfortable.

Everyone's comfort zone is different. Maybe it's public speaking, maybe it's driving a car, maybe it's fundraising, maybe it's going to a party where you don't know anyone. The list goes on and on.

> **Do one thing every day that scares you.**
> ~Eleanor Roosevelt

After saying it for one minute, practice it by doing something today that's outside your comfort zone.

50
A Deep(ak) Disappointment

We were loving Ecuador but knew our time there was coming to an end. We had planned it that way because six months prior, a client had introduced me to a woman who put together events surrounding spirituality and empowering women. She wanted to speak with me about the Wingman's Path. Turns out, she was putting together a panel discussion at the University of Virginia with the agenda to develop a strategy to encourage and educate women on how to utilize the power of spirituality and mindfulness to survive, and thrive, as they go through life's challenges, be it divorce, illness, loss of job, or any painful transition.

The main speakers were to be Deepak Chopra and Jon Kabat Zinn. She asked me to be on the panel. "Excuse me? You want me to be on a panel with Deepak Chopra and Jon Kabat Zinn?" I was incredulous.

Needless to say, I was honored, excited, and a bit unsure of my role. I mean, what could I add to the dialogue that would be more useful than anything Deepak or JKZ would bring to the conversation?

But over the next few months, I started to re-examine the transitional periods of my life and saw how they've helped me become "my own Wingman." I realized how far I have come from those dark days and how those miserable times became the springboard for my improved life.

> **Fall seven times, stand up eight.**
> ~Japanese proverb

The realization brought me a sense of confidence in my ability to contribute to this very important project. I thought that perhaps she needed some people who had hit bottom, and bounced back.

But being on the panel meant cutting our Ecuador trip in half. No problem. Of course I would. Jan wasn't so sure. Not that she didn't believe that I might be on a panel discussion with these two titans of the spiritual world...well actually that was exactly it, she didn't believe it. And we had to purchase airplane tickets. And they cost around $1,000 each. Me? I just so wanted to believe.

I called the woman a week before we purchased the tickets. "I'm purchasing tickets to return home two months earlier from South America than we were initially planning. Are you sure this thing is a go?"

"It's a definite," was her response.

Jan never totally bought in. With her beautiful command of the English language, she asked, "Are you sure she's not some sort of spiritual tease?" Actually, her language was a bit more colorful. But she agreed, so it was with an open heart and a bit of reluctance that Jan and I decided to cut short the Ecuadorian chapter of our great adventure, and return home in the hopes of helping others to successfully overcome their challenges.

It was at a Thai restaurant in Cuenca, Ecuador's second-largest city, when I received the email. "We have had further issues and have rescheduled the event for May at NYU."

Ughhh!

"What a bummer." I snorted and immediately realized she was full of it. May at NYU was just more bulls*&t.

"Tease," Jan replied with certainty.

The email was delivered along with my vegetarian Pad Thai at the same time some Peruvian boys started playing music right next to me. The food and music were great, but it didn't bring me any relief from the blanket of negativity that had enveloped me. You can imagine my disappointment.

"Do you want to talk about it?" Jan asked sweetly.

"NO!" I barked back at her, and we walked home in silence, me feeling saddened and a bit despondent. And you can now pile on guilty after the rudeness I exhibited toward my loving wife.

Two days later, I'm constantly doing Wingman's Path practices and still wasn't able to totally erase the sting of my disappointment. The thing is, I knew it. I knew it when I spoke with her. I knew it when we purchased our round-trip tickets. And I knew it before I received the email. There was no panel discussion.

Have you ever dealt with people like this? I've had these situations arise in my life before. OMG! As I wrote that sentence, I realized...I've had these situations arise in my life before.

Maybe it wasn't "people like this"! Maybe it's me. Maybe it's my vibration. Maybe I'm just too gullible. Change that, it's definitely me, it's definitely my vibration, and I definitely am too gullible.

Anyway, I had still bought in. Which added the feeling of foolishness to my disappointment. On the third day, as I awoke, I knew something more was needed. I was sliding down a dark rabbit hole. Jan wanted to help. We were planning to go to a museum that day. I told her to go alone, that I was bringing in the big guns to help me bounce back. "Don't worry, I've got this." She wasn't so sure, but in the early afternoon, she took off for the Pumapungo Museum.

I turned to Rumi, the famous 13th century poet, theologian and Sufi mystic. His moving poem, "The Guest House" is one of the best pieces of advice on dealing with negative feelings. Somehow, as I lay awake the previous night, the poem popped up on my feed as I numbly paged through Facebook.

> *This being human is a guest house.*
> *Every morning a new arrival.*
> *A joy, a depression, a meanness,*
> *some momentary awareness comes*
> *as an unexpected visitor.*
> *Welcome and entertain them all!*
> *Even if they're a crowd of sorrows,*
> *who violently sweep your house*
> *empty of its furniture,*
> *still, treat each guest honorably.*
> *He may be clearing you out*
> *for some new delight.*
> *The dark thought, the shame, the malice,*
> *meet them at the door laughing,*
> *and invite them in.*
> *Be grateful for whoever comes,*
> *because each has been sent*
> *as a guide from beyond.*

As I re-read the poem, for some reason, it reminded me of the time my departed brother, Stevie, and I were coaching a little league team. We had to make one last cut, which meant an eleven-year-old boy would have to play in the minors that year instead of the majors. His hopes were crushed, and his comment to my brother has stayed with me forever: "But Steve, it's the majors."

"But Rumi, it's Deepak," I whispered. Although I certainly didn't feel like inviting destructive and ugly emotions into my "house," after Jan left, I knew it was time. For I understood from experience that my disappointment could easily take me further down the dark rabbit hole. Inviting in my pain was the quickest way to accept it, and therefore be able to release it.

What to do?

I literally opened the front door of our little apartment and invited in my disappointment and my foolishness.

"Welcome," I laughed. "Come on in. Would you like a cup of Ecuadorian coffee"?

Disappointment answered, "Do you have anything stronger?"

I stood up, went to the cabinet, and grabbed some whiskey. If Rumi says to entertain them, entertain them, I will.

"Foolishness!" I called out. "Would you like some, too?"

"Of course," he replied.

I was smiling as I grabbed three glasses. It's good Jan went out, she would think I had lost my mind. Maybe I had, I mused, although, if it's good enough for Rumi, it's good enough for me. I poured each of us a glass.

I took my first sip, it was more of a swig. "I didn't expect you both," I began, "I—"

Before I could say anything else I was interrupted by Foolishness. "Really?" he challenged.

"So that's how it's going to be?" I replied.

"I'm just saying, you knew she was a tease. Our being here can't be a total surprise."

At this moment, I'm loving this practice and realizing Rumi may be onto something.

"Ok. Perhaps I did know," I answered him, or me, or whomever. "I'm still disappointed and feeling pretty foolish. Thank you very much."

"We know. Otherwise, we wouldn't be here."

Taking another swig, I asked, "Why are you here"?

"Why do you think we're here?" replied both of them.

"And who sent you?" I further queried.

"Who do you think sent us?"

I was getting the picture. "I think my Universal Wingmen sent you. I think you're here to let me know nothing ever goes perfectly. I think you're here to let me know to trust my gut, my intuition, myself. I knew it was too good to be true. I know I have something to offer, and perhaps one day, I'll be on a stage with the brightest minds, helping people. I also know this was not the time, and I knew it from square one. I think you're here to have me recognize exactly what I desire, that I would love to converse with Deepak and JKZ and other titans from the spiritual and self-help industry. I think you're here to let me know if that's what I want, I can have it, but I have some work to do before it is to be. I think you're here to let me know if that is what I desire, then I should start practicing it."

Actually, I had practiced it. Many days I had practiced seeing, feeling, acting, and believing I was part of that panel discussion.

"We know you practiced it," Disappointment assured me, "and you know when you did, you may have seen it, felt it, and acted it, but you really never believed it."

I did know it. I had practiced it often, and every time I did, I knew in my soul I wasn't up on that stage. They were right. I may have seen it and acted as if it were true. I even practiced the feeling of being there. But every time I practiced believing it, I could tell I didn't believe it.

I still felt bad. As I took another drink, I remembered my dad's words when I was flying into Las Vegas, "There is nothing wrong with feeling bad. As a matter of fact, feeling bad can be a great day. It can help you think about what you really want and help provide real clarity. Focus. Enjoy it."

Hmmm...what did I really want? Being on stage with the big guys of self-help and spirituality sounds good. But as soon as I said it, I knew it was just my ego speaking. Really, what I wanted was to continue this wonderful adventure Jan and I were on. Saying that out loud, I acknowledged the feeling of truth. I should never have even agreed to do the workshop as it interrupted our South American trip.

"Now you have your answer," assured both my negative guests.

Imagine that, me turning down the opportunity to be on a panel discussion with Deepak and Jon Kabat-Zinn because the timing wasn't right for me. That brought me a smile.

"Yeah, but think how great it would have been to be up there with them!" Disappointment suggested.

"It would have been," I grinned. "But it's just my ego. I'm letting that go. It will happen if it's supposed to happen. All is well. I'm in Ecuador. I'm traveling the world with my wife. I'm helping people. And I'm loving life."

Their time was up, and they knew it. "I'm grateful you both came by today. Tell my Universal Wingmen, thank you, I appreciate them staying in touch."

"You were still foolish to believe her," snickered Foolishness.

"I was, and I can live with that. It wasn't my first mistake, and it probably won't be my last." I finished my drink, put it down, then opened the door to our apartment, and led them out.

As I stood there for a few seconds, the elevator opened and off stepped Jan. "How was the museum?" I asked.

As we walked in, she replied, "It was great. I want to tell you all about it but first, how was your day? And what are these two glasses for?" She was looking at the two glasses of whiskey I had poured for my guests, Disappointment and Foolishness.

"They're for us," I proclaimed. "A toast. To my friends, Disappointment and Foolishness, for helping me see what I desire, and to you and me, for creating a life of our choosing."

We clinked our glasses and drank.

A Wingman Practice:

The Guest House

Read Rumi's, "The Guest House" over again.

As you read it, think of a pain, or embarrassment, or whatever difficult emotion is currently weighing on you. After reading the poem, invite those difficult feelings in, and be grateful for their arrival and all that they will ultimately teach you.

51
Guess Who Came to Dinner

Maybe everything does happen for a reason. By the time we departed Ecuador, I was over my disappointment, and we were making plans to travel to Malaysia, then Australia, Indonesia, and finally, South Korea, where I would spend some time with my friend and teacher, Zen Master Jung Bong Mu Mu.

What happened instead is I ended up chauffeuring my sister and brother-in-law around Providence. Little did I know this would lead me to receive my next Wingman's Path practice from none other than Jon Kabat-Zinn. Yeah, the same Jon Kabat-Zinn from the supposed panel discussion. Dr. Jon Kabat-Zinn, the brilliant founder of the Mindfulness-Based Stress Reduction program (MBSR), best-selling author, and internationally known meditation teacher.

Coincidence or some weird karmic serendipitous happening? You tell me.

Here's what happened. As we landed in Philadelphia, from Quito, Ecuador, sitting on the tarmac while waiting to deplane, I received the following message from my sister: "Need you in Providence, ASAP."

Turns out, my sister, Sandy, had had a couple fainting spells and wasn't allowed to drive for the next week. That coincided with my brother-in-law, Jack, tearing his bicep muscle and needing an operation within the next few days, so he, too, was unable to drive.

So, after just one day home in South Jersey, I took off for Providence, where I became "The Driver" for a week. I would take my brother-in-law to his office, then pick up my sister and we would go hang out with my mom at her assisted-living facility, and at the end of the day, go back to get my brother-in-law.

It's weird. I went from being with Jan 24/7 to not seeing her for three weeks.
Wait! Three weeks?
Why three weeks, instead of the one week I just told you about? Well, after the first week was up, as I was driving home to join Jan and head to Malaysia the next day, my sister called just when I entered the New Jersey Turnpike. Bad news: my mom had taken a turn for the worse. I called Jan to cancel our tickets, got off at the next exit, and headed straight back up to Providence. Mom's situation didn't look good. I was indefinitely grounded.

It was early March, so when I wasn't driving someone somewhere, I made the best of things by watching March Madness, college basketball's annual championship tournament. But one Friday evening, instead of us bringing in food and watching the beginning of the Sweet 16 playoffs, we went to a small dinner party where the guest of honor was Jon Kabat-Zinn.

Jon was in Providence, RI doing some workshops on Mindfulness-Based Stress Reduction for the faculty, staff, and students at the university in New England, where my brother-in-law, Jack, is a big-wig. He had initially declined, but when he told Sandy and me about it, I pleaded, "Jack, you owe me! I want you to say yes and tell them your driver must attend as well."

And that is how I ended up at dinner with Jon Kabat-Zinn: I was there as Jack's driver. Right time, right place sort of thing? Or was it a karmic reward for the whole panel discussion thing, and then our new trip, being canceled? You and I both know what it was though: my thinking about the panel discussion brought JKZ into my vibration. Prior to traveling to Ecuador, I had even purchased a book he had written to bone-up on his wisdom.

Whatever the reason, it was a fortuitous turn of events. This Wingman actually wound up seated right next to Dr. Kabat-Zinn at the table!. Sitting with us were Neuroscience Researchers, Professors of Religion, Wellness Leaders, my sister, Sandy, and my brother-in-law, Jack.

Funny side note to the panel discussion: when I mentioned to Jon, oh yeah, we were now on a first-name basis, how I was supposed to be on the panel with him at the University of Virginia, he said he didn't know anything about any panel discussion at UVA.

I called Jan after dinner and told her Jon's response. She snorted, "Tease."

Anyway, back to our dinner. Have you ever been in a really cool setting, like this dinner, and have your sister call you by your endearing family name? That's right, most people know me as Michael, or since my discovering the Wingman's Path, many people just call me Wingman, but now Jon Kabat-Zinn knows me as Mikey. Yep, like in the old TV commercial: "Give it to Mikey! He'll eat anything." Ahhh... family.

That was fine, though, because as I said, there I was, in the seat of honor, next to the guest of honor. How that happened is still a mystery to me, but the whole esoteric nature of life seemed to dominate the conversation so perhaps my privileged seating was just another example of such.

Mindfulness practice means that we commit fully in each moment to be present; inviting ourselves to interface with this moment in full awareness, with the intention to embody as best we can an orientation of calmness, mindfulness, and equanimity right here and right now.
~Jon Kabat-Zinn

When you live a nomadic existence with no permanent address, you would think you were always just "in the moment." But the truth is itineraries, reservations, and airplane tickets are planned and arranged usually months in advance. So, in the circumstances of being a Wingman and driver for my sister and brother-in- law, and a caretaker for my mom, all of my current travel plans had been thrown out the window. It was the perfect time to be reminded of the importance of Dr. Kabat-Zinn's primary philosophy to be present in this moment.

And with our trip postponed, our plane tickets canceled, and without a clear vision of what's coming next, I realized that this "be in the moment stuff," is easier said than done. But if there is one thing I've learned as a Wingman, it's that I can practice anything. So that's what I did. I practiced.

And as I practiced being in the moment, I realized you never really know what the next moment will bring. Just days earlier, I was driving home, getting ready to depart on another great journey. In a flash, I made a U-turn and was heading back up to Providence. Who could have foretold that because of that moment, that U-turn would have led to my dinner with Jon?

What capped off the evening was when Jon learned of my Wingman's Path practices, he gifted me a practice. He said, "Take 5 deep breaths and give yourself permission to be exactly who you are."

And so, I did. I took five deep breaths, and after each one, I said quietly to myself, "I give myself permission to be exactly who I am."

The next day, as I practiced it again I noticed it morphing. As I took a deep breath, I gave myself permission for whatever I desired. I took another and said, "I give myself permission to be happy." Then:

- I give myself permission to forgive myself.
- I give myself permission to be more loving.
- I give myself permission to be financially secure.
- I give myself permission to create a life of my choosing.

A Wingman Practice:

Jon Kabat Zinn's Wingman's Path Practice.

Take a deep breath and say quietly to yourself, "I give myself permission to..." and finish the sentence.

If you like, use Dr. Kabat-Zinn's exact words and give yourself permission to be exactly who you are. Or customize the practice and give yourself permission to be, do, or have whatever you desire.

Repeat four more times.

As you breathe in and out, and say the above words, feel the sensation of you giving yourself permission, and allow yourself to see, be, and love yourself for who you are in this very moment.

52
Today...

Everyone in my family was recuperating nicely. Sandy, after getting a bunch of tests, had been declared fine and was given the green light to drive; my mom had bounced back to being herself; and Jack had recovered from his surgery. All was well. So I left Providence and was back in New Jersey.

Which meant Jan and I were ready to take off once again.

The morning before we were to leave, I took a walk in my favorite woods. As I had done each morning since my dinner with Jon, I was giving myself permission for everything and anything. I thought back to the dinner party, the practice, and Jon's main message of being in the moment.

Right then, I most certainly wasn't in the moment. We were leaving the next day, and I was thinking of everything I had to do.

I have to do this, and this, and that, and that. My mind was racing, so I stopped and gave myself permission to be where I was, right then. As I did, I set the timer on my cell phone for one minute, thought of Monte, took a deep breath, and said, "Be here, now."

But I couldn't focus. I kept thinking of all I had to do that day. After a few breaths, and a few more, "Be here, now" statements, I looked around the woods. I observed the trees swaying and saw a few deer running in the distance. My timer beeped. I shut it off and stayed in the moment. It seemed like five minutes passed as I just focused on the woods. I was in the moment, and it felt great.

I was proud of myself for being able to shut out my distractions and congratulated myself for doing so. I then turned on the recording feature on my phone to make sure I didn't forget anything I wanted to do, and said, "Now you can think about what you want to do today."

Maybe it came from Dr. Kabat-Zinn's practice, but it was as if I gave myself permission to do what needed to be done. I was so thrilled I had turned on my phone's recorder because what came out of me wasn't my normal travel errands, such as packing, picking up some items from the pharmacy, unplugging things in the apartment, etc...But rather, a pearl of inner wisdom that became a promise to myself of what I would do "Today." It was like by centering myself in the moment, and then giving myself permission, I opened up a pathway to receive a new practice.

This is directly from my taped conversation with myself as I walked and talked.

- Today, I will give myself permission to be, do or have whatever I desire.
- Today, I begin a discipline of consciously practicing being positive.
- Today, I begin living my second life.
- Today, I begin connecting with my inner Wingman.
- Today I connect with my wiser self.
- Today, I really start making better connections.
- Today, I start living life exactly how I choose to live it.
- Today, I come from love.
- Today, is the dawn of a new day. I like that... It's the dawn of a new day.
- Today, I make certain to discipline myself to be the best I can be, to laugh more, to have more fun, to relax more, to enjoy the years I have remaining on this earth as best I can.
- Today, I will look for and see the best this earth has to offer.
- Today, I will help others.
- Today, is my day, my second life birthday.
- Today, I celebrate my second life birthday.
- Today, I'm playing with house money.
- Today, is my day to go the extra mile.
- Today, I will find something to appreciate in each moment.
- Today, I will seek to find the most joy in each moment.
- Today, I ask myself how I can have the most joy in each moment.
- Today, is going to be a great day.
- Today, is going to be a great day.
- Today, is going to be a great day.
- Today, I'm going to allow myself to feel fantastic.

- Today, I choose to feel great.
- Today, I will get myself into such a great feeling place; I will improve my relationships, my health, my productivity, my finances and the vibration I am sending out.
- Today, I will do better in each area of my life because I will be emitting a more positive frequency.
- Today, I am going to connect with me, with Michael, with who I am, and what I want.
- Today I am going to connect with all my universal wingmates.
- Today, I will be more open to allowing new pathways.
- Today, I will ask myself how, how can I be more open to allowing love, health, money and other positive energies to flow to me.
- Today, I will plant more seeds of positive energy. I like that. Today I will plant seeds of positivity.
- Today I will share a spark of positive energy with everyone I interact with.
- Today I will be grateful for everything that comes my way.
- Today, I will be thankful for today.
- Today, I will see more clearly what I can do to help others.
- Today, I will be confident in my abilities.
- Today, I will do my best at whatever I choose to do.
- Today, I will no longer look to the outer world, my situations, or my environment for my joy.
- Today, I will find the good in everything I see.
- Today, I will celebrate others for their joy.
- Today I celebrate the idea that you and I can create positive energy around us, or rather, attract more positive energy.
- Today, I will send out a positive energy vibration, and somehow in this world of "like attracts like", I will attract more positive energy.
- Today, I will attract more positive energy.
- Today, I will observe my vibration.
- Today, I will raise my vibration.
- Today, I will reap what I sow.
- Today, just like in nature, for every seed of positivity I plant, I will receive 10 x the positivity.
- Today, I will let go of any resistance to my happiness and success.
- Today, I will let it go.

- Today I will shake up any negative energy I'm feeling.
- Today I will allow myself to be positive.
- Today, I will look with wonder at that which is before me.
- Today, I will feel the magic.
- Today, I will embrace my challenges.
- Today, I will look for miracles.
- Today, I will keep my calm and keep my cool.
- Today I will find positives everywhere I am.
- Today, I will set the tone for my day and take responsibility for the energy I emit.
- Today, I will captain my team.
- Today, I will take at least one step in the direction of my desires.

Wow! What was all that? I had a feeling of being in a waterfall of positivity, with the wonderful sensation of gratitude and the light-filled energy of appreciation washing over me. What a fun practice this was! As I left the woods that morning, I felt...no, I knew I had reached the tipping point.

In chapter 11, I mentioned my original hypothesis: "...of my 50,000 thoughts. By practicing for just one minute, I was increasing the number of positive thoughts I was having, and thereby decreasing the number of negative thoughts. If I started with 40,000 negative thoughts and 10,000 positive thoughts, maybe tomorrow I could have 10,500 positive thoughts, and only 39,500 negative ones. And on and on until I reached what Malcolm Gladwell calls the tipping point. Sooner or later, I would reach the juncture where I would have more positive thoughts than negative thoughts..."

I had done it. I don't know how it could be proven scientifically, but I knew experientially, that I had reached the tipping point. I was now having more positive than negative thoughts each day. And I had momentum.

A Wingman Practice:

Today

Begin this practice with the word, "Today" and tell yourself what you want to accomplish for yourself today. You can start with the things on your to-do list that you will absolutely complete today and just keep going. Allow the words to flow.

If you're not sure what words to use, repeat the exact words I said. As you say each thing you want to accomplish, think about it, and see yourself achieving that. Only say things you honestly believe you will do. For example, when I said, "Today, I will look for miracles," or "feel the magic," or "connect with my Universal Wingmates," as I said those words, I practiced the feeling of seeing miracles, feeling magic, and connecting with the Universe. Whatever words you speak when doing this practice, as you say them, practice feeling the energy of them.

53
Travel Day

It's 22 hours after my *Today* practice in the woods, and I just woke up. I'm a bit confused until I see a screen in front of me. It says I'm 36,000 feet above the Pacific Ocean, speeding along at 529 miles per hour.

Oh yeah, it's a travel day. I'm on a plane. Jan and I were heading to Australia, then Indonesia, and beyond. Travel days are not my easiest of days. I've come to realize I have a lot of anxiety on those days. They're not usually days when I'm usually open to any new practices.

I'm still coming to grips with our new nomadic lifestyle. I've mentioned it before, but I believe it deserves to be repeated: I'm the guy who walks the same woods every morning, usually eats the same meal every day for breakfast, and watches "My Cousin Vinny" every time it comes on television.

I'm a routineer. I find my routine, and I stick to it. It's helped me to follow the Wingman's Path. Every morning I do a positivity practice for at least one minute. Each time I do, I take another step on the Wingman's Path. It's become the only routine that matters to me. I urge you to do the same. It's not the specific practice that you do, it's about being consistent and doing one minute of practice each and every day.

When a new practice is shown to me, I do it. Not blindly, but vibrationally. If the practice feels good to me, if it raises my vibration, I'll continue to do it. Interestingly, my routine practice wound up taking me away from my physical routines, and now I'm off discovering new places, connecting with new people, and exploring new cultures.

I've become an explorer. As I think those words, I feel my vibration rise. Hmmm...is this a new practice? The words, "I'm an explorer" slide easily through my mind.

"I'm an explorer." I like that.

I am an explorer. I've certainly journeyed outside my comfort zone. I've felt the nausea, but I've also felt the magic. Oh yeah! I have become an explorer. I am living my life as an explorer. The awesome part of that is when you live life as an explorer, everything becomes an exploration. Every new taste, sound, and view takes on new meaning. Every new connection becomes a new possibility.

It seems so unlikely to me. I've never been one to travel. I remember winning some fancy trips when I was in the financial industry and not even wanting to go.

The screen in front of us blinks, and I notice how much farther we have to go. I'm reminded of how far I've traveled. Not the physical distance. While that's been substantial, it pales in comparison to the distance I've traveled in my own mind.

I never thought of myself before as an explorer, but I am one. Friends frequently ask about my favorite location. My response is always the same: the last place I've been. I've loved them all. Each has something new and different to offer, the food, the spirituality, the people. Especially the people.

From our days spent in Chiang Mai learning, laughing, and opening our minds and hearts with Zen Master Jung Bong Mu Mu, to our hikes along the wild, windy, and wooly Cliff Walks in Ireland, to the crazy, chaotic, cacophony of sights and sounds that is the Saturday morning Chatuchuck market in Bangkok; I've loved them all.

However, I'm very appreciative of the fact that it's not my favorite trip that matters, but rather my most important. And that's the journey I take each day to connect with my highest self, with my inner Wingman. And while Jan might give me an eye roll if I verbalized that, in truth, if it weren't for my daily, one-minute excursions into the recesses of my subconscious, there wouldn't have been any trip to Australia. Or Indonesia. Or Thailand, Cambodia, Ireland, England, or Ecuador.

The best part of being an explorer is you don't even have to physically move. You don't have to climb Mt. Everest, you don't have to discover some new world, and you don't have to "Burn the boats." You just have to set your intention and open yourself up to the possibilities.

It is not the mountain we conquer but ourselves.
~Sir Edmund Hillary

"I'm an explorer." Each time I say it, it gives me a strong sense of courage and an explorer's feeling of confidence. They say a journey of a thousand miles begins with a single step. Well, my first step is always a Wingman minute.

Imagine living your life as an explorer. The same exact life you are living right now. No changes. Except for your mindset. As an explorer, would you become more curious? Would the routine things in your life become more interesting? Would you be more open? Would your everyday life become more exciting? And even if you go to the same office and do the same job every single day, would your attitude be different?

That's the thing about exploring; you never know what you might uncover. Especially inside your own mind. And that's been my most exciting journey by far. I've opened up my life to more. More possibilities, more love, more life.

> **Before enlightenment, chop wood, carry water.**
> **After enlightenment, chop wood, carry water.**
> ~Zen Proverb

For Jan and me, we've uncovered a whole new way to live. We still work, pay bills, have doctor's appointments, stressors over family and money, and all the other challenges we all face. Same as always. Or rather, as they say in Thailand, "Same, same, but different."

Because we're the same. But different.

The difference is our vibration. As we've raised our vibrational frequency, the Universe always matches our energy, and sends us back exactly what we are projecting. As we grew to send out higher and higher frequencies with our vibration, that's what we received in return. We now more often send out energy of optimism, confidence, and excitement, and the Universe always sends us back more reasons to feel optimistic, confident, and excited.

And when we send out energy of being an explorer, the Universe sends us back new things...not just places, but new ideas, new feelings, and new realities, to explore.

My journey of a thousand miles definitely began with a single step. Not a physical step, but a vibrational step, an understanding that the first journey I had to make, was to get beyond the walls I had built in my own mind. And those walls were very high.

But each day, I'd take one small step.

That's one small step for a man, one giant leap for mankind.
~Neil Armstrong

Looking back, I see how those small steps have become a giant leap. I'm now living life as an explorer. Maybe it's time for you to become an explorer in the journey of your life.

And start exploring the recesses of your mind.

A Wingman Practice:

I am an explorer.

Repeat the words, "I am an explorer" out loud for one minute. As you do, practice the feeling of having the courage, confidence, and conviction to discover the life of your dreams. Practice the feeling of setting your intention, developing a plan, and successfully conquering the mountains in your own mind

54
Sunrise, Amed, Bali

We arrived at the Sunshine Cottages in Amed, Bali. The people, both staff and guests, are wonderful. It has a nice feeling. A feeling of family.

A young lady named Sulis took our passports and recognized that she and Jan have the same birthdate, although almost 40 years apart. Her laughter was infectious. I'm not sure if it was her laughter, her belief in Hinduism, the prayer ritual she explained she did three times each day, or the fact that the temple, where many here seem to pray, is located right outside my room, but something opened up in me.

I thought perhaps it had to do with Sulis being Hindu, and us conversing about the rice she had between her eyebrows. It's a conversation I've had before, about the space between our eyebrows being a very special place, a place where all our energy is said to be concentrated. It is one of the chakras in our body and is considered to be the spiritual center of our body. A place we are said to be able to connect with our inner self, or as I prefer, our inner Wingman. Hindus apply rice to this area to help them focus their energy and improve their ability to connect.

When I started on this Wingman journey, it was because I wanted a better life, a happier life. I soon learned the only way to get a happier life was to develop a positive mindset. That lesson made me want to connect with the masters who taught it, and I developed a longing for a connection to them. I wanted direct guidance from my inner Wingman.

While I'd been advancing along the Wingman's Path, I realized that inner guidance mostly came from the lessons I learned, the people I met, the experiences I had. But, when I was in Bali...Bali was different.

In Bali, my inner Wingman contaced me.

I sensed it early in the morning, even before I awoke.

It felt like a graduation day. A "Congratulations" that I had made it. I had completed the first portion of the Wingman's Path. And instead of a diploma, I was given these words:

I am a creation of God. Like all of God's creations, I am a creator. I can create anything I desire. I have been given the tools to do so. Those tools are the ability to think it, feel it, act upon it, and see it so clearly that I believe it to be true. I can actually accomplish it by doing any of these four. By doing all four, I will create it even quicker. I am a creator.

Finally! After five and a half years, I had clarity. This stage of my education was finished. I now understood the feeling of "hitting the Spiritual Lottery."

The answers had actually been there all along. It's just that sometimes I get in my own way and forget that all I have to do is remind myself that I can create anything I desire by thinking it, feeling it, acting upon it, and seeing it clearly.

I imagine you forget that sometimes as well.

It's not surprising. With all our spirituality and divinity, we are still human, after all. And being human, it took me a long time to navigate this path.

However, that is in the past.

For as I sat there in the early morning, with the sun rising over the Bali Sea, I felt as though I would never again forget the power I have to manifest anything I desire. That was my gift that morning, a graduation present for completing this piece of the path, the "mother" of all Wingman practices. It was my reward for staying on the path, for sticking to it, for not giving up, and for successfully navigating the Wingman's Path.

How did I get there? How was I able to find, and successfully navigate, the Wingman's Path and hit the Spiritual Lottery?

"Practice, baby. Practice." For me, it was all about consistently practicing my Wingman Minutes to constantly raise my vibration. Just so we're clear once more, those practices are the Wingman's Path. And now you have traveled the path with me, hopefully feeling the power of these practices, and enjoying the stories of how each came to be.

You and me, we're creators. We can create anything we desire. Isn't that nice to know? Just saying it feels great.

A Wingman Practice:

I am a Creator

Repeat to yourself, for at least one minute:

"I am a creation of God. Like all of God's creations, I am a creator. I can create anything I desire. I have been given the tools to do so. Those tools are the ability to think it, feel it, act upon it, and see it so clearly that I believe it to be true. I can actually accomplish it by doing any of these four. By doing all four, I will create what I desire even quicker. I am a creator."

54
Thank You!

Great job on getting to the last chapter. You now have the tools in place to create a life of your choosing. I've found the most important tool is practice. Consistent practice. As my friend and mentor, the Venerable Zen Master Jung Bong Mu Mu told me:

Practice is all it takes to become enlightened.

You're not preparing to start, you've already started. Even better, you're well on your way, and you've got this. The exciting part is this is not the end of your journey, but the beginning of an exciting new chapter. Your goals, dreams, and desires are now within your reach. And once you're moving in the right direction, well, as Sir Isaac Newton will tell you, it's easier to keep moving in that direction. By finishing this book, you've already shown you can keep your momentum going when you choose to.

As for these practices, they're a fabulous base, but they don't have to be your only practices for bringing positive energy into your life. You'll find as your vibration continues to rise, you'll start recognizing new ways to practice. You'll be enjoying an ordinary conversation where someone will say something, and you'll recognize it as a statement, thought, or feeling that will help you improve your energy. Practice it and see if it helps you feel better. If it does, keep practicing it.

Since discovering the Wingman's Path, I keep coming up with different practices. People ask me how I come up with so many different practices. I believe I'm just practicing what I preach and following the laws of the Universe.

What I think, I become. So I think a great deal about how I can bring more positive energy into my life. Or like the *Lime-Green Cars* practice,

"What I look for, I find." When I look for practices that will help me raise my vibration, I find practices that will help me raise my vibration. And then it's just riding the wave and keeping my momentum going.

For the last practice in this book, I want to share the practice I do most often. It's my fallback practice. It's what I practice when I want to practice but can't think of which practice to practice. It happens often enough that I keep this as an excellent Plan B.

I say, "Thank You." I believe I practice gratitude more than any other practice.

> **If the only prayer you ever say in your entire life
> is thank you, it will be enough.**
> ~J. John and Mark Stibbe

I can't tell you how many mornings, during the early stages of my discovering the Wingman's Path, that I would take a walk and not be able to come up with a practice. Probably because my vibration wasn't as positive as it is now. On those days, I would just say thank you for one minute. Even when I didn't feel particularly thankful, it kept things easy for me.

And I like easy.

Thank you helps me keep consistent. My consistency helps me get, and keep, momentum on my side. When first starting out, it takes some work to get your energy moving in a positive direction. Once you have that positive energy rolling though, your vibration expands exponentially. You're no longer swimming upstream, you're now in the flow. Keep it going by practicing for at least one minute every day. As you do, creating the life you now want becomes easier and easier.

You've so got this!

Allow me to do my *Thank You* practice by thanking you for reading this book, for doing these practices, and for helping our Universe be a more positive place to be.

> **As they say on my own Cape Cod,
> a rising tide lifts all the boats.**
> ~John F. Kennedy

Thank you for being a part of the rising tide of positive energy. As I often say in my daily video practices, the more of us that share a spark of positive energy, the easier it is for each of us to hold onto that spark, and to share it with our loved ones, our family, our friends, our neighbors, and our community. Speaking of my daily video, please join me each morning for my Facebook Live daily video practice:

https://www.facebook.com/groups/WingmansPath/

I find it helps when we build our vibration together. The more we can surround ourselves with positive energy, the easier it becomes for each of us to raise our vibration and to achieve our goal of creating a life of our choosing.

A Wingman Practice:

Thank You

Repeat "Thank you" out loud or quietly to yourself for one minute. As you say the words, think about the things that you are thankful for. Practice the feeling of being thankful.

I remember working with one woman. She was in a rough space, and when I shared this practice with her she said, "Michael, what are you talking about? What do I have to be happy about? I'm hanging on here by a thread."

My answer helped solidify this practice and the frequency I want to be emitting when practicing *Thank You*.

I said, "Then you should be really thankful for that thread. Practice being grateful for that thread."

Whatever you can find to be thankful for, even if it's just waking up this morning, start emanating that energy, that "I'm thankful for that, and I'm thankful for that, and I'm thankful for that" vibration.

The more you can find to be thankful for, the more the Universe will send you to be thankful for. It's a nice cycle to be in. It's certainly made my life far more enjoyable.

Thank you for being on The Wingman's Path with me. I hope you enjoyed my journey to discovering it. Don't forget to keep practicing, to keep moving in the direction of your desires, and to remember to have some fun while traveling your path.

Further Reading

Here is a partial list of some of my favorite inspirational books. Many have been mentioned in the pages of this book and a few might be new to you. I found them helpful and thought you might too.

Ask and It Is Given: Learning to Manifest Your Desires, by Esther and Jerry Hicks
The Four Agreements: A Practical Guide to Personal Freedom (A Toltex Wisdom Book) by Don Miguel Ruiz
Conversations with God: An Uncommon Dialogue by Neale Donald Walsch
Think and Grow Rich by Napoleon Hill
The Magic (Secret) by Rhonda Byrne
Change Your Thoughts, Change Your Life: Living the Wisdom of the Tao by Dr. Wayne W. Dyer
E-Squared by Pam Grout
The Power of Myth by Joseph Campbell and Bill Moyers
The Wisdom of Florence Scovel Shinn by Florence Scovel Shinn
As a Man Thinketh by James Allen
Siddhartha by Hermann Hesse
One Minute Mindfulness by Donald Altman
Glad No Matter What by SARK
365 Prescriptions for the Soul by Dr. Bernie Siegel
You Are a BadAss by Jen Sincero
Be Happy!: Release the Power of Happiness in YOU by Robert Holden, PhD
Finding God in The Shack The Shack by Randall Rauser
Understood Betsey by Dorothy Canfield Fisher

Acknowledgments

My discovery of the Wingman's Path, and this book, would not have been possible without the many different Wingmates who shined a light for me.

I'd like to thank: my publisher, Lisa Shiroff, who took a chance on me and helped me believe this book was a possibility. I thank my mother, father, and brother Stevie, gone in body, but always in my heart: my sister Sandy, for her love and guidance throughout my entire life; my friend Cliff, who got me started on this path; my friend Rita, who helped me stay on it; my Law of Attraction Meetup group for their inspiration, knowledge and for allowing me to turn our meetings into Wingman's Path practice sessions.

In addition, none of this would be possible without my Wingmates on The Wingman's Path to Positivity Facebook group, for their energy, support, and enthusiasm in helping me keep my vibration high.

My deepest thanks to my daughter Alex, whose unconditional love got me through my darkest days; my son Lyle, for reminding me that we can achieve anything we set our minds to, and my step-daughter Evy, for always being in my corner and opening up the world to me.

And last, but always first, my wife Janet. Your love has changed my life and elevated me beyond what I thought imaginable. Thank you for loving, and believing, in me.

About the Author

The Wingman's Path to Positivity is Michael's first publication. The inspiration and ideas in his book were born out of his past blog, radio show, and ongoing Facebook group, The Wingman's Path to Positivity, where he shares daily, one-minute, motivational practice sessions from wherever he is in the world. When not traveling, Michael lives with his wife, Janet, in Southern New Jersey. They have three grown children and a new grandchild.

Follow Michael's live daily practices at:
https://www.facebook.com/groups/WingmansPath/

www.ingramcontent.com/pod-product-compliance
Lightning Source LLC
Chambersburg PA
CBHW032030290426
44110CB00012B/749